KNOWLEDGE
AS
DESIGN

KNOWLEDGE
AS
DESIGN

D. N. Perkins

LAWRENCE ERLBAUM ASSOCIATES, PUBLISHERS

1986   Hillsdale, New Jersey   London

Permission to reprint the following poems in Chapter 3 is gratefully acknowledged:

"The Span of Life" by Robert Frost, from *The Poetry of Robert Frost*, edited by Edward Connery Lathem. Copyright 1936 by Robert Frost. Copyright © 1964 by Lesley Frost Ballantine. Copyright © 1969 by Holt, Rinehart and Winston. Reprinted by permission of Henry Holt and Company, Inc.

"On the Vanity of Earthly Greatness" from *Gaily the Troubadour* by Arthur Guiterman, publisher E. P. Dutton, copyright 1936. Reprinted by permission of Lousie H. Sclove.

"My Papa's Waltz" by Theodore Roethke, from *The Collected Poems of Theodore Roethke*, copyright 1942 by Hearst Magazines, Inc., published by Doubleday & Company. Reprinted with permission of the publisher.

Illustrative completion of Theodore Roethke's "My Papa's Waltz" composed by John Ciardi, from *How Does a Poem Mean?* (Second Edition), p. 369, by John Ciardi and Miller Williams. Copyright © 1975 by Houghton Mifflin Company. Used by permission.

Lawrence Erlbaum Associates, Inc., Publishers
365 Broadway
Hillsdale, New Jersey 07642

10 9 8 7 6 5 4 3 2 1

Library of Congress Cataloging in Publication Data

Perkins, D. N., 1942-
Knowledge as design.

Bibliography: p.
1. Thought and thinking—Study and teaching.
2. Reasoning. 3. Knowledge, Theory of.   4. Imagery (Psychology) 5. Pattern perception. I. Title.
LB1590.3.P47   1986   370.15'2   86-13596
ISBN 0-89859-839-7
ISBN 0-89859-863-X (pbk.)

Printed in the United States of America

Fortunate in the teachers, formal and informal, that I have had, I dedicate this book to them

Contents

Acknowledgments

Two friends and colleagues, Catalina Laserna and Omar Carrizales, contributed greatly to the initial development of the ideas explored in this book. Catalina Laserna, an anthropologist, worked with me in writing and testing the inventive thinking sequence for Project Intelligence, which produced the *Odyssey* thinking course. There we first recognized the importance of the concept of design. We jointly gave a workshop in Colombia, her native country, where the conception moved significantly closer to its present form. Since that time, we have continued to collaborate. Omar Carrizales, a professor of mathematics at the Universidad Central in Caracas, Venezuela, spent a sabbatical year at the Harvard Graduate School of Education, during which we had extended conversations about knowledge as design and the general problem of developing students' thinking. Many of the examples presented in this book directly reflect discussions with Catalina and Omar.

As already mentioned, the ideas in this book grew out of my work on Project Intelligence. Special thanks go to José Buscaglia for getting me involved and providing good counsel throughout, Mario Grignetti for his sensitive responses to the evolving inventive thinking lessons, Ray Nickerson, director of the project, for his provision of elbow room as well as good advice, and Margarita de Sánchez, for her astute practical perspective on thinking skills programs and their implementation.

Several individuals provided valuable responses to the draft of this book. Vernon Howard, Israel Scheffler, and associates of the Philosphy of Education Research Center at the Harvard Graduate School of Education offered helpful feedback. Ken Hawes in particular supplied fine-grained reactions to a number of points. Howard Gardner, co-director with me of Harvard Project Zero and colleague of many years, mused over the first several chapters in helpful ways. Jonathan Baron of the University of Pennsylvania went over the manuscript, producing apt advice chapter by chapter. Inabeth Miller, then at the Harvard Graduate School of Education and now at the Boston Museum of Science, offered trenchant thoughts on the slant accessibilty of the book. Julia Hough, my editor at Lawrence Erlbaum Associates, supplied sensitive guidance chapter by chapter, section by section.

While this book is far from a direct report of research or curriculum development work, it has benefitted from knowledge I have gained through such activities. Consequently, I would like to acknowledge the government of Venezuela and Petroleos of Venezuela, which supported Project Intelligence, and the Spencer Foundation and the National Institute of Education, both of which supported a line of research into the development of informal reasoning especially reflected in Chapters 6 and 7. My thinking also was informed through my work at the Educational Technology Center of the Harvard Graduate School of Education, functioning with funding from the federal government.

Let me add the standard disclaimer that, of course, the ideas expressed here do not necessarily reflect the positions or policies of the supporting agencies.

Finally, my wife Ann, two sons Teddy and Tommy, and daughter Alice were willing respondents to trial balloons of many colors as these notions evolved. Warm thanks for their ready help and support.

Introduction: The Giving and Getting of Knowledge

We wish for what comes hard. You can see that in our literature and religion, our myths and folktales. For instance, how many novels have you read or movies have you viewed about the joys of eating? Not many, in part because this joy comes fairly easily for most of us. On the other hand, sex, money, and power remain staples of novelists, directors, and their audiences. Sex, money, and power do not come as easily, so people find the fantasy endlessly engaging.

This book concerns a rarer field for fantasy—the giving and getting of knowledge. We wish for knowledge too. I construe knowledge broadly, including facts, concepts, principles, skills, and their intelligent, insightful, and sensitive use. I have in mind active knowledge that one thinks critically and creatively about and with, not just passive knowledge that does little but await the final exam. Knowledge—especially active knowledge—counts among those things that do not come easily. So, although we may not cherish it quite as much as sex, money, and power, we have some literature and religion, myths and folktales about this hunger also.

There was Moses, for example. Moses went up into the mountain, faced God, and brought back His word. The particular wisdom of the ten commandments was a gift from God to Moses, and from Moses to us all. What a fine idea about something that does not come easily—knowledge as a gift. Jumping forward a few thousand years, there is Stanley Kubrick's classic 2001: A Space

Odyssey. Remember how, at the beginning, the godlike monolith stands on earth to impart intelligence to a tribe of simians. They sniff curiously about the base of this blank alien shape. Then it begins to sing a one note tune that hurts their ears, shocks their heads, crinkles their brains, wakes their minds up. Soon and for the first time, a bone is seen as a club. They have the gift of insight.

Both these narratives carry a moral about our hunger for knowledge and how to fulfill it. Real knowledge (wisdom, insight, and so on) is so difficult you cannot get it for yourself. You have to get it as a gift. Like many stories on many matters, such tales marry our fears to wishful thinking. In reality, knowledge does not come as easily as a gift. Learning is a sometimes inspiring but too often onerous challenge. In reality, teachers cannot give wisdom as handily as God gave it to Moses or the monolith to the simians. Teaching also is an occasionally smooth but often labored process. This book concerns ways to make more tractable the teaching and learning of knowledge and its critical and creative use.

Who should worry about all this and why? Well, who are the givers and getters of knowledge? We all are—you, I, your and my sons and daughters, parents and grandparents, nephews, nieces, aunts, uncles, enemies, friends, acquaintances, partners, school-mates, playmates, workmates, bedmates. Giving and getting knowledge is a core survival strategy of humankind. This is an old point. Take a couple in cashmere sweaters, put them out in the wilderness, and they probably will not make it for a month. They are far less well equipped with anatomy and instincts for survival than the ignorant buzzard whose shadow crosses them at noon. They are not even good enough at what humans are especially good at—learning—to get themselves out of the bind.

But give them a start, a minimal mass of knowledge, enough to survive, and they and their descendants will start to build it up and pass it along. Civilizations such as Egypt or Greece were made not out of pyramids or Parthenons but principally out of knowledge built up and passed along. The technological world today, on the surface a construction of microchips and prestressed concrete, is underneath an edifice of knowledge. To be sure, the talent for building up knowledge that has brought us this high in some ways threatens to tip us over the brink of disaster. Short of that disaster, we will never be done learning. Indeed, we hardly dare to be done, since now we need to learn our way out of messes we have learned our way into.

So the travails of teaching and learning should be the concern of us all. In fact, they always have been to a significant extent. One way or another, any society makes serious provision for teaching and learning. In industrialized societies, this takes the form of schools that try to get across a body of scientific and humanistic knowledge. Unfortunately, we have had only middling success.

For instance, you may remember your own frustrations. Perhaps you recall crouching over a college desk, busily transcribing the professor's blackboard notes, bothered by the itch in the back of your mind that said you did not really understand. Later you worked it out — painfully. Or you may remember when you read an article on the binary number system that gives computers their basic operating language. Binary to decimal conversions were tractable, but you never did get straight how to translate big decimal numbers into binary. Or you may bring to mind the poems by Emily Dickenson you read in ninth grade; you would have tried your hand at writing a couple in that spirit, but there was no discussion about how to do such things nor any occasion to try. Or perhaps you recall wanting to get off your chest some of the inconsistencies of English spelling; but the teacher was not ready to treat such anomalies as an interesting phenomenon worth discussing. Or perhaps you remember how you wondered why a minus times a minus number yields a plus number, or how the history course with the flood of facts scared you off at the end of the third week.

More frustration about middling success can be found in the spate of recent reports about precollege education in the United States. We hear the litany of ills repeated from perceptive voice after voice: Students cannot write. They can learn the number facts, but they cannot solve problems. They can read the words but they cannot think about the words analytically nor draw apt inferences from them. Some students do better, of course, but some of them do worse. Too many are getting passive knowledge instead of active knowledge, knowledge they store and retrieve but do not know how to use. In short, the learning of facts proceeds well enough but critical and creative thinking languish.

Sometimes in more acid moods, I like to put it this way. Education too often amounts to truth mongering. Truths are sold to learners as givens to be learned, without context, without critical perspective, without creative application. In gentler moments, I recognize the source of the problem: Education for genuine understanding and critical and creative thinking is a hard and in some ways *technical* enterprise, calling for theories and tools of teaching and learning suited to the challenge. Truth mongering is a relatively unsubtle and nontechnical endeavor, so naturally much of teaching and learning drifts into that pattern.

But in recognizing the trap, we need not be resigned to it. This book is impatient with truth mongering. It concerns the universal human enterprise of transmitting knowledge. It hopes that this enterprise can be much more immediate, penetrating, and empowering than the status quo suggests. It explores some notions about how to do the giving and getting of knowledge better, in schools and out of them, in homes and out of them, on the job and off it, wherever you happen to be, whatever you need to learn or teach.

1 Knowledge as Design

The classic British science fiction author H. G. Wells once wrote a story about a man who wishes the world would stop turning. Troubled and in need of time, the hero of his tale wants tomorrow to come a little later. The conceit of Wells' narrative is that the fellow gets his wish, but from that moment on all consequences follow according to natural law. The Earth stops turning, but the atmosphere does not. Enormous winds sweep down forests and farms. The oceans also keep in motion, heaving up onto the land, demolishing homes and factories. Bridges and skyscrapers, not part of the Earth, retain momentum, toppling over of their own impetus.

This whimsey about the price of idle wishes invites a like parable about human invention. Suppose that, tired of TV commercials and trendy boutiques, someone wishes that there is no such thing as design. After all, for most of us, design is a rather special word — the enterprise of admen, architects, and fashion czars. But broadly construed, design refers to the human endeavor of shaping objects to purposes. Let us, like Wells, follow rigorously the consequences of this wish. The clothes vanish from our bodies, never having been invented. The floors and pavements on which we walk slip away into nothingness. We find no books, no artificial lighting, not even a primitive hearth. We wander around the wilderness, mouthing at one another. And perhaps, if language itself can be considered a design, we do not even understand what the mouthings mean.

1

WHAT IS DESIGN?

This parable dramatizes how pervasive and important design is: Our sophisticated lives depend utterly upon it. If building up and passing along knowledge is one characteristic of the human way, another is embodying knowledge in the form of a tool to get something done. A knife is a tool for cutting, a bed a tool for sleeping, a house a tool for sheltering, and so on.

In general, one might say that a design is a structure adapted to a purpose. Sometimes a single person conceives that structure and its purpose — Benjamin Franklin as the inventor of the lightning rod. Sometimes a structure gets shaped to a purpose gradually over time, through the ingenuity of many individuals — the ballpoint pen as a remote descendant of the quill pen. Sometimes a structure gets adapted by a relatively blind process of social evolution, as with customs and languages that reflect human psychological and cultural needs.   But notice that in this book we do not use another sense of design: regular pattern that serves no particular purpose, as in ripples on sand dunes.

If knowledge and design both are so central to the human condition, then a speculation looks tempting. The two themes might be fused, viewing knowledge itself as design. For instance, you could think of the theory of relativity as a sort of screwdriver. Both are human constructs. Both were devised to serve purposes — the screwdriver physically taking apart and putting together certain sorts of things, the theory of relativity conceptually taking apart and putting together certain sorts of phenomena. That seems promising; at least "knowledge as design" poses a provocative metaphor. Indeed, perhaps knowledge is not just *like* design but *is* design in a quite straightforward and practical sense.

KNOWLEDGE AS INFORMATION
VERSUS KNOWLEDGE AS DESIGN

What is knowledge? Fuzzy as it is, the question has some importance. How we think of knowledge could influence considerably how we go about teaching and learning. A stolid formula tends to shape how we see knowledge and the giving and getting of it: knowledge as information. The theme of knowledge as design can break the familiar frame of reference, opening up neglected opportunities for understanding and critical and creative thinking.

Through learning at home, at work, and in schools, we accumulate a data base of information that we can then apply in various circumstances. For instance, you know a friend's phone number, the layout of your town or city, the rules of chess, your favorite foods, when Columbus discovered America, the Pythagorean theorem, the capital of Russia, Newton's laws. You have this information at your disposal and may call upon it for whatever you want to do with it.

But can we consider knowledge in a different light, as design rather than information? That would mean viewing pieces of knowledge as structures adapted to a purpose, just as a screwdriver or a sieve are structures adapted to a purpose. You know your friend's phone number—so you can call when you need to. Moreover, your knowledge is well-adapted to the purpose; the number is only seven digits long and well-rehearsed, so you can remember it readily. You know the layout of your town or city—so you can get to work, to your home, to the airport, wherever you want to go. Again, your knowledge is well-adapted; if you have lived in a place a while, you probably have a rather comprehensive "mental map" of the area that you can apply not only in finding places you normally go to but in navigating to new locations in the same area. Similar points can be made about knowing the rules of chess or your favorite foods.

For these examples of everyday practical knowledge, knowledge as design does make sense, but how about more academic knowledge? When you ask yourself what the purpose of a piece of knowledge like "Columbus discovered America in 1492" or the Pythagorean theorem is, you may not have a ready answer. Treating *that* sort of knowledge as a design—as a structure adapted to one or more purposes—does not come so easily.

The question is how to interpret the shortfall. Possibly knowledge as information is the right way to think about academic knowledge. On the other hand, perhaps academic knowledge can be thought of as design, but the "information attitude" toward knowledge that pervades teaching and learning in academic settings has let to our accumulating knowledge stripped of its design characteristics. In academic settings, we often treat knowledge as data devoid of purpose, rather than as design laden with purpose. To recall a theme from the introduction, much of the academic knowledge we hold shows a symptom of truth mongering—knowledge disconnected from the contexts of application and justification that make it meaningful.

If all this is so, by pushing the point one should be able to see academic knowledge as design after all. Indeed, sometimes the case that academic information has—or should have—a design character is easy to make. The theory of relativity was already mentioned. Consider its ancestor, Newton's laws. These have a fairly transparent purpose: organizing a diverse set of observations in order to explain phenomena of motion, anything from the trajectory of a baseball to the orbits of the planets. Also, the laws have a parsimonious and powerful mathematical structure well-adapted to this purpose.

"Important facts" such as when Columbus discovered America pose a more difficult challenge. One might question whether the facts have that much importance after all. However, connected to significant purposes they at least take on somewhat more meaning. For instance, milestone dates like 1492 are pegs for parallel historical events. What was happening in Europe at about that time, or in the far East? For another, 1492 and other milestone dates in American history provide a kind of scaffolding for placing intermediate events. What happened in America between 1492 and the next milestone date? In such roles, a date functions not just as information but as implement, in particular a tool for grasping and holding information. What was mere data becomes design.

There is a tempting analogy here with Stanley Kubrick's *2001*. What is an old bone—just an object in the environment, or a tool? Surely Kubrick's simians knew about bones long before the monolith, but not bones as clubs. Bones were simply objects lying around. But with the help of the monolith, the simians saw how a bone could be used as a weapon. Something like this applies to academic information also. To be sure, we have a fair amount of mere information sitting in our mind's attic that does little more than wait and weather there, like old bones. But when a piece of data gets connected to purposes, it becomes design-like. In this way, all information potentially is design. Of course, not very datum we have functions as design or even can do so readily. All of us keep in storage a great deal of passive information, one might even say dead information. But that is part of the problem. There is little point in teaching and learning that provides primarily dead information.

In summary, knowledge as design makes sense. One can see both practical and academic knowledge through that lens. In various contexts and for various reasons, you might prefer one construal or the other for knowledge — information or design. In the context of teaching and learning, knowledge as design has much to offer. Knowledge as information purveys a passive view of knowledge, one that highlights knowledge in storage rather than knowledge as an implement of action. Knowledge as design might be our best bet for a first principle in building a theory of knowledge for teaching and learning.

FOUR DESIGN QUESTIONS

All this is okay as far as it goes, but a mere attitude will not carry us very far unless we can elaborate it into a method. "All right," a cautious voice complains. "You want to call the concept of ecology, Boyle's law, and the Bill of Rights designs. But that's pretty easy and only mildly illuminating. What do you do to follow up?"

What we need is a way to use the theme of design systematically as a tool for understanding knowledge. To put this another way, we need a theory of understanding reflecting the theme of design. And perhaps there is one. Here are four questions that help in prying open the nature of any design.

1. *What is its purpose (or purposes)?*
2. *What is its structure?*
3. *What are model cases of it?*
4. *What are arguments that explain and evaluate it?*

Consider, for instance, an ordinary screwdriver. Here you know the answers. You certainly know about purpose: It's for turning screws. Other purposes could be mentioned too, such as prying open paint cans, but we focus on the most common purpose here.

As to structure, you can give me a general description of it, outlining its major parts and materials — the plastic or wooden handle, the metal shaft, the flat tip, and so on. In general, the term structure is used loosely and broadly to mean whatever components, materials, properties, relations, and so on, characterize the object in question. As with purpose, there may be different ways of describing structure; we simply pick one that is natural and illuminating in the context.

As to models, you can show me or draw me examples of screwdrivers. You can demonstrate how to use one. In general, a model exemplifies in some concrete way the design or how it works.

As to arguments, you can explain why it should work. In particular, the handle lets one grip and twist. The flat tip nests into the screw and allows one to turn it. You can also give some pros and cons about its design. For instance, sometimes an ordinary screwdriver does not provide enough leverage to turn screws in hardwood. Sometimes it slips and scars a wood surface. Note that under evaluation we include side effects pro or con, such as scarring wood, as well as effectiveness in the principle objective, turning screws. In summary, your understanding of the design of an ordinary screwdriver includes knowledge about purpose, structure, models, and argument.

Moreover, if you do not understand those four things about a design, you do not understand the design fully. For instance, consider the sample design in Figure 1.1. The pictured model lets you

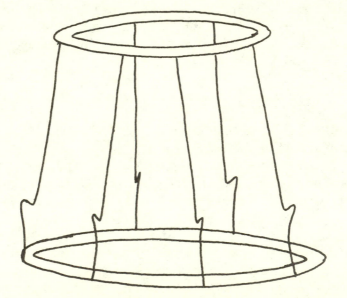

FIG. 1.1. A mystery design

see much of the structure of this design. Here is some further information about its structure: It is made entirely of steel and has a width of about six inches at the bottom.

Even with all this information, however, you probably do not feel that you understand the design, because you do not have answers to the questions about purpose or arguments. As to purpose, the gadget is a toaster, designed to hold toast over a gas burner. That much of a clue probably lets you figure out some arguments for yourself. Why should it work? The gas flame will toast the pieces of bread as they sit against the wires, supported by the bends near the bottom. With another moment of thought, you can begin to see some pros and cons. For instance, one has to turn the bread in order to toast both sides.

As in this example, so in general: It appears that understanding a design thoroughly and well means understanding answers to the four design questions. Note that there is nothing very novel or esoteric about this notion. The four design questions simply articulate the sort of understanding we all achieve about such ordinary objects as scissors, thumbtacks, belts, shoes, and chairs. They also spell out points we commonly pay heed to when teaching and learning in many concrete contexts such as carpentry or motor repair. The four design questions offer a guide to doing more consciously and carefully what we often do intuitively anyway.

But do the questions apply to a piece of knowledge as well as they apply to a screwdriver? The issue is crucial, since we need a theory of understanding that encompasses knowledge of all sorts, from the most concrete to the most abstract. Let us test the matter. For a first example, consider your knowledge of what a traffic light means. The knowledge has a purpose: to allow you to judge when it is safe and legal to proceed. It seems natural to interpret the structure of the knowledge as these constituent rules: Green means go; red means stop; yellow means proceed with caution. You can give models of the knowledge — a picture or a demonstration at the next traffic light. And, finally, you can give arguments for the utility of having such rules — the arguments of experience or a citation of the legal code, for two instances.

Perhaps the design questions suit such pragmatic knowledge as what to do at a traffic light but not more abstract knowledge. Consider Newton's laws again. One certainly can ask after purpose — to integrate and explain data about the motions of bodies from baseballs to planets. A useful rendering of structure would be the laws themselves, considered one by one. (Instead, you could take the component words of the laws as the elements of structure, but this would not be an illuminating choice; if you pick the individual laws as your elements of structure you can ponder under argument how each law contributes to the ensemble, but if you pick each word you choose a grain too fine to allow an illuminating account of the whole). Model cases include the solar system and how the laws explain the orbits of the planets. Arguments include an explanation of how the laws work together to give a complete account of a range of dynamic phenomena and an evaluation of the evidence for and against Newtonian mechanics.

Simple facts seem the hardest sorts of knowledge to view as design. Will the design questions serve there? Consider the fact that George Washington was the first president of the United States. This piece of knowledge could have various purposes, one of the most important being to give us an anchor point in history, as with Columbus's "1492" mentioned earlier. Classifying historical events by presidential administration is a neat way to organize the course of American history. As to structure, it may be useful to think of two components: "George Washington," which identifies a certain individual, and "first president of the United States," which identifies a role that individual played. Regarding models, one can find movies and books that dramatize the period and Washington's presidency. We also have complex mental models of what it is to be a president — the responsibilities, benefits, power, and so on. Regarding arguments, we have plentiful evidence that Washington was indeed the first president, and we can explain how this fact might help us to organize our historical knowledge by providing an anchor point.

Furthermore, as in the case of the screwdriver and the toaster, unless you understand answers to the four design questions, you do not really understand the fact that George Washington was the first president of the United States. If you lack the structure, you lack the fact itself and so of course do not understand it. If you see no purposes for this piece of knowledge, you also lack a kind of understanding, the kind that sees what to do with things. If you lack models of it, including mental models, you will not be able to make the sorts of inferences that are a routine part of understanding something. Finally, if you lack arguments, you do not understand the grounds or motivation for the fact.

To be sure, our understanding of a fact is often shaky in one or more of these respects. But this is only to say that we get along with partial understandings much of the time. The aim of the four design questions is to guide understanding by providing four subcategories of understanding that spell out what it means to understand a design comprehensively. The questions apply to almost any knowledge you might want to understand.

THE CUTTING EDGE: AN EXAMPLE IN DEPTH

The weather signs are encouraging. The design questions offer a guide to understanding designs in general and knowledge in particular. Moreover, the examples already given suggest that often it is rather easy to answer the design questions. This has some importance, because, to help with the giving and getting of knowledge, the design questions should be easy to use in most cases. To double check this point, imagine thinking through the four design questions for such school topics as these:

The organization of the U. S. Senate.
A deceptive practice in advertising.
The organization of a paragraph.
The form of an Italian sonnet.
The rate × time = distance formula.
The heart as a pump.

For most people with a bit of background knowledge, such topics yield up answers to the four design questions handily. In our teacher roles, we might teach such things by way of the four design questions; in our learner roles, we might work through the four questions for ourselves by gleaning information from texts and other sources and applying a little common sense.

There remains the matter of depth. Do the design questions offer a guide to understanding in situations of some subtlety and complexity? A lot hangs on the answer, because, although much that we teach and learn is relatively straightforward, a certain portion is not. Let us put the issue to a test.

Consider, for example, the cutting edge, a design so common and taken for granted that most of us never think about it. Can the design questions provide a framework for presenting the cutting edge in a way that makes the underlying principles clear?

What is the Purpose?

Any kitchen, workshop, barn, or armory presents a study in the diversity of the cutting edge—knives, axes, planes, lathes, chisels, cleavers, razors, sabers, bayonets. And it is not difficult to make the list longer. The cutting edge, with its generic purpose of cutting substances from butter to steel, is one of the basic human inventions. Most animals survive by adapting to their environments. But, to a remarkable extent, human beings survive by adapting their environments to themselves. The cutting edge is one of the basic tools for doing so.

What is the Structure?

Perhaps a knife provides the handiest example of a cutting edge. In an ordinary kitchen knife, one finds the basic structure of this ancient tool. There is not much to it—a chunk of metal smoothly tapered to a sharp edge. The cutting edge presents about as simple a structure as one finds anywhere.

What are some Models?

A visit to your kitchen should provide several.

What is the Argument?

The questions have been easy so far. Evaluative argument, too, would be fairly easy—the conveniences of cutting edges versus their dangers. It is when we turn to explanatory argument and seek the principles behind the cutting edge that the mystery emerges. Why does a cutting edge cut? "Because it's sharp," is the first answer to come to mind. But a little thought shows that this does not give much of an answer. It simply pushes the question one step further back: Why does sharpness foster cutting? In fact, the simple structure of the cutting edge is a little misleading. At least three distinct principles conspire to help the cutting edge to do its job.

The Principle of the Wedge.   First of all, the tapered profile of
a knife blade makes it a kind of wedge. A wedge is a way of amplifying muscle power. Anyone who has driven a nail or a stake with
their wedge-like points has experienced the power amplification the
wedge provides. Imagine what it would be like to drive a nail or a
stake with a blunt tip.

A quick look at the mathematics of the wedge is worthwhile.
Like the lever, another basic tool, the wedge purchases greater
force at the price of distance. Figure 1.2 illustrates how this happens. Suppose you push the wedge four inches to the right with a
certain force. The wedge only spreads whatever it is separating one
inch, because of the taper. But it accomplishes that one inch
spread with four times the force. Notice that this amplification
reflects directly the geometry of the wedge. As in the picture, a
wedge four inches long and one inch wide at the base gives you a
four to one power amplification.

What kind of power amplification do you get from the wedge
shape of a typical knife? This is again just a matter of geometry. It
is not even necessary to employ sophisticated measuring instruments
like micrometers, since you can measure roughly the length and
base of the wedge in a kitchen knife using a memo pad. A quick
application to a small paring knife in my kitchen reveals a taper 47
sheets long and a thickness at the base of 8 sheets. The taper is
about 6 times longer than the base, for a power amplification of 6.

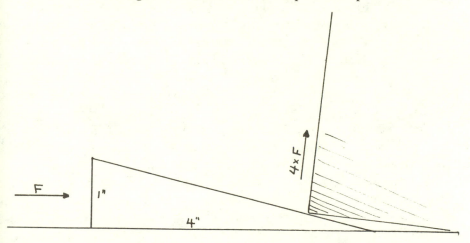

FIG. 1.2.   Amplification of force by a wedge

That probably overestimates the amplification some, since it looks as though the taper is slightly more rapid toward the edge. But we have a rough estimate at any rate.

Concentration of Force. There is another kind of force amplification at work in the cutting edge, as you can illustrate with some ordinary household objects. Press the head of a large nail into your hand with moderate force. The pressure of the flat surface hurts very little. Now do the same with the head of a small nail. Here the pressure of the head may bother a little. Now do the same with the head of a pin. This easily can hurt quite a bit.

The difference cannot reflect the wedge effect, since in all cases you used the flat head rather than the pointed tip. Rather, as you move from large nail to small nail to the head of the pin, the same moderate force becomes applied over a smaller and smaller area — first the area of the large nail head, then the area of the small nail head, and finally the area of the pin head. One might say that the same force was condensed to become more and more intense.

As in the case of the wedge, the mathematics of this is a matter of ratios. This time it is ratios of areas. If the area of the head of the pin is one sixth the area of the nail head, the force will be six times as great throughout that area. Using this principle, you can calculate the amplification achieved by a sharp knife rather than, let us say, a knife with no sharpness at all, a knife as thick at the blade as at the back. The knife considered earlier was 8 sheets thick at the base. Suppose it was 300 sheets long (the length does not matter since it cancels out anyway). Then the area of the unsharpened blade is 300 × 8. The knife looks pretty sharp, so let us guess that the edge of the blade is in fact about 1/2 a sheet thick, for an area of 300 × 1/2. That is 1/16 the area for a power amplification of 16.

Those who have some background in physics will recognize that it is possible to talk about this more precisely. We have been lumping together force and pressure. The proper thing to say is that the force your hand applies to the knife results in a pressure between the cutting edge and the object, pressure measured in pounds per square inch or some other ratio of force per unit area. Naturally, the smaller the area receiving the same force — the sharper, that is, the cutting edge — the higher the pressure.

Scratching. So far, two kinds of force amplification seem to serve the cutting edge — the wedge effect, which works to spread apart forcefully the substance being cut, and the concentration effect, which works to press the edge forcefully against the substance being cut. But everyday experience with knives teaches that these two factors do not explain cutting completely. It is a commonplace that if you simply press a knife against your hand without making any slicing motion, the knife will do no harm.

The missing principle is *scratching*. How scratching helps a seemingly smooth edge to cut can best be understood by considering some related examples. First of all, imagine you are scratching a piece of wood with the tip of a nail. A groove in the surface of the wood results. Notice that the scratching effect depends on having a point and, to some extent, a wedge-shaped point. That is, it depends on the two force amplifiers discussed already. Now imagine how a saw cuts wood. To a first approximation, a saw is a row of nails, all scratching at the surface simultaneously. The saw cuts deeper because there are many points scratching at once.

Two kinds of knives obviously work like this — bread knives and steak knives. Both have visible teeth that scratch their way through substances. In reality, all knives operate this way. The seemingly smooth edge of an ordinary knife is far from smooth on a microscopic scale. Every irregular protrusion on its surface becomes a point that helps the knife to scratch through substance. You can have some confidence in this idea exactly because experience teaches that good cutting requires a slicing motion. There must be a physical reason why that slicing motion helps. The reason, apparently, is that it makes the knife work more like a saw.

Scratching also gives you more control over the knife, which in turn makes cutting easier. If the material is tough, you can press down only a little as you saw back and forth. This means that the microscopic irregularities dig only a little into the material, so the entire force of the back and forth motion of your arm gets concentrated on the limited contact the irregularities make with the material. If the material is not so tough, you can press down more. The microscopic irregularities make much more contact with the material, distributing the force of your back and forth motion more widely and hence getting less force per irregularity; but since the material is not as strong, the less force is enough. You cannot make such adjustments while pushing down alone and not sawing back and forth; you make them by both pushing down with a certain force and sawing back and forth with a certain force to suit the toughness of the material.

In summary, the cutting edge depends on three factors to do its job. (1) the force amplifiers of the wedge and concentration effects operate at the macro level of the knife's tapered sides and thin edge. (2) The same force amplifiers work at the level of the microscopic irregularities along the edge of the knife when a sawing motion is used. (3) The wielder's independent control of downward force and back and forth force allows cutting with little effort materials of very varied strength. This picture of the cutting edge reveals considerable complexity underlying the deceptive simplicity of a tapered shape that, recalling our first answer, "cuts because it's sharp."

It is worth noting that models play a helpful role throughout this account of the cutting edge. To be sure, there was a short separate section labelled models. However, all the informal mental and physical experiments, drawings, and allusions to particular examples from common knowledge and experience involved models as well. Broadly speaking, a *model* is any example or other representation that makes a concept more accessible by rendering it concrete, perceptual and vivid. True, the most typical model is a model of structure, an example that makes the structure vivid. But, as with the discussion of the cutting edge, one can have models that dramatize purpose or argument also.

THE THEORY OF NATURAL SELECTION:
A SECOND EXAMPLE IN DEPTH

The example of the cutting edge tested an issue: Can the design questions help us to get clear about something of some subtlety and complexity? The results seem encouraging. Subtle features of the cutting edge were brought out but in a way that naturally involved principles of physics. Come to think of it, physics can be found at work constantly not just among atoms and planets, but in the everyday world about us, among the knives, tacks, jacks, pans, spoons, shovels, rakes, and chairs. As illustrated, we can easily carry analysis of the physics of ordinary objects to the level of mathematics. How motivating to see physics at work that close to one's hand!

But the analysis of the cutting edge started with a concrete design and worked toward more abstract knowledge by way of argument. Can the design questions help when we begin with a subtle abstraction? We have to test again. As urged already, any theory is a design. Consider Darwin's theory of natural selection. Most people might recall the general purpose of the theory, but the structure, good model cases, and the arguments all are likely to be vague. Perhaps the design questions can pry open this piece of knowledge for our understanding.

What is the Purpose?

Nature presents us with a bewildering variety of life forms ingeniously adapted to their ways of life. There are, for example, bird bills for spearing fish, for crushing seeds, or for sipping nectar from the hearts of flowers. There are spiders that spin webs, that stalk their prey like panthers, even one that casts a web like an entangling net. The problem for science is to offer a causal account of these marvels of adaptation. How did they come to be? Charles Darwin sought to do that job of explanation with his theory of natural selection. His theory, like any theory, is a tool for producing explanations of a certain range of phenomena, and hence a design.

What is a Model Case?

Consider this model case, loosely adapted from an actual event in England. Many years ago, a species of white moths frequented a forested area made up of trees with whitish bark. The moths were not exactly the same color. Some were a little darker, some a little lighter. But no moth had a very dark color and most matched fairly well the color of the bark. Birds living in the forest fed upon the moths, albeit with some difficulty since they were nearly invisible against the bark.

The advent of the industrial revolution upset the situation. The soot from nearby factories began to coat the trees. What happened then will be clearer if we have numbers to stand for the darkness of moths. Let us say that 1 is white, 10 is black, and the numbers between measure increasing greyness.

In the first generation of the factories, the moths ranged in color from 1 to 3. But the tree bark had turned a little darker. The birds that fed upon the moths could see the lighter colored moths more easily against the darker bark, and so ate most of them. So the moths left to breed the next generation were mostly 3's.

You might think that the next generation would all be 3's, like their parents. However, there was a sprawl beyond the parental range. The next generation of moths showed greys 2, 3, and 4. The trees were still getting darker. The birds came and ate mostly the more visible moths of greys 2 and 3, leaving the 4's to breed the next generation.

Again the next generation showed a sprawl relative to the parents. Although most of the parents were 4's, the young moths ranged in color from 3 to 5. Again the birds came, eating mostly the 3's and 4's, and leaving the 5's to breed the next generation.

The pattern should be clear by now. Gradually, the moth population became darker and darker, as the birds gobbled up the lighter members of each generation while the darker members remained to breed the next generation. In the course of a few years, the forest was filled with dark moths — moths about the same color as the sooty trees — when originally there had been no dark moths at all.

What is the Structure?

This model case illustrates three key principles in the structure of the theory of natural selection. First of all, there is *inheritance*. The young moths have more or less the same greyness as their parents. Of course, the principle applies generally to all life: Offspring have more or less the same characteristics as their parents. Secondly, there is *variation*. The offspring of the moths do not always have exactly the same color as the parents, but range somewhat around the parents. In general, the offspring in any species display minor differences from the parents. Finally, there is *selection*. The birds select the lighter colored moths to eat, leaving the darker ones to breed the next generation. In general, it is commonplace in nature that some factor in the environment—a predator, availability of a certain sort of food, temperature, amount of water, and so on—makes a characteristic advantageous for survival and breeding.

What is the Argument?

As with many situations in science, the argument for the theory of natural selection has two sides. On the one hand, does the logic of the theory hold together? In particular, do the key features of inheritance, variation, and selection predict the result—gradual adaptation? On the other hand, does the empirical evidence support the theory? Specifically, do the observations of biologists and paleontologists support the theory of natural selection? The latter calls for a long technical discussion out of place here. Perhaps it will be enough to illustrate knowledge as design if we look only at the former—the logic of Darwin's theory.

The points to be made are two. First, the features of inheritance, variation, and selection are sufficient to explain evolution. That is, taken together, they predict evolution. Second, the theory has no excess baggage: Each feature plays a necessary role in the explanation.

The argument for the first point amounts to a reprise at a general level of the story of the moths. Suppose we have variation of some characteristic. Also, suppose we have selection for more of this characteristic. Then the parents of the next generation will have more of that characteristic, because the other potential parents will not, by a large, survive and breed. Now suppose we have inheritance. Then the parents will pass more of that characteristic on to their offspring. But remember again that we have variation. The offspring will have the desireable characteristic in varying degrees, making way for another round of selection where those that have the characteristic to a lesser degree are less likely to survive and breed. Accordingly, over many generations, an accumulative effect will occur.

As to the lack of excess baggage, it is easy to see why each of the three principles is required. Taking the model case of the moths again, suppose inheritance did not occur. Then, in the first generation, the birds would still eat the whiter moths, leaving the 3's to breed the next generation. However, no inheritance means that the characteristics of the offspring are not constrained by the parents. So the offspring of the 3's would not be mostly 3's, but instead would reflect the demographics of the original population — 1's, 2's, and 3's, with maybe a couple of 4's due to variation but no progress toward a dark population. So inheritance is necessary.

Now suppose that selection did not occur — no birds. Then 1's, 2's, and 3's would all become parents of the next generation. Indeed, the 3's might produce a few 4's along with 2's and 3's as offspring, but again there would be no significant shift toward a dark population. So selection is a necessary part of the process.

Now suppose that variation did not occur. Then the birds would eat most of the 1's and 2's and the darker 3's would breed the next generation. But, without variation, all the offspring would be 3's and their offspring in turn 3's. The population could never get any darker. So variation also is a necessary part of the process.

Quite apart from the empirical evidence for the theory of evolution, these arguments highlight its logical elegance — the three elements of inheritance, selection, and variation sufficient taken together to explain evolution, and each one of them necessary to make the theory work.

KNOWLEDGE AS DESIGN: THE ARGUMENTS

Have you notices that knowledge as design has been used to present itself? In the introduction, the purpose was addressed: teaching and learning for better understanding and critical and creative thinking. Then in this chapter the structure was outlined: the notion of knowledge as design and the design questions about purpose, structure, models, and argument. Numerous model cases have appeared, including the two extended ones about the cutting edge and natural selection. Some arguments for knowledge as design have been mentioned along the way but now a focus on argument is timely. Why specifically should this simple theory of knowledge promote understanding and critical and creative thinking in teaching and learning contexts?

Many reasons come straight out of the discussion so far. Treating knowledge as design treats it as active, to be used, rather than passive, to be stored. Grasp of purpose, structure, model cases, and explanatory and evaluative arguments figures in understanding anything thoroughly by definition. Lacking a sense of these, we do not really and comprehensively understand the thing in question. Moreover, attention to argument can help to identify uncertainty and weed out falsity. In this age of information glut, attention to purpose can help to decide what to learn and what not to learn, what to teach and what not to teach. Knowledge acquired with understanding equips learners to use it more flexibly, modifying it to suit novel applications; knowing a formula without understanding inevitably limits its application to the rituals learned with it.

Knowledge as design and the four design questions highlight the critical and creative thinking behind knowledge, emphasizing knowledge as constructed by human inquiry rather than knowledge as "just there." Moreover, the four design questions provide a framework for teachers and learners doing their own critical thinking about knowledge and creative thinking in making knowledge and products of mind generally. In particular, all four questions and the argument question especially offer a framework that teachers and learners can use for critical analysis. Examples in later chapters show how the design questions can be used as a guide to writing poems, writing essays, designing experiments, and other sorts of creative endeavors. Also, knowledge as design reveals provocative connections between different disciplines by making salient commonalities and contrasts in the kinds of purposes, structures, model cases, and arguments employed.

What about the psychological foundations of knowledge as design? The notion of knowledge as design and the design questions incorporate a number of principles, concepts, and concerns that have emerged in the contemporary psychology of mind. They need to, in order to guide the giving and getting of knowledge. For example, one current theme in the writing of some psychologists is the problem of "inert knowledge"—knowledge at the opposite pole from knowledge creatively applied. Research shows that learners commonly acquire a store of knowledge they can retrieve in quiz situations, but which they do not bring to bear in situations calling for active problem solving. This is a serious problem in medical education, for example, where volumes of anatomy and physiology absorbed by medical students lie inert when they face actual problems of diagnosis and treatment. The emphasis on purpose is just one among several features of knowledge as design that should combat the problem of inert knowledge and foster its creative use.

More generally, the importance of purpose to understanding finds support in studies where understanding hangs on appreciating what something is for and also in the general importance of means-end analysis in human thought, where, for example, a chess player or a solver of problems in mathematics reasons out an approach by considering what moves might serve the goal at hand. As for structure, any number of psychological inquiries have examined the learning of structures in various senses and highlighted their importance. The emphasis on models echoes studies showing that overt models can mediate understanding and that mental models — ways of envisioning a particular concept or situation — play a crucial role in human understanding. As to arguments, a body of psychological research on formal and informal reasoning and its hazards informs the better practice of critical thinking.

For yet another link with psychology, the design questions should abet even the most trivial side of learning, sheer memory. Research on memory has demonstrated repeatedly that organization, imagery, and meaningfulness foster memory. The four design questions provide an organized approach to understanding any design, one that vests the design with meaning through emphasis on its purpose, structure, models, and argument. Models offer visualizations and dramatizations, both providing imagery. While not dwelling on the psychological literature, from time to time in the coming chapters I make reference to it in connection with these themes.

Further argument for knowledge as design turns to education itself and its frustrations. One way to look at the problem focuses on practical and professional knowledge versus school knowledge. From early times, practical knowledge had a design character — purposeful knowledge about what sorts of stones made good cutting edges, what sorts of branches made fine clubs, where water could be found, what seeds would grow, what to make an oar or a sail of, how to build an arch. Today at both everyday and technical levels the same can be said. For the professional mathematician, an established theorem is a tool of inquiry. For the professional scientist, a theory is a tool of explanation. For the professional historian, an historical generalization is a tool for organizing historical events. Of course, the design perspective is largely tacit and unarticulated, an automatic part of how the professional uses technical knowledge and how all of us use our everyday knowledge.

A time arrived in human history when specialized knowledge about nuclear physics, the sonnets of Shakespeare, or ancient Greece was to be given over to nonspecialists, as part of a general education. A problem of packaging occurred: What should the nonspecialist be told? The simplest thing was done—as used to be said on *Dragnet*, "Just the facts, M'am." By and large, knowledge came to be presented as received or given, not much supported by arguments or linked to its purposeful role as an implement of inquiry or other sorts of creative and critical action.

How can we characterize this shortfall more sharply? One might say that our learning often suffers from *disconnected knowledge*— knowledge disconnected from purposes, models, structure, or argument. That is, most learning situations neglect one or another of the design questions. In consequence, we emerge from those situations without a full understanding of the knowledge we have encountered. The perspective of knowledge as design nudges us all, in our varied roles as teachers and learners, to remedy that neglect.

RESTORING CONNECTIONS

Conventional schooling suffers from numerous problems of disconnected knowledge, but it need not. Although conventional schooling only constitutes a part of learning, we do well to consider this special case both because it plays a central role in most people's learning and because its chronic problems of disconnection cry for repair. A number of examples follow.

Connecting to Purpose

Let us look more closely at a piece of information we touched on before: Columbus discovered America in 1492. We all dutifully learn that fact early in our educations. What most of us do not learn are purposes for knowing this and like facts. To put it another way, we learn dates and events as information, but not as design. Too much of instruction in history comes disconnected from the purposes that give history significance as a discipline.

"Purpose" should be taken broadly here to include significance, import, role in integrative theorizing, and the like. A purpose for dates was mentioned earlier: The dates of milestone events in history serve as an organizing framework. What about Columbus's voyage as an event? It can be invested with import in a number of ways, through a number of questions for students to ponder. For example, was Columbus's voyage pivotal historically, or interesting only because it was "the first?" What analogies appear between voyages of discovery then and now? Do we still *have* voyages of discovery? Are there any besides space exploration? How are they different from Columbus's venture, and why? If straightforward physical exploration has fallen prey to an over-explored world, have other forms of exploration — say scientific inquiry — come to take the place of such adventures? And do they really?

Voyages of exploration, seeds of war, the rise and fall of civilizations, key technological innovations, the fate of dynasties, how geography shapes politics, and endless other pages from history and histories are natural food for question-raising, analogy-making, theorizing, and other sorts of venturesome thinking. Lacking this link to inquiry, historical facts become threads without a tapestry. They stand disconnected from the contexts that make them meaningful. Some history instructors and history books take this problem to heart and try to deal with it. But many do not.

Oddly enough, mathematics, the most logical of disciplines, falls prey to problems of disconnection from purpose quite as much as history, the most empirical. Consider, for example, the Pythagorean theorem, which states that the sum of the squares of the two legs of a right triangle equals the square of the hypotenuse. Mathematics instruction routinely presents and proves this theorem. But that same instruction typically leaves the theorem disconnected from its import.

In fact, the Pythagorean theorem is a key design for much of mathematics. To name some connections, without really explaining them, in trigonometry, the theorem underlies crucial trigonometric identities — for example the identity saying that the square of sine X plus the square of cosine X equals one. In analytic geometry, the theorem becomes the basis for defining distance in a two-dimensional Cartesian coordinate system. The distance from point A to point B is the square root of the sums of the squares of the differences in the coordinates of A and B — because those differences form two sides of a right triangle. A generalization of the formula applies when we have not two, but three or more dimensions. Indeed, the n-dimensional formula can be demonstrated by repeated applications of the Pythagorean theorem. All of this in turn contributes to other developments: the vector cross and dot products, for example, the correlation coefficient from statistics, or, from calculus, the formula for integrating to determine the length of a curve.

Of course, mentioning these connections in passing will not make them clear to a person unfamiliar with the mathematics. The problem is to explain in advance the import of the Pythagorean theorem. Because mathematics builds complex edifices out of not so simple bricks, it is a challenge to forecast for learners the edifices the bricks will yield before the bricks themselves are thoroughly familiar. Because this is hard, usually no such effort is made. Abstractions are introduced, the purposes of which only become plain as those abstractions get built into a system they themselves help to define.

Recognizing the reality of the dilemma, however, does not require giving up on it. On the contrary, the premise of the design perspective on knowledge is that mathematics instruction must strive ingeniously, by way of models and analogies perhaps, to anticipate the applications of concepts and theorems. Not to do that leaves too much of mathematical machinery unmotivated for the learner.

Connecting to Models

The laws of Newton provide a classic example of disconnection from models. Contemporary psychological and educational research has shown that even students taking college physics courses maintain entrenched misconceptions about the motion of bodies in space. They have an intuitive physics that mismatches the correct Newtonian one.

Here, for example, is a simple thought problem that gives many people trouble.

> A rocket glides along in free fall at several hundred miles per hour. Wanting to head off in another direction, the pilot rotates the rocket so that it points at right angles to its direction of motion and fires. In what direction will the rocket travel? (See Figure 1.3.)

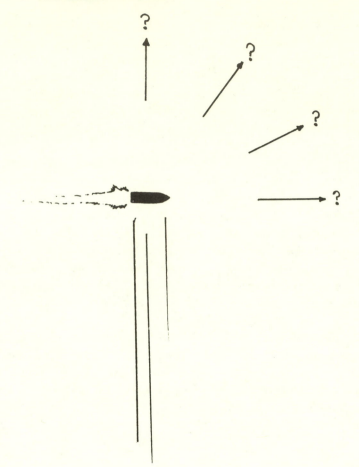

FIG. 1.3. Trajectory of rocket upon firing at right angles to direction of motion?

Many people expect that the rocket will start off at right angles to its original direction of motion, rather like a car turning a corner. But this answer neglects the behavior of objects in free fall. The newly fired rocket indeed accumulates motion at right angles to the original direction. But the original motion is still there too. Where, after all, would it go? The resultant net motion amounts to a compromise between the original direction and a right turn. The rocket goes off at an angle between the two, an angle depending on the intensity and duration of the blast. (See Figure 1.4.)

The answer conflicts with the intuitive physics of many people. The problem lies in part in our ordinary experience of the world. In most motion that we see, frictional forces dominate. For exam-

FIG. 1.4.   Trajectory rocket will follow.

ple, an object certainly does not keep moving in the same direction with the same velocity, as Newton's laws prescribe; because of friction, it simply stops in a few seconds. Velocity "wears out" quickly, so to speak. A life filled with such experiences makes a right angle turn a reasonable prediction, a prediction backed by years of perception. After all, if space were full of friction, the forward motion of the rocket would quickly "wear out," and a blast at right angles would indeed take the rocket off at a right angle, unmodified by the original motion.

Since life misleads us, education must do better. For example, computers can generate better models, an approach that some educators have explored. The students encounter, on the display of a computer, a frictionless world of objects that behave as Newton's laws dictate. The students can try the experiment mentioned earlier, among others. They can turn a rocket at right angles to its path of motion, blast away, and see what happens. One can also present displays where the learner can vary the degree of friction, to see how objects behave differently when friction dominates and when friction plays little or no role. After some experiences with such model cases, the students presumably develop a much better sense of what Newton's laws really imply.

We can also look harder for better models in everyday experience. In sports there are situations aplenty where objects behave in a rather Newtonian way. Suppose, for example, that you are tackling a football player from the side. In what direction will the collision send you and him? If you imagine your way through the event, your experience will answer: off at a diagonal—a compromise between the direction of your tackle, and the direction of his run. Or imagine you are playing basketball. Someone on the opposing team takes a shot at the basket, and you swat the ball from the side. Does the ball fly off perpendicular to your hand? Of course not. It caroms off at an angle.

As here, so in general we can try harder to mine the ordinary world of experience for appropriate models. Whether by rummaging in everyday experience or constructing novel models, the aim is the same: to connect abstract physical principles to concrete experienced manifestations of them, so that the import of the principles will be understood in an intuitive way.

Connecting to Structure

Of the four design questions, the one about structure receives the most attention in conventional schooling. Usually, a teacher of English, mathematics, history, or physics takes some pains to lay out explicitly the concepts being taught. However, there is a situation both within and outside of school where structure often gets neglected: when the teacher provides a model by demonstrating his or her own skill. For instance, artists sometimes teach students by modeling for them the process of painting, sculpting, or throwing a pot. A coach may demonstrate how to work on a trampoline or shoot foul shots. Within the academic disciplines, a math teacher may sometimes demonstrate how to think through a math problem, the English teacher how to think in planning an essay.

Providing demonstrations is a case of modeling, and a powerful instructional move. But sometimes such models come without a concomitant laying out of structure. There is a deep problem of communication here: Many models are ambiguous. When you see them, it is not entirely clear what features of them count the most, unless an accompanying explanation of structure highlights those features. Recall, for instance, the model of the moths, the birds, and the factories for natural selection. Imagine that the description had not singled out and emphasized the principles of selection, inheritance, and variation. The import and generality of the model would have been much less clear.

When models come disconnected from structure, this may signal simple neglect. But it often reflects a genuine difficulty in knowing what structure to present. You can model bicycle riding for your son or daughter, but what do you tell them to make clear the structure of what they should do? Similar problems arise no matter whether the demonstration concerns solving math problems, painting a picture, or some other skilled performance: Often demonstrators do not have good descriptions of performances they can easily display. Their very status as experts aggravates the problem. So far are they from the experience of learners that they often have forgotten which aspects are obvious, which obscure. Moreover, much of their own skill has become automatized so they do not know how they go about the activity in question as well as they did when they were learners.

So the learner gets a model without a good structural description, which may help some, but not as much as a model with structure. To connect to structure, the teacher has to strive toward a simple and telling description of the modeled activity, however little the teacher's own need for such a description.

Connecting to Argument

History as normally taught presents problems not only of disconnection from purpose, but disconnection from argument. How do we *know* that "Columbus sailed the ocean blue in fourteen hundred ninety two?" Because we have been so informed, but not because we have any better grounds for belief than the authority of the textbooks.

The risk is not that the textbooks might be wildly wrong. I suppose that most of the time they are right. Unfortunately, students learn history while not learning much historical reasoning — the patterns of inquiry that historians use to establish what happened and its import. Often an historian must labor mightily through circuitous means to confirm an historical fact, not to mention an historical generalization. Yet the usual way of presenting history conceals the mindwork behind it.

Some might say that there is a good excuse. Perhaps history is too specialized an area of inquiry for students. After all, most students can hardly hope for access to original materials regarding the French revolution or the early development of the steam engine.

However, This doubt identifies history with previous decades and centuries. Suppose instead that a group of students set out to reconstruct what happened at a town meeting two months ago. All the features of historical reasoning come at once to the fore. There is the quest for sources — newspaper accounts, witnesses to the event, perhaps a tape recording or even a videotape of the proceedings, official records, and so on. There is the quest for objectivity. Most witnesses were participants, perhaps participants with axes to grind. What axes? Do the witnesses agree? Do their disagreements follow fault lines of political difference? Then there is the quest for significance. Amidst a maze of minor issues addressed at this town meeting, what ones stand out as important? What general style or bias dominated the meeting? How did the meeting match or mismath the style or bias of past meetings? Do we see innovation, stagnation, retrenchment?

These questions pose challenges ranging from straightforward to very difficult. That, of course, is the point. Relatively recent events provide plentiful opportunities to *do* history. Obviously, none of this means that we should discard traditional history for the sake of historical reasoning, shifting our attention entirely to recent town meetings and neglecting the French revolution. But, for the moment at least, the risk surely lies in the other direction — not making enough of historical reasoning, rather than making too much of it.

Biology is another discipline where argument deserves more attention. Students learn *that* the blood circulates, but not how this became known, in one of the classic breakthrough episodes of medical inquiry. Students learn *that* genes encode the structure of living organisms, but little about the evidence for this bizarre claim that the complexity of a human body and brain lies dormant in a spiral structure of microscopic size.

Yet there is no need to neglect argument. Evidence for phenomena like the circulation of the blood can easily be given. Moreover, it is relatively easy to engage students in biological reasoning. For instance, ecology offers a rich range of occasions for reasoning about the adaptation of organisms.

Here, for example, are three "think" questions in ecology.

1. Why do we find sessile animals (animals that stay attached to surfaces, like mussels or barnacles) in the water, but not on land?
2. Why do terrestrial animals lay far fewer eggs than aquatic animals?
3. With question 2 in mind, consider the case of terrestrial insects: They lay a great many eggs and hence seem an exception to the usual terrestrial strategy. Why?

I will always remember how one individual in a workshop reacted to these questions. As here, the questions were presented as a way to promote reasoning: The participants were asked to think out answers. This particular fellow complained, "But we don't *know* anything about sessile animals! How can we possibly deal with such a question?"

His reaction illustrates a fundamental problem in educational practice. Most educators will agree that sooner or later in the course of instruction students need to learn to reason with what they know. But the usual conception, if anyone would dare to state it baldly, runs like this: "First you learn the facts. Then you learn to reason with them." In contrast, knowledge as design says, "Don't just learn the facts as data. Learn the facts *as* you learn to reason with them." Reasoning is not so locked into prior knowledge of the official facts that one cannot develop both at the same time. The ecology questions demonstrate this point. Everyone brings to such questions considerable general knowledge and common sense.

Take the first question, for example. Why should sessile animals occur in the sea, but not on land? Well, what difficulties would a land animal rooted to the spot encounter? It could not hunt or forage for food. It could only wait. Why should waiting for your dinner be a viable strategy in the sea but not on land? Does your dinner come to you any more readily in one place than the other? Perhaps so. In water, the currents constantly bring food past sessile animals. The buoyancy of water allows water to carry a far greater cargo of food than air does. With door to door delivery of groceries, staying in one place makes sense, so the opportunity arises for some species to enjoy various advantages linked to staying in one place—for instance, heavy protective shells that would not be mobile anyway, or maintaining position in the nourishing soup of tidal areas or silty currents.

These reflections of the lifestyle of sessile animals grow not from any special biological knowledge, but from common sense and common experience. We all know that creatures must eat. We all have some familiarity with the basic properties of a liquid medium. To be sure, a more technical knowledge base would allow deeper and more subtle reasoning. But a good start can be made at one.

A Report Card

As the above examples make plain, the design questions provide a guide to connected knowledge. They remind us to attend to all of the four aspects—purpose, structure, models, and argument—one or more of which we might otherwise omit. This can happen in any context of giving and getting knowledge, formal or informal, private or public. It certainly happens in formal education. Let me underscore this point by presenting a brief report card on the typical handling of a few subject matters in elementary and secondary school—and all too often even at the university level.

Mathematics. Often strong on argument, presuming the arguments are understood. Falters frequently for lack of vivid models. Very explicit on the structure of the content, but often neglects the structure of how to do things—the problem solving process. In serious trouble with purpose, because of a genuine, but partially surmountable, difficulty of describing the later role of concepts and results just being introduced.

History. Often strong on models—specific examples of historical events. Structure is explicitly laid out; often, in fact, there is too much of it to keep track of; it is not organized enough. Weak on connection to purpose. How do various historical events and trends connect to others; what to they imply for modern times? Weak on argument. Students learn little about the justifications for important historical claims and get hardly any practice with historical reasoning.

Biology. Structure is laid out explicitly. Often strong on models, through diagrams, dissections, and so on. Often strong on purpose, through discussion of the functions of various parts and processes. But weak on argument.

Physics. General purpose should be clear — to explain physical phenomena. However, the phenomena to be explained may seem minor matters rather irrelevant to life; students need to feel more vividly how infused life is with the laws of physics. Often strong on structure and argument, through mathematical derivations and the discussion of key experiments. Often weak on models, especially when our intuitive understanding of physical events conflicts with theory. Vivid models are needed to displace our naive concepts.

Literature and Art. Strong on models; students spend most of the time reading or looking at particular worthwhile examples. Mixed on purpose. Sometimes the role of the arts in society and in the lives of individuals is sensitively addressed, sometimes not. Mixed on structure, because of the descriptive and interpretive difficulties works of art often pose. Poor on evaluative argument. Although students encounter critical opinion, they often embrace the position that critical judgment solely reflects idiosyncratic taste. They receive virtually no exposure to the special ins and outs of aesthetic argument.

If your most or least favorite subject matter was left out, it is only because these examples should suffice to make the general point. Report cards like this are earned by nearly any subject one might name. Most subjects as normally taught suffer from significant problems of disconnection within themselves. In addition, instruction rarely deals in connections between the subject matters by way of commonalities or contrasts in purpose, structure, models, or arguments. Consequently, subject matter knowledge means somewhat less than it might and sticks in learners' minds as indifferently as it does.

WHAT YOU CAN DO

Perhaps there is something new in speaking of knowledge as design. But there is nothing new about the four design questions taken separately. Consider purpose, for instance. Many a good teacher takes care to clarify the purpose of a piece of knowledge, and many a learner asks, although not always receiving an answer, "What's it good for?" In our teacher roles we routinely provide structure and often models or arguments. And if we do not, learners often call for them.

The potential of knowledge as design and the design questions comes not from any new slant on knowledge they introduce but by making explicit an old intuitive time-tested slant. While as teachers and learners we sometimes spontaneously treat knowledge as a purposeful structure and pay heed to models and arguments, all too often we do not. Knowledge as design crystallizes our best impulses into explicit method.

What, then, can you do in your role as a teacher or learner? Every chapter of this book addresses that question, so a full answer certainly cannot surface here in the first chapter. However, already the following practices should make sense.

As a learner in a formal or informal setting, you can:

- *Watch out for the problem of disconnected knowledge.* You can test your own understanding of concepts, principles, and so on, with the four design questions. Can you answer them all for the piece of knowledge in question? Moreover, can you think of *new* model cases, to be sure you are not just functioning by rote?

- *Guide your study of a particular piece of knowledge by the design questions, searching out answers to each one.* Sometimes you may discover that your source of knowledge — for instance, a textbook — neglects one or more of them. In that case, you may find answers in other sources or devise your own answers; at worst, you will know where the gaps in your understanding lie.

- *Look to the lessons of ordinary objects,* thinking about the arguments that explain how their structure serves their purpose according to principles of physics, economics, or other disciplines, as in the case of the cutting edge.

- *Ask yourself to be critical and creative about knowledge,* analyzing pieces of knowledge with the design questions, constructing new model cases, and even improving or creating knowledge, guided by the design questions.

In your teacher roles, you can:

- *Watch out for the problem of disconnected knowledge.* You can check your own understanding of what you are teaching by answering the four design questions yourself. You can ensure that your instruction deals with all four.

- *Follow the design questions in presenting a topic,* as was done for the cutting edge and Darwin's theory of natural selection. You can teach whatever you were going to teach anyway, using the framework of the design questions. (By the way, in presenting a piece of knowledge, purpose should come first to establish a frame of reference. Structure or models comes next — whichever seems to serve the need for clarity best in the particular case. Arguments appear either at the end or in alternation with points about structure, because arguments explain and evaluate the structure in relation to its purpose.)

- *Use the design questions with learners of any age down to around four or five.* Of course for young learners you would choose simpler things or concepts, use simpler and shorter explanations, and avoid vocabulary problems. For instance, instead of "purpose," you might say "What's it for?"; instead of "structure," "What's it like — parts, what it's made of, and so on?"; instead of "models," "What's an example?"; instead of "argument," "How is it supposed to work?" and "Does it do a good job?"

- *Use the design questions with learners of almost any ability level.* Knowledge as design is not only or even especially for bright students. It is for anyone in a learning situation.

- *Take advantage of everyday designs to disclose deep principles at work.* The discussion of the cutting edge is an example.

- *Engage your students in design analysis, asking for purpose, structure, model cases, and explanatory and evaluative arguments.* You can pose fairly accessible questions — the analysis of a chair, for example — or more challenging ones — why sessile animals are found in the sea but not on land, for instance.

- *Teach your students the notion of knowledge as design and the design questions, to equip them with this tool of thinking and learning.* The same applies to any other strategies you want to convey. There have been experiments comparing direct instruction in thinking strategies with instruction in which teachers simply tried without comment to model the desired thinking strategies by their own actions and through examples. The first style of instruction gets much better results.

As teacher or learner you can remember this:

- *Apply knowledge as design and the design questions flexibly.* Does a particular point fall under purpose or argument? Sometimes this is ambiguous, so place the point by whim. How do you analyze the structure of a beachball or a referendum? You invent a breakdown into parts or aspects that proves illuminating in the context. Knowledge as design invites generative application, not rigid formulaic use. Accept the invitation!

The examples in this chapter give the flavor of the quest, but each teacher and learner must be his or her own cook. More exploration of the opportunities follows in the chapters to come, along with ways to apply knowledge as design to reading, writing, argument, and other mindful activities. To be sure, a seasoning of realism is crucial. No art of teaching and learning, including knowledge as design, will make the giving and getting of hard knowledge quick and easy. But knowledge as design should make the enterprise more mindful, manageable, and motivating.

2 Design Colored Glasses

In philosophy, there is a concept called *natural kinds*. A natural kind is a category apparent to our perception. Flowers, for example, make a natural kind—they bear an obvious resemblance to one another and not much resemblance to other things. Trees are another natural kind, fish another, stars another.

What about an example of a non-natural kind? Here is the definition of three-year property quoted from the Internal Revenue Service instructions for Form 4562, *Depreciation and Amortization*. Three-year property "includes section 1245 class property that:

- Has a midpoint class life of 4 years or less, or

- Is used for research and experimentation, or

- Is a race horse more than 2 years old when you place it in service, or any other horse that is more than 12 years old when you place it in service."

Usually, when writers want to illustrate what a non-natural kind is, they make one up. But here occurs a natural example of a non-natural kind—several things classed together in a seemingly arbitrary way.

Natural kinds are easier for the mind to deal with than non-natural kinds. One trouble with viewing the world in terms of design—wearing design-colored glasses, so to speak—is that design is not a natural kind. An amazing diversity of things can be seen as designs. Here is a deliberately disparate list:

Screwdrivers	Eyelashes	Microchips
Potato chips	Beethoven's *Fifth*	Ear trumpets
Taste buds	The Dow-Jones	Vectors
Penicillin	*Hamlet*	Saber-toothed tigers
TV sitcoms	Elections	Caesar salads
Puns	The wheel	Epitaphs
Sine waves	Numbers	This list

Despite the diversity, design-colored glasses are worth wearing. But because of the diversity, and a few other factors, one has to learn to see through them. If you are a wearer of real glasses, you know that a new pair takes some getting used to. At first, things blur a bit. As you move your head, the world seems to move too. Seeing clearly through design-colored glasses takes some getting used to as well.

To assist with that, this chapter provides a tour of a few familiar objects and ideas, along with suggestions about how to view them from the perspective of knowledge as design. If you are teaching something, learning something, or just pondering something, the strategies discussed here should help you to think about it in terms of design.

At the same time, the most important strategy of all is: *Be inventive*. As urged in the last chapter, knowledge as design and the design questions should not be viewed as a rigid system that can only apply in one way. To treat knowledge as design in such a manner would be to defeat its generative intent. The design questions allow great flexibility. When it is not at first obvious how to put them to work—for instance, when the strategies outlined below do not help or you do not remember a strategy—*be inventive*. Make up a strategy of your own.

HOW TO RECOGNIZE A DESIGN

Perhaps the broadest question concerns which things are design and which not. It almost seems that *everything* is a design.

Not quite. More insight is gained by distinguishing between *designs* and *nondesigns*. As mentioned in the last chapter, a design refers to a structure adapted to a purpose. A screwdriver has a structure adapted to a purpose—turning screws. A symphony also has a structure adapted to a purpose—engaging the aesthetic attention of an audience. A theorem also has a structure adapted to a purpose—characterizing an important property of a mathematical system.

In contrast, an atom has a structure, but not a structure adapted to a specific purpose. The same can be said for the solar system, with its well-organized array of nine planets in neat elliptical orbits. The weather likewise has a structure, but again not a structure adapted to a particular purpose. In general, natural phenomena lack structures adapted to a purpose. They simply happen. Natural phenomena are *nondesigns*.

A wheel and a foot both have structures adapted to the purpose of transportation. By our definition of design, they are both design. But they differ one from another in a very important way. Human beings invented the wheel, adapting it with intelligence to its purpose. In contrast, no one designed the foot, the structure of which reflects instead a long biological process of natural selection. One can think of the foot as a design but a design without intention.

We can put names to this contrast by speaking of *deliberate designs* versus *natural designs*. Deliberate designs are structures adapted to a purpose by the calculating act of a maker or group or series of makers. Accordingly, deliberate designs include computers, poems, pliers, hairdos, sitcoms, and so on. Natural designs are structures adapted to a purpose by some 'blind' natural process, without the calculated shaping of any group or individual. One such natural process is Darwin's natural selection. Another is social evolution, as, over the course of generations, languages, customs such as how to greet friends or behave toward strangers, and social institutions such as marriage or styles of friendship change to suit better the needs of a culture. (Of course, some biological and social changes are mere nonadaptive drift; moreover, natural designs, like deliberate designs, may be quite imperfect.)

In summary, to tell whether something is a design at all, you can ask, "Does it have a structure adapted to a purpose?" Beyond that, you can distinguish between natural and deliberate designs by asking, "Did the adaptation come about through deliberate planning or a 'blind' natural process?"

Some Objections

Having discovered a three-way distinction between nondesigns, natural designs, and deliberate designs, we should explore the argu-

ments in favor of that distinction and against some other alternatives. Someone might object, "You can call the pattern in a crystal
or the wandering loops of a river seen from the air a design. How
does that fit?" Basically, it does not. In everyday English, people
sometimes call whatever makes a regular visual pattern a design,
regardless of adaptation to purpose. But that really is a different
meaning of the word design. As with other words like *cape* (article
of clothing versus geographic formation) and *saw* (past tense of *see*
versus what you cut wood with), *design* is ambiguous. Wanting just
one of its usual meanings, we have to keep the other out of the
way.

Another reasonable objection runs as follows. "The solar system
is adapted to a purpose in a sense — the purpose of supporting on
its third planet life, including ourselves. So perhaps the solar system
should be considered a design after all." But this position takes
"adapted" in a sense more generous than we really want. Although
the solar system turned out to be an effective life-support system,
nothing in its physical history selectively shaped it toward such a
function. Likewise, atoms are well-suited to be the building blocks
of matter and life itself, but no process selectively shaped them in
that direction. Things or situations that just happen to serve a
function, without any sort of selection or shaping involved, do not
count as being adapted to a purpose or function.

People sometimes also object to treating feet, fins, and so on as
"natural designs." "Since there is no designer," they say, "there
should be no design." This reservation certainly has a point. Really,
natural designs are borderline cases. On the one hand, they lack a
designer. On the other hand they *do* have a structure adapted to a
purpose. The question becomes what to do with the borderline
cases. If we leave them out, the design perspective does not directly
address such things as feet, fins, languages, and customs. So we
miss an opportunity to provide connected knowledge by means of
the design questions. If we count the borderline cases as designs,
the design perspective will include feet, fins, languages and customs. So let us count the borderline cases as designs to make the
design approach more comprehensive. To avoid confusion, we can
make a distinction between *deliberate* designs and *natural* designs.

Finally, someone might object, "So *much* is a design it can't be
very illuminating to look at the world in terms of design. Design-
colored glasses aren't selective enough." This point has merit too.
Indeed, it is not very interesting to go around picking out

designs—"This is. This isn't. This is. This isn't." But wearing design-colored glasses provides insight not merely by sorting out designs from nondesigns, but by going on to apply the design questions, defining purpose, thinking about structure, finding models, and exploring the argument. Looking through design-colored glasses means taking those steps too, the steps by which we understand a design.

(Incidentally, notice that the definitions of nondesigns, natural designs, and deliberate designs were presented by way of the design questions themselves. First came the purpose—to tell whether something was a design or not. Next came structure and models—the actual definitions along with a number of examples. Finally the arguments themselves appeared. Knowledge as design continues to offer a framework for presenting its own details.)

HOW TO DEAL WITH A NONDESIGN

Much of learning directly concerns designs such as governments, theorems, experiments, short stories, and so on. Despite the diversity here, the design questions foster connected knowledge by providing an immediate and unified way to think about such designs. However, people also study nondesigns like atoms, solar systems, and the weather. What should you do, then, to explain the heliocentric theory of the solar system to your son or daughter or class, using the design perspective?

You should *not*, of course, treat the solar system as a design. But you can instead treat claims and theories *about* the solar system as designs. For instance, consider the claim that the earth and the other planets orbit around the sun. What purpose does this claim have? It is designed to organize a plethora of informal and scientific observation about seasons and the movement of the planets against the fixed stars. What structure does the claim have? Here you might want to talk about the nine planets and their distances from the sun. For a more advanced discussion, you might want to talk about their elliptical orbits and Kepler's laws of planetary motion. What arguments support the claim and its elaborations? This calls for reviewing the evidence and contrasting how well that evidence is accounted for by the earth orbiting the sun versus the sun orbiting the earth.

Generalizing from the example, anyone can treat a nondesign like the atom, the solar system, or the weather by treating not *it* but claims *about* it as designs. The most pragmatic argument for this policy is that it allows treating nondesigns like the solar system within the design perspective. "However," someone might object, "isn't the design framework simply too roundabout in such situations? Why not treat the solar system directly, instead of dealing clumsily with claims about the solar system?"

Despite the roundaboutness, focusing on claims offers something in return. It treats knowledge as design, as a construction rather than as a given. It presents "the earth orbits around the sun" not as a simple fact to be learned and understood, but as a proposal about nature, the grounds of which must be examined. Remember: Perceptually, it is not at all evident that the earth orbits the sun. Historically, Copernicus's heliocentric concept of the solar system became a renowned scientific breakthrough. We grow so comfortable in our rote knowledge that the earth orbits around the sun that we forget how unobvious and non-commonsensical a proposal it is.

In general, treating a scientific fact as a claim designed for the purpose of explaining a complex array of phenomena restores to scientific knowledge its tentative, hypothetical character. It provides connected knowledge, highlighting the connection between knowledge and argument. Such a treatment should promote a realistic and useful understanding of the nature of inquiry.

HOW TO COPE WITH AN ABUNDANCE OF DESIGNS

Nondesigns pose one problem; an abundance of designs poses another. Imagine, for instance, that you are addressing the political history of the United States with the help of a large map. What do you treat as the design? Should it be the actual map, with its conventions for depicting borders, rivers, roads, and so on? Should it be the geographic partitioning of the states, an half-deliberate, half-natural design reflecting two century's worth of political jockeying. Should it be the political design implicit in the organization of the states? Or something else yet? The answer, of course, is that it could be any of them, depending on the exact points you want to make. So:

> *Strategy number one: Choose for the design whatever comes closest to the points you want to make.*

But suppose you begin by taking as your design the geographic partitioning of the states. You explore that organization and now want to move on to the United States as a political organization. Now you seem to be stuck with the wrong design after all. So:

> *Strategy number two: Change designs as often as circumstances require, but announce it, so everyone always knows what the design of the moment is.*

Another example

Here is another application of strategies one and two. You are explaining a piece of mathematics, the formula for the sum of this series:

$$1 + 2 + 3 + \cdots + n = n(n+1)/2$$

You want to prove the formula by a method called mathematical induction. Which do you take as the design—the formula or the method of proof?

Strategy one applies: What is your focus? Are you trying to teach about mathematical induction, or are you trying to teach about sums of series? If it is sums of series, the formula is your design; mathematical induction is your method of argument for the design. If your focus is mathematical induction, then that method of argument is your design; the formula and the application of induction to it provide a *model* of induction.

Strategy two applies if you want to do both. You might begin by focusing on the formula. You go through the usual treatment: What is the purpose of this formula? What is its structure? What are some model cases of application? What arguments are there for the formula? Here, you give the inductive argument.

Then you want to shift gears. You say, "This argument is one example of a general method of argument called *mathematical induction*. Let us put aside the formula for a while and focus on the method of argument. What is the general purpose of mathematical induction? What is its general structure? What arguments are there for mathematical induction itself as a valid method of proof?

Multipurpose Designs

Another kind of abundance in designs occurs when the same design has two or more rather different purposes. There are several designs in one, so to speak. For instance, some hats serve for protection either from rain or from sun. Certainly your explanation and evaluation will differ according to the purpose you have in mind, and you might even highlight different features of structure.

The gist of the strategies just discussed applies: Choose the purpose that best represents the point you want to make and announce when and if you switch to discussing another purpose. You may also want to underscore tradeoffs between multiple purposes as part of the intrinsic tension that commonly arises in designs. For instance, the hat heavy enough to protect against rain may be a little hot for ideal sun protection. Just such tradeoffs commonly lead to more specialized designs: one hat for sunny weather, another for rainy. Of course, such specialization involves a tradeoff too: You buy and bother with two hats rather than one.

What argument recommends the tactics discussed? Actually, the argument is all common sense. Strategies 1 and 2 and their extension to multipurpose designs are straightforward tactics for managing a messy situation—take the most important thing first; when you change, be sure that everyone knows it; and, when there are important tradeoffs, discuss them. Someone might complain that all this gets complicated. True, but the complications are not the fault of a design perspective: They are there in the world. Interrelated and multipurpose designs are part of reality; we cannot expect that complexity to go away, but we can treat it systematically.

HOW TO THINK ABOUT EVERYDAY INVENTIONS AS DESIGNS

Does it matter whether you are applying the design perspective to a cutting edge, the theory of natural selection, or the Pythagorean theorem? Yes and no. No, because the same quartet of questions about purpose, models, structure, and argument applies. Yes, because there are some useful tips on how to think about such very different things as everyday inventions, theories, and theorems in terms of their designs.

Consider, for instance, the world of everyday inventions like knives, thimbles, doorknobs, and handkerchiefs. The purposes of such everyday hardware usually pose no mystery, since we use these inventions routinely and know their roles in life. That same familiarity acquaints us with their structure. A good strategy for thoroughness in surveying structure recommends attention to three things: *parts, materials,* and *shapes.* For example, consider an ordinary table fork. What parts can you identify? There is the handle, also the palm-like part of the fork between the handle and the tines, and the tines themselves. What material can you identify? Stainless steel. What shapes can you identify? The tapering shape of the handle, the slightly curved shape of the palm, and the curved, pointed shapes of the tines.

Teaching experience has shown that the headings of parts, materials, and shapes make a useful guide for thinking about the structure of ordinary inventions. Lacking this organization, people leave out a lot. For instance, in the case of the fork, they might comment on the handle and the tines, but not say anything about the palm, the stainless steel, or the shape of the handle. The closer look at structure prompted by attention to these three sorts of attributes pays off for the argument question as well, because each part, material, or shape identified invites evaluative and explanatory arguments.

HOW TO COVER EXPLANATORY AND EVALUATIVE ARGUMENTS

The fourth design question asks after both explanatory and evaluative arguments. Explanatory argument—or just plain explanation—aims not to debate but to explicate. It responds to the question, "Why is this the way it is?" For instance, why the handle? To hold the fork with. Why the palm of the fork? It helps to hold fine-grained food like rice. It also provides a strong base to support the tines. Why the tines? They stick into certain sorts of food to pick it up. They also allow liquids to drain off between them. Why stainless steel? Because it is strong and does not tarnish. Why pointed tines? Because they stick into the food better. Why a tapered handle? Because it fits the hand better. As these examples illustrate, such questions ask about the functions of whatever elements of structure you have identified.

It is generally useful to ask the "why this way" question in a comparative manner—"Why is this the way it is rather than some other way?" For instance, why stainless steel rather than, say, wood? Well, wood is cheaper, but softer, so it would not wear as well. Wood also absorbs liquids and would be harder to clean. Why have several tines rather than a single point? They hold better. Also, food would spin around a single point and hence be harder to handle. Also, the tines together create a cupping effect (remember how they bend upwards). A single tine could not do that. In general, comparison tends to generate insights.

Straightforward explanation poses few problems in familiar cases. Even young children can handle it. For example, I have led my four year old son Tom through simple design reviews of objects like toy cars. He can perfectly well answer "why this way" questions like these. Why does the car have a roof? *To keep the rain out.* Why does the car have windows? *So you can see to drive.* Why does the car have wheels? *So the car will go.*

Evaluative argument concerns less how the design is meant to work and more whether it works well. For instance, what advantages and disadvantages does an ordinary table fork have? It spears food better than knives and spoons do. You can cut with the edge of a fork better than with a spoon, but worse than with a knife. A fork cuts well enough for soft foods. The tines of a fork present more danger than spoons, perhaps more than table knives, which usually are quite dull. And so on.

If you want a thorough evaluation, there are tactics to make sure that the ground gets covered. One tactic turns back to whatever analysis of structure you have made. You can assess every single element of that structure. Another complementary strategy for thoroughness is to make a list of standards suited to the sort of design in question. For concrete designs such as forks or tires, the following list works well:

1. Gives good results
2. Easy to use
3. Safe
4. Durable
5. Attractive
6. Comfortable
7. Reasonable cost

For instance, you might ask whether the fork delivers food to the mouth effectively (gives good results), handles easily (easy to use), has tines not too sharp (safe), does not bend or rust readily (durable), has a pleasant appearance (attractive), balances well in the hand (comfortable), and comes at a good price for forks (reasonable cost). A different sort of object invites different interpretations of the criteria. For a tire, you could ask whether the tire does its basic job of keeping the car rolling (gives good results), goes off and on readily (easy to use), does not blow out or skid (safe), lasts a long time (durable), presents neat whitewalls (attractive), gives a cushioned ride (comfortable), and comes at a good price for tires (reasonable cost).

Sometimes the contrast between explanatory and evaluative remarks seems slight. Suppose you say, "The handle of the fork allows holding it easily." This explains the function of the handle, which is explanation, but also praises the handle for serving well, which is evaluation. So which is it? The fact is that mildly evaluative sentences like this one might appear in either sort of argument. The difference lies in the nature of the whole activity. As mentioned already, explanatory argument aims at explanation of the elements of structure, and stating what the elements contribute often involves mildly evaluative positive comments. In contrast, evaluative argument focuses on assessment, with strong pro or con comments throughout. So look to the aim of the whole argument, not to any particular sentence.

Taking It Further

So far in this section, explanatory argument seems quite simple. However, one can go on to make what might be called a *deep explanatory argument*. Deep explanation seeks to understand a design in terms of basic underlying principles. For instance, the discussion of the cutting edge in Chapter 1 referred to basic principles of physics such as the wedge.

Much the same can be done with the fork. Why, for example, does a fork have pointed tines? Both of the principles of force amplification discussed in the first chapter apply—the wedge effect and the force concentration effect (pressure). Why does a fork have four tines rather than one? To offer greater holding power by providing more surfaces that create friction with the piece of food you have speared. Also, one tine would allow the food to spin. A basic principle of geometry enters here: Two points determine a line. As a special case, at least two tines on a fork (and you do sometimes see only two on cooking forks) prevent objects from spinning.

These examples do not mean that fundamental principles always suggest themselves readily or illuminate the design in question. For instance, why does the handle of a fork taper? As noted earlier, to fit the hand better. But what fundamental principle of physics or anything else explains "fitting better?" One might do something with the concept of congruence from geometry, but it seems a bit forced. For another example where fundamental principles fall flat, why does a fork have curved tines? At the surface level, to better cup food, of course. For an underlying principle from physics, you might say, "To create a potential well." But then you have to explain the concept of a potential well. Moreover, whereas a spoon has a garden variety potential well, the fork has an odd one — front and back but no sides. That is, a fork curls upward front and back, but not to the sides. So you need to say even more to explain just what sort of a potential well a fork has. It may not be worth the trouble.

On the other hand, a search for basic principles can yield some surprising insights, especially after a person has accumulated a repertoire of basic principles to think with. For instance, my eleven year old son surprised me one day when, after talking about things like forks, we got to discussing a fan. "Why does a fan blade push the air," was one of my questions. "Because," suggested Ted, "it works like a wedge." What a surprising idea! But of course he was right. The same principle that wedges wood apart when you drive a nail wedges air forward when you turn on a fan. And science makes more sense when youngsters realize that such principles are at work constantly in the most mundane circumstances, holding together the daily life we take so much for granted.

We reviewed three kinds of arguments — explanatory, evaluative, and deep explanatory. All three types are of course themselves designs suited to certain purposes. It is fair to ask: "What are the arguments for these types of arguments?" That is, why should these types of arguments serve especially well?

The basic advantages of (surface) explanatory and evaluative arguments are simplicity and accessibility. Even young children can grasp the point and method of such arguments in simple cases. Yet, such arguments have immense practical importance. Common sense explanatory and evaluative arguments underlie everyday decision making and design activities, for instance deciding what to serve to guests this Sunday and designing in your mind what sort of house you would like to live in and then, shopping in the real market, deciding whether particular houses come close enough.

The basic weakness of the two is that they do not cut very deeply. They do not lead the thinker into an encounter with fundamental principles. So we make deep explanatory arguments, too. Our knowledge includes general principles, in the case of mechanics, basic concepts such as the wedge or the lever. Also, sometimes we can discern basic principles simply by generalizing from one or more particular designs. Explanation can be sought in terms of these fundamentals. The power of abstraction and generality is the reward, while the price is that deeper digging is harder digging. In teaching and learning situations, one needs to choose what kinds of argument to use according to the requirements of the situation.

HOW TO THINK ABOUT PROCEDURES AS DESIGNS

Civilization depends not only on things but on procedures as well. To be sure, clocks, calculators, and computers enable us in many ways. But the technology would do nothing without the procedures to use it and keep it in repair. For instance, besides the clock there is the procedure for reading it, and not an easy procedure to learn if you remember the difficulties youngsters have. Calculators relieve us of hand arithmetic, but you have to learn how to use the calculator itself.

As structures adapted to purposes, procedures are, of course, designs. If you are teaching, learning, or simply thinking about a procedure, you can look at it through design-colored glasses. The purposes of familiar procedures we know from experience. For unfamiliar procedures, of course, it is important to make the purpose plain if you are explaining the procedure. Just as with any design, a procedure loses meaning when disconnected from its purpose. Many rote procedures taught in schools seem arbitrary or pointless because the instruction has not richly enough filled in and fleshed out the purpose.

What about the structures of procedures? Remember that for everyday inventions, examining parts, materials, and shapes fostered thoroughness. Procedures do not have materials and shapes, but they do have parts—the steps to be followed. Basically, procedures are made out of steps. Some procedures simply proceed step by step from beginning to end. Others jump around in complex ways.

Computer programs are a special case of procedures, where the programmer spells out in a formal language exactly what steps the machine must follow. Computer programs often include sequences of steps that are repeated until some condition is met; these are called loops. Computer programs also often include steps that direct the computer to go on to one sequence of steps under one condition, and another under another. These are called conditional branches.

As just mentioned, some everyday procedures jump around in complex ways. Loops and conditional branches arise routinely not just in computer programs but in everyday procedures also. For instance, you sort the laundry until the basket is empty—a simple loop. You go directly to the phone, turn to your address book, or get out the telephone book according to whether you know the number by heart, have it noted down, or need to look it up—a simple conditional branch.

Looking at a Procedure: Supermarket Shopping

Of course, most everyday procedures are not as explicit as computer programs. When looking at them through design-colored glasses, we can make a detailed description with many steps or a sketchier one with fewer more inclusive steps, depending on our aims and interests. What is it like to describe an everyday procedure in middling detail? Take a procedure we all have model experiences of, shopping in a supermarket. Perhaps the following steps lay out the basic structure pretty well.

1. You tour the aisles until you have selected all you want.
2. You take your groceries to a short check-out line.
3. You wait in line until you get to the clerk.
4. The clerk totals up your purchases.
5. The clerk presents you with the bill.
6. You pay the bill.
7. The clerk or a bagger bags your groceries.
8. You take your groceries away.

The shopping procedure turns out to be a fairly simple sequence of steps. However, there are hints here and there of loops. For instance, "You tour the aisles until you have selected all you want" is a loop expressed in a single step. "You wait in line until you get to the clerk" is another one.

For this everyday example, explanatory argument may seem dull: "Why do you tour the aisles? To select your groceries." However, it gets more interesting and yields more insight if you adopt a strategy of comparisons. For example, you can ask, "Why tour the aisles for your groceries *instead* of having someone get them for you?" This leads to an interesting range of cases. A clerk usually assembles your purchase in a fish market or a meat market. Why do super-markets handle the matter differently? In part, because they want to save on labor. In part, because a customer should not be handling directly meat and fish that might eventually be purchased by another — and indeed supermarkets often have special sections where meat and fish are packaged to your individual order. Clerks in the prescription section of drugstores also assemble orders. Here the reason is different: Handling restricted substances, they cannot very well let customers help themselves. Such comparisons highlight the diverse adaptations of procedures in different commercial settings to their special circumstances.

As to evaluative argument, it is easy to list positive and negative features of the supermarket shopping procedure. You have little clerical help. Balancing that, you have a very large selection, something that would be impossible if clerks had to run around fetching everything for everyone. From the supermarket owner's perspective, your tour of the store has the advantage of fostering impulse buying. That may be a negative feature for you, or you may enjoy it. Waiting in line to pay is a nuisance. But at least most supermarkets have express lines for people who are only buying a little. And so on.

Deep explanation also deserves attention. What basic principles underlie the design of the supermarket shopping procedure and account for its smooth effective functioning? Certainly one is the principle of the queue, a fundamental human invention for delivering a service in a fair and orderly manner. There is a whole mathematical theory about various designs for queues and their relative efficiencies. Money contributes another strand to the fabric. Money, of course, is a design for facilitating trade. It works here, as throughout virtually any contemporary civilization, to make the transfer of goods an efficient and orderly process.

Another more particular premise behind the design of a supermarket is what you might call the "self-service principle." The organization of a supermarket has the customer doing most of the work, with services that have to be delivered by the personnel concentrated at a limited number of stations. Supermarkets contrast with more traditional markets, and, as noted earlier, meat markets and fish markets, in their dedication to the self-service principle. Are there other cases of self-service and non-self-service versions of the same basic enterprise? Yes. Examples include cafeterias versus restaurants, self-service versus regular gasoline stations, and libraries where you browse through the aisles versus libraries where you request a book by the catalog number.

These three are mentioned only as a sample. The everyday procedure of shopping in a supermarket depends on a host of subtle and clever principles made invisible by familiarity. Quotidian though it is, we do not understand the procedure of shopping in a supermarket in a fully connected way. To be sure, shopping in a supermarket may be a procedure of only passing interest. But the underlying principles such as queues, a medium of exchange, and even the more specific self-service style, show up so often in such a diversity of contexts that they bear real significance.

HOW TO THINK ABOUT A FORMAL PROCEDURE

Like everyday life, schooling is full of procedures. Some of these are formal knowledge that students must learn, for example, the algorithms of arithmetic. Long division is an interesting case in point, because it is not so readily understood.

The purpose of long division is familiar enough: to calculate the quotient of two large numbers.

The structure of long division is best approached by a model case, worked step by step. We want to divide 4127 by 23. The usual steps look like this.

$$
\begin{array}{llll}
\text{a.} & 23\overline{)4127}^{\,1} & \text{b.} & 23\overline{)4127}^{\,1} \\
& & & 23
\end{array}
$$

a. $\dfrac{1}{23\,)\,4127}$

b. $\begin{array}{r} 1 \\ 23\,)\,\overline{4127} \\ 23 \end{array}$

c. $\begin{array}{r} 1 \\ 23\,)\,\overline{4127} \\ \underline{23} \\ 18 \end{array}$

d. $\begin{array}{r} 1 \\ 23\,)\,\overline{4127} \\ \underline{23} \\ 182 \end{array}$

e. $\begin{array}{r} 17 \\ 23\,)\,\overline{4127} \\ \underline{23} \\ 182 \end{array}$

f. $\begin{array}{r} 17 \\ 23\,)\,\overline{4127} \\ \underline{23} \\ 182 \\ 161 \end{array}$

g. $\begin{array}{r} 17 \\ 23\,)\,\overline{4127} \\ \underline{23} \\ 182 \\ \underline{161} \\ 21 \end{array}$

h. $\begin{array}{r} 17 \\ 23\,)\,\overline{4127} \\ \underline{23} \\ 182 \\ \underline{161} \\ 217 \end{array}$

i. $\begin{array}{r} 179 \\ 23\,)\,\overline{4127} \\ \underline{23} \\ 182 \\ \underline{161} \\ 217 \end{array}$

j. $\begin{array}{r} 179 \\ 23\,)\,\overline{4127} \\ \underline{23} \\ 182 \\ \underline{161} \\ 217 \\ 207 \end{array}$

k. $\begin{array}{r} 179 \\ 23\,)\,\overline{4127} \\ \underline{23} \\ 182 \\ \underline{161} \\ 217 \\ \underline{207} \\ 10 \end{array}$

Putting it into words, at (a), you figure out the first digit of the answer; (b) you multiply times the divisor, writing the answer underneath; (c) you subtract; (d) you bring down the next digit from the dividend; (e) you figure out the next digit of the answer;

(f) you multiply times the divisor, writing the answer underneath; (g) you subtract; (h) you bring down the next digit from the dividend. And so on.

The example also illustrates the broader structural elements of the long division algorithm. In the first row, a b c d, you get started. The second row, e f g h, demonstrates the basic loop of long division, the loop that you repeat over and over, continuing to figure out the next digit of the answer, multiply, subtract, and bring down the next digit of the dividend. The last row, i j k, shows what happens at the end—you run out of digits to bring down and so you are finished.

The question remains, why does this ritual work? We need explanatory arguments for the various steps in the ritual.

Those arguments are best approached by way of another model, a variant way of dividing designed to flesh out and illuminate the normal process of long division. For a start, the connection between division and subtraction is worth remembering. "What is the result when we divide 4127 by 23?" simply means "How many times can we subtract 23 away from 4127?" Let us begin with a one digit approximation. We can subtract 23 from 4127 about 100 times. How much does that leave left over? We can figure it out as follows. We find we have 1827 left over.

$$
\begin{array}{llll}
& \quad\ \ \overline{100} & \quad\ \ \overline{100} & \quad\ \ \overline{100} & \quad\ \ \overline{100} \\
\text{A.} \ 23\overline{)\,4127} & \text{B.} \ 23\overline{)\,4127} & \text{C.} \ 23\overline{)\,4127} & \text{D.} \ 23\overline{)\,4127} \\
& \qquad 2300 & \qquad \underline{2300} & \qquad \underline{2300}
\end{array}
$$

beginning to subtract (saving the easy 0's):   18   left over: 1827

Now we have to estimate how many *more* 23's we can subtract off from the 1827 that is now left over. Again, let us make a one-digit approximation—about 70. How much is left over this time? We can figure that out as follows. We find out that 217 is left over.

$$
\begin{array}{llll}
& \quad\ \ \overline{70} & \quad\ \ \overline{70} & \quad\ \ \overline{70} & \quad\ \ \overline{70} \\
\text{E.} \ 23\overline{)\,1827} & \text{F.} \ 23\overline{)\,1827} & \text{G.} \ 23\overline{)\,1827} & \text{H.} \ 23\overline{)\,1827} \\
& \qquad 1610 & \qquad \underline{1610} & \qquad \underline{1610}
\end{array}
$$

beginning to subtract (saving the easy 0):   21   left over: 217

Now we have to estimate how many more 23's we can subtract off from the 217 that is now left over. We see that there are about 9, and need to find out again what is left over, as follows.

$$
\begin{array}{lll}
& \quad\ \ \overline{9} & \quad\ \ \overline{9} & \quad\ \ \overline{9} \\
\text{I.} \ 23\overline{)\,217} & \text{J.} \ 23\overline{)\,217} & \text{K.} \ 23\overline{)\,217} \\
& \qquad 207 & \qquad \underline{207} \\
& & \qquad \overline{10}
\end{array}
$$

Finally we have 10 left over. Since we cannot subtract away any more 23's, we are ready to total up. On the first round, we subtracted off 100 23's from 4127. On the second round, we subtracted off 70 more from what was left over. On the third round, we subtracted off 9 more from what was left over. Because each time we only made a one digit approximation, 100, 70, and then 9, the numbers turn out to be easy to add up—179. We still have 10 left over, which we call the remainder.

Of course, the steps of this procedure correspond to the steps of the usual procedure. This procedure amounts to an expanded version of the usual procedure, hence the capital letter labels A, B, C, instead of a, b, c. By looking at the expanded procedure, we can see the usual procedure as a streamlined way of finding out how many 23's can be subtracted away from 4127.

We can even go through the usual procedure reminding ourselves of the streamlining. It would sound like this. At (a) let us figure out about how many 23's go into 4127—about 100, but no point in writing 0's, so we will just write 1 in the third place. At (b), let us begin to figure out how much is left over; but again, no point in fiddling with 0's, so we will leave them out. At (c) we subtract off the 23 from 41, keeping in mind it is really 2300 from 4127. At (d), we start to fill in the other two digits of the subtraction—the 27. But then we decide not to bother with it all. Instead of 1827 left over, 1820 is close enough. And no point in writing 0's, so we will just deal with 182, but positioned one place leftward so we do not lose track of the place position. And so on.

Thus the expanded procedure illuminates one of the particularly obscure steps in the normal algorithm—"bringing down." Bringing down the next digit turns out to be a straightforward subtraction obscured by the facts that the leftward digits are subtracted first (step c) and, when the subtraction is carried further (step d), the rightward digits are dropped, settling for a temporary approximation that is good enough.

There is more to be explained here, of course. For instance, why is it safe to make the approximation and take 1820 instead of 1827? That question will be left as an exercise; Can you show that dropping the rightmost digits upon bringing down will never lead to a different answer? At any rate, this much should be enough of a sketch to allow us to see the usual division algorithm as a streamlined version of a much more understandable process.

This point leads naturally into an evaluative argument. The usual division algorithm is a perfect example of a tradeoff. You gain one thing, but you lose another. You gain efficiency by suppressing zeros and some other tricks. But you lose a clear sense of why you are doing each step. Obviously, the usual division algorithm suits the purpose of hand computation well. But it does not provide connected knowledge, failing to make clear the basis of the computational procedure. To do so, one needs to expose the usual division algorithm for what it is—a clear but cumbersome design re-designed for efficiency at the cost of clarity.

HOW TO THINK ABOUT CLAIMS AS DESIGNS

Claims are simply statements that such and such is the case. Although we do not ordinarily think of claims as designs, they are one of the most important sorts of designs that we have. We embody ideas from the most trivial to the most precious in the form of claims we advance to others or even just to ourselves. Civilization in its diverse aspects rests upon claims religious, historical, political, scientific, ethical, contractual, and so on. Yet to see a claim as something not so remote from such handware as a screwdriver or a pencil may seem to be a difficult squint through design-colored glasses. Certainly, the view of claims as designs needs some explaining.

The purpose or purposes of a claim vary quite a bit with the kind of claim. A scientific theory has the purpose of explaining and predicting a certain range of phenomena. The theory of evolution, for instance, aims to explain and predict biological adaptation. In contrast, a mathematical theorem aims to state concisely a mathematical claim of import in some larger system or range of application. The Pythagorean theorem, for example, asserts a relationship between the sides of right triangles with import for trigonometry and for the use of Cartesian coordinate systems, among other things.

The diverse claims found helter-skelter in newspapers, magazines, lectures, and even casual conversations serve a whole range of purposes, some more and some less explicit and focused. Advertising claims, for example, serve the purpose of getting people to buy products and services. Claims about the efficacy of one or another social policy characteristically serve the purpose of recommending for or against it. Historical claims about Vietnam may aim at drawing parallels with other past or contemporary situations, and may well serve to warn against similar political entanglements. A neighbor's claim about the activities of the neighbor one house further on may serve no purpose other than idle entertainment.

In general, the purpose of a claim is its import or significance, the aim with which the claim was mentioned in the first place. Often, of course, no one states the purpose of a claim; you have to figure it out from context.

It is important to look hard for the purpose of a claim exactly because we tend to get distracted by the truth of the claim. As urged in the introduction, education tends toward "truth mongering," working hard to impart truths but not so hard to impart significances. To recall an example, the math teacher or text rarely attempts to recount in advance how a newly introduced theorem will play a part in a larger mathematical structure or development. History instruction seldom emphasizes the far-reaching import of historical facts. In the words of the last chapter, much of the content of education comes disconnected from purpose.

In considering the structure of claims, we do well to remember that here, as always, there is no universal law about how to analyze the structure of something: One chooses an analysis illuminating for the case at hand. Some claims divide naturally into subclaims. For instance, Darwin's theory of natural selection included subclaims about inheritance, variation, and selection pressure. Some claims depend on concepts that should be separated out from one another for clarity. Some claims involve a generalization fleshed out with details. Each detail can be considered a piece of the claim, elaborating its structure. In general, look for a meaningful illuminating decomposition into parts or aspects of some sort. If the claim is so straightforward that you cannot find an *illuminating* breakdown into parts or aspects, you can simply skip it and take the claim whole, as one unitary structure.

How can we investigate the explanatory and evaluative arguments behind claims? Broadly speaking, explanatory arguments can be handled much as before. In evaluation, however, there is an interesting distinction to be drawn. It is worthwhile to examine both *truth* and *relevance*. For instance, in the case of the Pythagorean theorem, you can argue for the truth of the theorem, starting from the axioms of Euclidean geometry. At the same time, you can argue for the relevance of the theorem to trigonometry and analytic geometry. In the case of "Columbus discovered America in 1492," you can argue for the truth of the historical claim. Also, you can argue for the relevance of the historical claim in organizing our perception of history. (Or perhaps you find it serves that role poorly; then you would want to argue against, rather than for, its relevance.)

In the case of an advertising claim, you can consider arguments regarding the truth of the claim and also arguments regarding the relevance of the claim to selling the product. As with many designs, you can gain more understanding by pondering alternative designs, alternative advertising claims here, and comparing them on truth and relevance. In the case of Darwin's theory of natural selection, you can argue whether or not in empirical fact natural selection gives a true account of evolution. But also, you can argue whether it is relevant logically to explaining evolution. That is, *would it* explain evolution, given appropriate empirical evidence? That was the sort of argument about evolution given in Chapter 1. No empirical evidence about the theory was reviewed, but simply its logic, showing that its key premises of inheritance, variation, and selection indeed could explain evolution. Again, as with advertising campaigns, you can contrast Darwin's theory with competing theories for a comparative appraisal of truth and relevance.

What recommends considering arguments about both the truth and relevance of a claim? For one thing, the need to build a bridge between the structure and the purpose of a claim. The fit of a claim with its purpose always involves more than a question of truth. Even if true, does the claim have the scope, pertinence, bearing, reach, power, or whatever else it might need to do its assigned job? Another reason to consider both recognizes that truth plays a varying role in the overall effectiveness of a claim. Sometimes truth is essential. For instance, a scientific theory logically relevant to explaining a certain phenomenon but shown to be false by experimentation does not do its job. Sometimes truth does not count for much. If an advertising claim proves relevant to selling a product, the truth of the claim may hardly matter at all to the vendor, assuming the vendor can evade the laws about truth in advertising. Of course, from the perspective of the buyer truth does count: The buyer is well-served by advertising claims that are true and informative.

HOW TO THINK ABOUT FAMILIES OF DESIGNS

So far, looking at the world through design-colored glasses has meant looking at it design by design. There are times when a panorama serves better—thinking in terms of *families* of designs. To put it another way, you can understand a design better by seeking connections not only to its own purpose, structure, models, and argument, but to relatives of the design as well.

Consider a model case, fasteners. Fasteners are objects with a common purpose—fastening. Members of the fastener family come easily to mind: tacks, nails, string, hooks, glue, paperclips, screws, adhesive tape, latches, locks, pins, thread, buttons, belts, zippers, shoelaces, and so on. Besides listing contemporary members of the fastener family, it is interesting to name ancestors such as grass ropes, leather thongs, or wooden pegs.

All fasteners share the general purpose of fastening, but each serves a particular variation of that general purpose and displays an appropriately adapted structure. A tack, for example, has a large head and a short point; it is designed to fasten lightly and temporarily, and to be driven with the thumb. Its style is the quick fix. A nail, in contrast, has a small head and a long shaft; it is designed to hold permanently and, needing to penetrate deeper, has to be driven with a hammer. A tack and nail are close kin, despite these differences. Glue comes from another branch of the family altogether. Like the nail, glue generally aims at permanence. Unlike the nail and the tack, glue depends for its effect on adhesion rather than penetration and friction.

In referring to adhesion versus penetration, we approach deep principled argument. As with the cutting edge, we begin to ask, "What physical principles underlie and guarantee the success of this design?" In fact, it is interesting to try to lay out the principles behind fasteners. Although fasteners come in an incredible diversity, there do not seem to be many basic principles. Here are some:

Adhesion: A sticky substance, which may or may not dry, does the fastening, as in glue or adhesive tape.
Penetration: A fastener penetrates the things being fastened, as with a bolt or nail.
Friction: Friction, usually increased by a tight fit, keeps something in place, as with a nail or screw.
Squeezing: Something is held tight by forces from one side and the other, as with a clothespin or tightened nut and bolt.
Encircling: The fastener wraps around whatever it fastens, like a string or an elastic.

Some fasteners apply several of these principles at once. For instance, a nut and bolt penetrates. Friction keeps the nut from spinning loose once you tighten it. When tightened, the nut and bolt squeeze what they clamp between them. Other fasteners, like glue, exercise only one principle. The following table lists several common fasteners, showing what principles they use.

Fasteners							
		nut &		safety		Scotch	paper	rubber
Principle	screw	bolt	tack	pin	pin	tape	clip	band
Adhesion						X		
Penetration	X	X	X	X	X			
Friction	X	X	X		X		X	X
Squeezing		X					X	X
Encircling				X				X

There are at least two other less common fastening principles. Can you think of one?

In general, it is often illuminating to look at a family of designs rather than just a single design. One can list ancestors and contemporary members of the family. The design questions about purpose, structure, models, and argument can be applied to investigate the similarities and differences among the fasteners. When a systematic look seems worthwhile, one can use tables to lay out comparisons.

With these strategies for exploring families of designs in mind, what are the arguments for them? Why, for example, might you want to examine the "ancestors" of contemporary designs? Because a look at the ancestors gives a sense of perspective on the accomplishments of civilization. Why might you want to compare and contrast the purpose, structure, and arguments of contemporary members of the same family? Because the similarities and differences highlight the elaborate and fine-tuned technologies we have developed. For another reason, comparison and contrast lead toward the recognition of abstract principles, such as basic methods of fastening. Why use tabulations? To lay out in an organized manner complex relations in a family of designs. Why do all this in the first place? Because the result is a more encompassing and integrative understanding of the family of designs in question. No great subtlety in these arguments. It's all common sense.

HOW TO THINK ABOUT A FAMILY OF PROCEDURES

Just as you can have families of everyday inventions like fasteners, so you can find families of procedures or claims. In fact, theorems or scientific theories are two very general families of claims with considerable importance. Since these families of claims have been discussed at least in passing, let us look at a family of procedures.

Consider the family of procedures for sharing resources. The general purpose of such designs is to allow many people the use of the same resource. Examples abound: libraries, roads, parks, public drinking fountains, rental cars, public beaches, and so on. At first it may seem odd to think of renting a car or borrowing from a library as a design. But these procedures are structures adapted to a purpose. In fact, procedures for sharing resources are ingenious and important designs for the smooth functioning of a complex civilization.

With a little thought, you can begin to see some of the structural features that mark out different kinds of resource sharing. One important distinction is *use on site* versus taking away. We use on site a beach, a zoo, a drinking fountain, a computer. We take away a rented car or a borrowed book. Another contrast concerns arrangements for a *fee* versus *no fee*. We pay a fee for the use of apartments, rented cars, turnpikes. We pay none (directly) for schools, libraries, parks.

Yet another distinction concerns formal *sign-up* or *sign-out* arrangements versus simply using the resource *anonymously*. We sign out library books and rental cars, sign up for the use of an auditorium or reserved seat at a concert. In contrast, we use roads, parks, and zoos anonymously.

With these three contrasts in mind, it is interesting to ask which of all the logically possible combinations occur. Is the universe of possibilities thickly or thinly populated? We can explore that question by laying out the possible combinations and seeking examples of each:

On site examples
    Sign-up examples
        With fee: Renting an apartment, concert hall, studio, reserved seats.
        No fee: reserve books in a library, music rooms at a university.
    No sign-up examples
        With fee: attending a concert, zoo with admission, skating rink, circus.
        No fee: park, free zoo, free concert, public roads, drinking fountains.
Off site examples
    Sign-up examples
        With fee: renting a car, boat, chain saw, bus, typewriter.
        No fee: Borrowing from a library, record library, pool of athletic equipment.
    No sign-up examples
        With fee: rare or none, because of risk of loss or theft.
        No fee: informal borrowing of book, tool from acquaintance.

As the chart shows, ways to share resources came in almost all varieties possible. Only one combination suggests no immediate examples — off site use, with fee, and no sign-up. Being an arrangement for a fee, such a loan normally would occur between strangers. The lack of a sign-up makes the risk of loss to or theft by a stranger too great.

Having examined the comparative structure of some different strategies for sharing resources, we should take a brief look at the arguments for such strategies. In broadest terms, the same argument applies to all. When any one person only gives limited use to a resource, it makes no sense for that person to maintain the resource for himself or herself alone. A more careful look discloses that each of the three dimensions mentioned above — on site versus off site use, fee or not, and sign-up or not — has its own particular purposes and arguments.

For example, on site use is often explained by resources impossible or inconvenient to transport, like apartments or recording studios. Here the argument is physical necessity. On site use also often reflects valuable portable resources, such as rare books. Here caution provides the argument; such resources need protection against loss or theft.

Fees have the purpose of paying for the resource and, frequently, making a profit. In private enterprise, both purposes are always served, the argument being, "Otherwise, why bother to offer the resource at all?" When a government makes the resource available, whether and what fee should be charged always can be argued in two directions. Relevant questions include: Is it practical to collect a fee from users? (Imagine officials collecting one penny tolls for the use of sidewalks.) Is the resource in such general use or so much an individual right of a sector of the population that the government should pay for it outright?

Signing up or out sometimes serves purposes of security, as with books. Here again, the argument concerns avoiding losses. On the other hand, sometimes the purpose is simply systematic sharing of a scarce resource, as in signing up for the use of a studio. The argument in this case cites the confusion that results if several people arrive at once to use the same resource, and the inequity if one person takes possession of a resource for an inordinate period.

These examples and points show how the many procedures for sharing resources constitute a connected family of designs relatively fine-tuned to a diversity of special needs and circumstances. Although one might not realize it at first thought, the procedures for sharing resources reflect a well-developed social technology, a repertoire of ways for getting things done smoothly, safely, and to mutual benefit. Such insights are likely whenever we take seriously an everyday procedure we rarely contemplate and view it in the context of a family of procedures.

HOW TO GO WILDLY ABSTRACT

Just for fun, let us reduce the world to four families of designs: fasteners, conductors, containers, and transformers.

Taken most literally, fasteners are things like paperclips and clothespins. But stretched into metaphor, fasteners include things like handshakes, wedding rings, and business contracts. In metaphorical generality, fasteners encompass whatever binds one thing to another.

Taken most literally, conductors are substances that conduct electricity. But stretched into metaphor, conductors include pipes that conduct water, radio and television waves that conduct signals, speech that conducts messages, trucks that conduct produce. In metaphorical generality, whatever transports or conveys anything in any sense is a conductor.

Taken most literally, transformers are gadgets for changing the voltage of alternating current. But stretched into metaphor, transformers include schools, inventors, messiahs, and petroleum refineries. In metaphorical generality, transformers encompass whatever shapes something to a purpose by transforming it.

Now we can try on a very specialized pair of design-colored glasses, one tuned to see the world as fasteners, containers, conductors, and transformers. To avoid omitting things that might give these glasses trouble, let us start with, say, letter *m* entries in the dictionary and take all nouns referring to familiar concrete objects.

Macadam — roads are made of this; it is part of a conductor.

Macaque — a form of life, the macaque would be most of all a transformer, a complex chemical and electrical factory.

Macaroni — as a food, macaroni is a container of energy.

Macaw — another form of life, another transformer.

Mace — a weapon, a way of destroying life, another grimmer sort of transformer.

Machete — a tool for work or destruction, a transformer.

Machine — a transformer of things and energy.
Machine-gun — another grim transformer.
Macramé — a container of aesthetic pleasure.
Macrocosm — The container of everything.
Magazine — a container of information.
Maggot — a biological transformer.
Magician — an entertaining transformer.
Magistrate — a judicial transformer.
Magnet — finally, a fastener, our first one on the list.

Let us stop with the first fastener and do something else — parts
of the body.

Eye — carrying information to the brain, a conductor.
Ear — another conductor.
Mouth — a conductor of food to the stomach. And a transformer,
since it grinds up the food. And a transformer again, since it
shapes words. There is no reason why a single thing cannot have
multiple functions.
Brain — a container and transformer of information.
Knee — a conductor, part of your transportation system.
Hand — fastener when you hold on to the railing, container when
you protect something in it, conductor when you carry something
in it, transformer when you make something with it.

Perhaps the hand is the ultimate design. The hand does it all.
Can you think of another design that does all four?

Or stretch your mind even more. Perhaps *everything* does all
four if we allow very metaphorical and indirect ways of fastening,
containing, conducting, and transforming. Try that idea out on
several items from the lists above.

This plan for mapping the world, exotic and idiosyncratic,
should make it plain that design-colored glasses provide no narrow
recipe for thinking and learning. By yourself, you might look at
Darwin's theory of natural selection or fasteners or the world
mapped into four families of designs and arrive at something a little different or very different from the examples described here.
Design-colored glasses are made to help beholders to see along certain lines. But beholders contribute their share to perception, too.
What gets seen depends enormously on the vision of the person
looking.

WHAT YOU CAN DO

As a learner or a teacher dealing with any subject, in formal or not so formal settings, individual or group, you have found in this chapter answers to some natural questions about how to apply knowledge as design. You can make use of knowledge as design in many situations. In particular, you can:

- *Distinguish between nondesigns, natural designs, and deliberate designs, in order to decide what can be treated as a design.* Examples would be, respectively, cumulus clouds, the fin of a fish, and a sailboat.

- *Approach a nondesign by focusing on claims about the nondesign as designs.* In so approaching a nondesign like cumulus clouds or a crystal lattice, you highlight the constructive creative character of our knowledge about them.

- *Handle situations that involve several interrelated designs by focusing on one design at a time.* You should choose the one most central to your immediate aim and note explicitly when you switch.

- *Explore the arguments about a design by way of explanatory and evaluative arguments.* In particular, you can use (1) explanatory argument, explanation for short, that addresses straightforwardly how the structure suits the purpose or purposes, (2) evaluative argument, evaluation for short, that assesses how well the structure suits the purpose and what other advantages and disadvantages the design has, and (3) deep explanatory argument, deep explanation for short, that discloses deep principles of physics, economics, logic, or any other domain at work in the design.

- *Understand concrete designs through a design analysis that for structure highlights parts, materials, and shapes.* Such an approach suits well such objects as hubcaps, transistors, pencils, or bathing suits.

- *Understand everyday and formal procedures through a design analysis that for structure breaks down a procedure into steps.* You may find loops, conditional branches, and other elements that give the steps a complex structure. Comparison of steps with alternatives often highlights the logic of the procedure.

- *Treat claims as designs.* You can apply a design analysis to supposed facts, theories, advertising assertions, and so on by considering the purpose of the claims, taking for structure any component claims or concepts, choosing for models examples or instances of the claim, and considering for argument both the truth of the claim and the relevance of the claim to its purpose, that is, the effectiveness of the claim in serving its purpose.

- *Encompass a greater range by considering a family of designs that share a similar purpose.* You can ponder how and why various members of the family resemble one another or differ.

- *Play with analogy and families of designs.* Remember "How to Go Wildly Abstract."

- *Above all, be inventive in seeking ways to apply knowledge as design and the design questions.* The questions were chosen to serve flexibly our quest to understand things and ideas creatively and critically. If you think you see a way to apply them but are not sure whether it is "right," go ahead and see how it works out.

3 Words By Design

Fourscore and seven years ago our fathers brought forth on this continent a new nation conceived in liberty and dedicated to the proposition that all men are created equal—the first words of Abraham Lincoln's Gettysburg Address, one of the most eloquent brief utterances in the English language. The Gettysburg Address is, of course, a design. It was a structure well adapted to the purpose of dedicating the cemetery at Gettysburg in the midst of the Civil War.

Besides being a design, Lincoln's Gettysburg Address speaks *about* a design. Just as a paragraph explaining Newton's laws is both itself a design—for communication—and talks about a design—Newton's laws, so Lincoln's Gettysburg Address is a design that deals with another design. Remarkably, just as ideal textbooks present fully connected knowledge, so did Lincoln, advancing in some three-hundred words a certain structure in service of a certain purpose, with models and arguments.

To be sure, the dramatic Lincoln did not settle for ticking off points one by one in linear order—purpose, structure, model, arguments. But the points are there, every one of them. The purpose he urges upon the audience and the nation appears most clearly at the very end of the address, as its conclusion: *that these dead shall not have died in vain, that this nation under God shall have a new birth of freedom, and that government of the people, by the people, for the people shall not perish from the earth.*

The structure to further this purpose emerges just before, Lincoln urging that each citizen dedicate himself to the cause for which so many had died: *It is for us the living rather to be dedicated here to the unfinished work . . . dedicated to the great task remaining before us . . .* It is dedication, then, that will help to save the nation.

With a renewed nation as the purpose and dedication as the structure to achieve it, Lincoln wove into his plea for dedication the argument for it—that we cannot adequately honor the sacrifice of those who died at Gettysburg other than by our own continued striving. *But, in a larger sense, we cannot dedicate, we cannot consecrate, we cannot hallow this ground . . . It is for us the living rather to be dedicated here to the unfinished work which they who fought here have thus far so nobly advanced . . . That from these honored dead we take increased devotion to that cause for which they gave the last full measure of devotion.*

As to model, Lincoln's models of dedication, were, of course, the dead of Gettysburg.

Yet Lincoln knew nothing of knowledge as design. Strange that we find him answering the four design questions, questions articulated here more than a century later.

But no, not strange. As urged in the first chapter, the only really fresh aspect of knowledge as design is my putting the four design questions together into a pattern with a name. The need for stating purpose, structure, models, and argument lies inherent in the nature of understanding and the requirements of communication. The gifted voices among us have often had the savvy to present knowledge in a fully connected way. In our roles as readers or writers, or teachers of reading and writing, we do well to follow knowingly what they did naturally.

READING BY DESIGN: CONTENT

We read a discursive text for what it says and, ideally, for what we think about what it says. We read to understand, remember, appraise critically, and make creative connections. This multiple challenge poses a perennial problem for us as learners, whether we are learning in classes, on the job, or for the fun of it. A strategy to guide the reading process would be a help; knowledge as design offers one.

Let us begin with a model. What might happen with an actual piece of reading? I choose a short article from *Time* with the totally intriguing title: *Zombies: Do They Exist?*

I sit with eleven year old Ted to read through this article and untangle its threads, using the design questions. We have done this several times before. It goes something like this.

Dave: What design or designs are talked about here, that you can base your reading on?

Ted: I don't know yet.

Dave: Can you make a start by looking at the title?

Ted: Oh yeah. I guess the article says that zombies exist — under the title it says "Yes, says a Harvard scientist, who offers an explanation."

Dave: So what kind of a design do you have?

Ted: A claim.

Dave: Fine. Go ahead.

Ted: On a brilliant day in the spring of 1980, a stranger arrived at L'Estere marketplace in Haiti's fertile Artibonite Valley. The man's gait was heavy, his eyes vacant. The peasants watched fearfully as he approached a local woman named Angelina Narcisse.

Dave: What's going on here? How would you classify this.

Ted: It's an example of a zombie, a model.

Dave: Okay. So the design in question is. . . ?

Ted: A zombie.

Dave: That's fine. But wait a minute. What was the design you started with?

Ted: Oh yeah. The claim that zombies exist.

Dave: Well how does the model fit into that?

Ted: It's evidence that they exist. I mean, if you have one, they have to exist. (As mentioned in earlier chapters, often an example serves as both model and argument.)

Dave: So now we have two designs going — zombies, and the claim that zombies exist.

Ted: Right.

Ted continues reading and classifying. Soon he comes to a new paragraph.

Ted: This incident and four others in recent years have sparked the most systematic inquiry ever made into the legendary voodoo phenomena of zombiism. That's a new design. Structure of the search for zombies.

Dave: Right. Go ahead.

Ted: According to Haitian belief, a zombie is an individual who has been "killed" and then raised from the dead by malevolent voodoo priests known as "bocors." That's structure of zombies. *Though most educated Haitians deny the existence of zombies, Dr. Lamarque Douyon, Canadian-trained head of the Psychiatric Center in Port-au-Prince, has been trying for 25 years to establish the truth about the phenomenon, no easy matter in a land where the line between myth and reality is faintly drawn.* That's more structure of the investigation.

And so on. After reading the whole article, sometimes with prompting from me about how to classify things and sometimes not, and with quite a bit of help on vocabulary, we end up with four key designs: the claim that zombies exist, the process of investigation, the procedure for zombie making, and zombies themselves. The article intermingles information on the four.

Later on, we try to reconstruct what we read, recalling which designs proved key and reviewing the answers to the design questions.

What did we learn, for instance, about zombies as a design? *Purpose:* Zombies were used for labor. People were made into zombies as punishment for some supposed wrong. *Structure:* Zombies were dazed, drugged, weak, with vital signs hard to detect. *Model:* Some cases were described. *Argument:* How well did zombies serve their purpose? As workers, not very well. They were too weak. As retribution, the article did not say. Pretty well I bet.

What did we learn about zombie making? *Purpose:* same as above. *Structure:* You administer a drug made of a toad, a puffer fish, and human bone (for show). The drug puts the person into a near-death state, with hardly any detectable breath or heartbeat. Apparently dead, the person is buried. If the person is dug up within a few hours, he can be awakened somehow. They did not say how. Then another drug is given that puts the person in a trance state. The person is led off to a plantation to work as a slave. They do not say whether you have to keep giving the drug to keep the person in a trance or not. *Model:* Just the blow by blow account. *Argument:* Haitian witch doctors report this procedure. Also, the trance drug contains a strong hallucinogenic. The drug that induces the near-death state contains the same chemical as that which occasionally kills Japanese eating improperly prepared puffer fish. Japanese suffering from such an attack exhibit much the same near-death symptoms.

Suppose we want to go further, not only synthesizing what the text said but exploring what we think about what the text said. We can extend the argument to appraise critically the evidence and explanations reviewed. Can we find out more concerning the physiological plausibility of the process of zombie making? Are there supporting parallels in any other cultures? In the spirit of connected knowledge, we can also make connections to families of designs and, in general, to other interesting contexts. How does zombie making as a strategy of social control compare and contrast with other frontal assaults like brainwashing? As a way of altering mental and physiological functioning, does zombie making have any potential medical applications?

With this example in mind, let us try to sum up a general strategy.

Strategy for "Reading by Design"

1. *Select key designs to read for.*

   As you start to read an article, chapter, or even a section, look for *one or a few* key designs to read for.

   You may find it useful to look at the title, introduction, *and* conclusion to find designs that play a key role.

   Remember, a design can be a concrete invention, a procedure, an institution, a claim, and many other things.

   Pay special attention to claims, since much writing is organized around claims

   If you have your own agenda, separate from the author's, choose a design *you* want to find out about; then read to discover whether the text speaks to it.

2. *Read to answer the design questions.*

   Pause periodically as you read to review in your mind the design questions for your key designs: What have you learned from the text about purpose, structure, model cases, and arguments?

For a close reading, pause frequently and review carefully; for a more holistic reading, pause less frequently.

You do not have to read from beginning to end; if you want, you can skip around looking for answers to design questions.

You do not have to read every word; that depends on your need.

You often will find that the text does not answer all the design questions. Try to bridge the gaps with your own knowledge and inventiveness, elaborating purpose, structure, models, or arguments yourself when the text does not provide them.

If you find the text worthwhile as you read, *always* review your chosen designs and answers to the design questions after finishing the article, chapter, or section, if you are reading by sections. Try to think of models not mentioned in the text, an effort that tests your understanding. This review fixes what you have learned in your mind.

3. *For critical thinking, extend the argument.*

   Try to extend the arguments in the text about the key designs. Look for their weaknesses, question their confidence, add your own perspective.

   You can do this as you go or at the end for sure.

4. *For creative thinking, make remote connections.*

   Connect the key designs to families of designs by generalization, or by analogy to any other related context.

   You can do this as you go or at the end for sure.

   My own rule of thumb: For each design, make three interesting connections to something outside the immediate context of the reading.

Now why should "reading by design" help a learner's reading of discursive texts? Broadly speaking, because selecting designs to read for and organizing your reading and reviewing according to the design questions provides a systematic approach that highlights connected knowledge. The attention to extending arguments and making remote connections in steps 3 and 4 above builds in critical and creative thinking. Even by the measure of sheer memory, reading by design scores well: All these activities require processing the text in ways that abet memory.

But does reading by design always apply? Almost always. The design questions suit the content of most nonfiction because nonfiction usually concerns designs—designs such as zombies, the stock market, or procedures for confirming compliance with nuclear test ban treaties, for example. Recalling that claims are considered designs, the design questions almost have to fit because, whatever else nonfiction deals with, it almost always advances claims of one sort or another. For instance, the claim that zombies exist was one key design for the zombie article.

Is reading by design too much work to be worth the bother? It is as much work as you need it to be and make it to be. You can follow the strategy superficially with very little effort, after getting used to it. All depends on how deeply you want to probe the text in question, a decision for you to make.

Despite the guidance it provides, reading by design will be hard at first for many young readers. The difficulty reflects not awkwardness in the system but the genuine challenges of understanding texts. For instance, when you discover that a reader has trouble identifying the arguments for a claim in an article, you are finding out that your reader has not really been grasping the logical connections before. For the young reader, reading by design does not so much streamline an existing and reasonably effective process of understanding as it moves someone who probably has been reading mechanically toward much more mindful reading. Thus, reading by design offers no quick fix. It calls for a fair amount of practice that fuels a gradual development of skill.

Comparison with Another Reading Strategy

If reading by design seems a reasonable strategy for reading nonfiction, how does it compare with other strategies of similar purpose? A good example of a competitor is an old and heavily researched method called the SQ3R plan. The mnemonic stands for "Survey, Question, Read, Recite, and Review." You *survey* the title, headings, captions, and so on to discover the basic organization of the text; skim once more, generating *questions* concerning the topics you have identified; *read* to answer the questions; go over the major headings and captions again, at each point recalling your questions to try to *recite* answers from memory; finally, you *review* by going over the text quickly one more time. Research has shown that this procedure boosts memory for the text substantially.

So why the design questions and not SQ3R? Try them both, by all means. SQ3R offers a sensible process, but one without a basis in a theory of knowledge like knowledge as design. Consequently, SQ3R does not help you with what sorts of questions to ask about the knowledge in the text, questions provided by the design framework. You might favor reading by design because it offers an explicit way of orienting to a text (choose key designs), a systematic approach to understanding (answer the design questions), and emphasis on critical and creative thinking (extend arguments and make remote connections).

READING BY DESIGN: ORGANIZATION

The style of reading sketched in the foregoing trades on the fact that most nonfiction texts are *about* designs: They discuss designs or defend claims, which are also considered to be designs. But such texts are interesting in another way as well. Besides being *about* designs, they are themselves designs—designs for communication. Another challenge to our understanding of texts, nonfiction *and* fiction, asks how they work as communication tools.

Exploration of a text as itself a design proceeds like any other design analysis. An ordinary newspaper article makes a nice case in point. What would you discover if you were thinking through the design of a newspaper article? You might say something like this:

The purpose is quick, efficient communication of current information.

As to structure, newspapers belong among the most highly heirarchized forms of text because so many topics find room on the same pages. The individual article constitutes a key level of organization in this heirarchy. Important structural features of an ordinary newspaper article include the headline. A headline presents the theme of the article and often tries to compress the message of the article into a few words. For instance, consider this typical headline from one of the many cycles in U.S.-Soviet arms discussions: *U.S. Negotiator Urges New Arms Proposal.*

The introductory paragraphs, another structural feature, convey compactly the gist of the new information the article has to offer. For instance:

> The Reagan administration is considering a recommendation from its chief negotiator on medium-range missiles that the United States make one more proposal before the expected walkout of the Soviet Union from the Geneva talks.
>
> Well-placed officials disclosed that Paul Nitze has urged that the proposal include: . . .

The introductory paragraphs shade into follow-up paragraphs that elaborate details and provide background information on earlier events. For instance, on the expected walkout:

> Soviet President Yuri V. Andropov suggested that the Soviet Union would walk out of the talks if deployment proceeds next month.
>
> Sources say Nitze contends that Moscow wants the United States to reject the latest proposal made by Andropov last week in an interview with Pravda . . .

Enough text appears on the headline page to tell the gist of the story, but usually the text continues on a later page.

As to argument, what reasons recommend such a structure for newspaper articles? The headline allows the reader to scan a page quickly, selecting those articles of greatest personal interest. A newspaper, unlike most books, operates on the tacit assumption that readers may only read a fraction of its contents. Accordingly, in contrast with a book, newspapers feature many bold headlines.

Just as readers of newspapers are not expected to read every article, so they are not expected to read any one article completely. Accordingly, articles contain a compact statement of the most recent information up front in the first few paragraphs. It is presumed that the interested reader will follow the article to the back pages of the newspaper.

In summary, the principal argument for the structure of newspaper articles (and indeed the whole newspaper) comes down to efficiency of sampling. That is, the structure serves to present material in such a form that individuals can find and follow their interests as far as they please, garnering more complete information the further they proceed.

Fiction as Design

The newspaper example shows how the design questions help with understanding not just the content but the format of nonfiction. But, content aside, the design questions apply just as well to fiction, too. Such readings do not usually focus on designs in their content as much as do nonfiction texts. But they in themselves certainly *are* designs—designs with such purposes as engaging aesthetically, entertaining, and even edifying the reader.

Good poems are superbly refined examples of design. For a long time, my favorite source about the design of poetry has been John Ciardi's *How Does a Poem Mean?* Maybe my sympathies were with a design perspective years ago, when I had never entertained such notions explicitly, because the very name of Ciardi's book tells you that he takes seriously the mechanism of a poem—not just *what* it says, but *how*. The concepts Ciardi presents in the course of his book give us names for different kinds of structure in poetry. (A caution here: The word "structure" in the design sense covers more than literary critics usually mean when they speak of structure. Because the design sense of structure includes virtually any relevant property, diction or rhythm or pace would be an element of structure just as much as sonnet form or ABBA ABBA.)

Then can knowledge as design help us to understand a poem and perhaps even to respond to it more strongly? Let us begin by examining a poem Ciardi discusses, using one of his concepts and the language of the design questions. The poem runs as follows:

The Span of Life

Robert Frost

> The old dog barks backward without getting up.
> I remember when he was a pup.

What is the purpose of a poem? Broadly speaking, to engage, to move the reader in some direction, to provoke thought. Then what impact does this particular poem seek? Plainly, we are meant to contemplate starkly juxtaposed youth and age, beginning and end, entry and exit. Plainly, we are meant to hold a compressed awareness of this polarity not just as it applies to dogs, but also to ourselves. In fact, the notion of a model applies: The mini-drama enacted by the poem serves as a model, exemplifying a fundamental and troubling feature in life.

What are we meant to feel? Does the poem leave us overwhelmed by the tragedy of hopeful birth come down to dismal age and death? Perhaps not. The very casualness and simplicity of the lines undercut such melodrama. It seems more that this is a part of life, perfectly ordinary, perfectly mundane. Taking my own reactions as a litmus, the poem expresses a somewhat stoic, contemplative, and untroubled perception, and all the more inventive for being so.

We could explore the structure of this small poem by way of many windows. Let us choose just one: Ciardi's concept of *fulcrum*. Ciardi has this to say about his notion:

> Note that neither line is a poem by itself. It is not a poem to say "The old dog barks backward without getting up." That much is only a statement. Nor is it a poem to say "I can remember when he was a pup." That much is only a comment. But a poem does happen when the two lines are said one after the other. It must follow that the poem exists in the countermotion of the two lines, in the way the second line (in this case the comment) makes something of what has been established in the first line (in this case the statement). Nor do the two lines simply run together: There is some point of balance between the end of the first and the beginning of the second, a pause, a meditative silence like a rest in music.

This pause Ciardi calls the *fulcrum* of a poem, finding one not only here in this model case, but in many other poems as well. Let us make an evaluative and explanatory argument for this structural feature of Frost's poem. Does the fulcrum serve the poem well, and how? In describing the concept of fulcrum, Ciardi already has provided most of the argument. As he notes, neither of the two lines by itself would make a poem of *The Span of Life*. The fulcrum enriches, coupling statement with comment, thesis with antithesis, making more complex and pungent.

But more than that, it seems to me that *this* fulcrum offers something special. In longer poems, a fulcrum may be a strong structural feature having its impact along with other features. But in Frost's remarkably compressed poem, the fulcrum utterly dominates our reaction. In fact, going one further than Ciardi, who points out that neither half makes a poem, you might say that neither half even makes half a poem. In a longer poem, if you take either half you have something sounding like poetry, although incomplete. For this poem, if you take either half alone you have nothing particularly poetic at all. The fulcrum generates virtually all the poetry in the poem. So let us take stock. Can we probe the design of a poem with the design questions? The answer seems to be yes. In fact, beyond Ciardi's fulcrum concept, much more could be said about the delicate tuning of this short poem's structure to its purpose. Do we thereby come to respond to the poem more intensely? Here people will differ more. Some people seem to feel that any kind of an analysis dulls their appreciation. It is true, of course, that an analysis does not *feel like* the sensitive experiencing of a poem; an analysis, after all, is not supposed to *feel like* its object but to analyze its object. So the real question should be: When you go back to the poem as an experience, after analyzing it, is your re-experiencing sharpened? I find that mine usually is: I react to the poem more strongly and in a more nuanced way. I suspect that many people think analysis spoils experiencing because (a) they expect the analysis to *feel like* the experience, which it is not supposed to, and (b) they stop with the analysis, neglecting to re-experience.

In summary, there are two distinct purposes to analyzing a poem. One is to appreciate it as a marvelous engine, designed to move and illuminate; another is to sharpen our experiencing of the poem as we read it. Knowledge as design serves the first of these purposes well, and the first is itself a worthy one. Whether knowledge as design or any other scheme serves the second well may be more controversial. I have cast my vote.

READING BY DESIGN: CRITICAL CONCEPTS

Not only are texts like Frost's poem designs, but designs for analyzing such texts in turn are designs. In particular, Ciardi's concept of fulcrum amounts to such a design. Perhaps we can take our exploration of texts a step further by abstracting from the introductory poem, as, of course, Ciardi himself does. The general concept of fulcrum is our design. Can we investigate and appreciate it better as such?

The concept of a fulcrum has a straightforward purpose: It names and leads us to attend to an important structural feature of poetry. Accordingly, it helps us to understand how the poem works. It may thereby sharpen our experiencing of the poem, an independent question. As mentioned above, in my view critical concepts often do.

A model case of a fulcrum was just discussed. As to structure, in the case of a concept, structure would mean the definition or meaning of the concept. Ciardi offers the following compressed characterization: *A poem is one part against another across a silence.* That silence is the fulcrum.

But the structure of Ciardi's concept turns out to be more complicated than you might think. Need a poem have only one fulcrum? By no means. Ciardi allows that a poem can have a complex heirarchy of fulcrums. Finally, what if a poem contains no obvious fulcrum? Ciardi finds such cases. He suggests that the fulcrum occurs after the last line. The most straightforward applications of the fulcrum concept pose few problems for argument. What doubt can there be when a poem presents a counterpoised structure so blatantly as does Frost's *The Span of Life?* But these additional notions seem less straightforward. Let us scrutinize them one at a time.

Consider first Ciardi's proposal that a poem can have many fulcrums. The idea of one fulcrum per poem has an attractive neatness about it. Why open the door to such complications? Simply because certain poems offer several contrasts that seem so fulcrum-like it would be odd to withhold the name. In other words, we feel led on by our intuitive sense of what a fulcrum is to extend its meaning to include multiple fulcrums. A delightful example follows.

On the Vanity of Earthly Greatness

Arthur Guiterman

The tusks that clashed in mighty brawls
Of mastodons, are billiard balls.

The sword of Charlemagne the Just
Is ferric oxide, known as rust.

The grizzly bear, whose potent hug
Was feared by all, is now a rug.

Great Caesar's bust is on the shelf,
And I don't feel so well myself.

The poem certainly has a major fulcrum in Ciardi's basic sense. The fulcrum falls between the next to last and last lines. All of the poem through the next to last line concerns the mighty of the world and their utter downfall. The last line suddenly reduces the topic to an insignificant individual and, in the same stroke, reduces the terrible downfall to something just as insignificant—"I don't feel so well myself."

So far so good. But what should we make of those juxtapositions that mark every line, for instance, the contrast between "The tusks that clashed in mighty brawls/Of mastodons" and its antithesis "are billiard balls?" We could withhold the term fulcrum and call it something else. But the fulcrum concept seems to fit our intuitive sense of a fulcrum except for the fact that we are dealing with only a pair of lines in a larger work.

Make no mistake about it. What to do comes down to a design decision, not a logical necessity. One can keep the concept of fulcrum for main fulcrums only, or follow impulse, opt for generality, and extend the concept to include cases like the mastodons. Ciardi's choice, and a persuasive one, was the latter.

This seems fairly straightforward, but Ciardi's proposal that all worthwhile poems have a fulcrum, which may even come *after* the end of the poem, is harder to swallow. He offers a clever argument though, again by means of a model that tries to get us to perceive that oddly positioned fulcrum.

His example is Theodore Roethke's *My Papa's Waltz*, a poem that portrays in the deceptive guise of a rhythmic dance a child's stark terror at being danced about the room by his drunk father.

My Papa's Waltz

Theodore Roethke

The whisky on your breath
Could make a small boy dizzy;
But I held on like death:
Such waltzing was not easy.

We romped until the pans
Slid from the kitchen shelf;
My mother's countenance
Could not unfrown itself.

The hand that held my wrist
Was battered on one knuckle;
At every step I missed
My right ear scraped a buckle.

You beat time on my head
With a palm caked hard by dirt,
Then waltzed me off to bed
Still clinging to your shirt.

Ciardi acknowledges that the poem presents no change of tone, but a steady intensification. But "imagine," he writes, "as a horrible example, that the poet had written an additional summarizing stanza in his first draft, and imagine that it had run to some such sad stuff as the following:

Ah, that was long ago.
Now, his first terrors shed,
This dancer turns to go
Calm, to the fearless dead.

" . . . Had such a stanza existed one would have had no hesitation in placing the fulcrum between it and the preceding poem," and, "For silence, too, is a communication when placed in context. Thus *the fulcrum exists outside the poem, between the enacted experience and the silence that follows it*" (italics Ciardi's).

Ciardi takes an interesting stand here, deploying the powerful modeling strategy of created examples. He does this often in the book, suggesting new lines, deleting lines, or revising lines to make a point of contrast.

But, to give a personal reaction, I am not convinced. Yes, Ciardi's ending creates an obvious fulcrum. But the poem as written has no such ending. To be sure, a powerful silence follows the poem as written, but the worth of calling the point between the poem and the silence a fulcrum is less sure. I do not feel the intuitive pull to generalize the term fulcrum to the silences after poems, though I did feel the pull to generalize the concept to multiple fulcrums, as in *On the Vanity of Earthly Greatness*. There only remains the formal motive of making the fulcrum concept apply to every poem, even where it does not seem to. But, since the application seems forced, perhaps the gain of having a universally applicable term does not pay for the strain of the forcing.

On the other hand, we can grasp Ciardi's way of using "fulcrum" and proceed to use it likewise. And it is *his term*. He has some right to set his own convention.

Again, as in the case of generalizing to multiple fulcrums, you have to see the matter as a design decision. No logic compels or forbids calling the pivots between some poems and their following silences fulcrums. Rather, the question comes down to which convention yields the more powerful and illuminating design for understanding poetry. The moral: We see that knowledge as design offers an avenue to understanding critical concepts as constructions of the literary mind and appreciating some of the tradeoffs involved in their making.

WRITING BY DESIGN: ESSAY THEMES

Some people scratch their heads and wonder why students emerge from a dozen or more years of schooling without adequate writing skills. There is no great mystery in this. Characteristically, schooling provides some practice with writing, but very little direct instruction about handling the several challenging dimensions of setting thoughts to paper.

It is helpful to keep in mind four dimensions of writing: theme, organization, expression, and mechanics. That is, to write well, you should (1) have something to say — theme; (2) say it systematically — organization; (3) say it expressively — expression; and (4) say it correctly from the standpoint of spelling and grammar — mechanics. Knowledge as design can help with each of these, but in this section we take on only the first one, having something to say.

To make a point, you must find a point to make. This is the first creative challenge of writing. The ideas that people write down do not serve themselves up magically, but emerge from thinking. Many approaches to writing instruction suffer here, because, although they help the student who has a point to express it, they fail to recognize that finding something worth saying poses one of the most troublesome roadblocks of writing. Once you advance beyond simple narratives — the "what I did on my summer vacation" approach — the going gets tough. How is the writer to discover the generalization, the analysis, the evaluation, the opinion, on which to build a piece of cogent prose?

The design perspective proposes a clear approach to this problem. Its simple recommendation is: Write about an interesting design (or family of designs).

For instance, any interesting claim that has relevance and calls for support makes a reasonable focus for an essay. This includes claims historical, social, psychological, political, scientific, and more. Such a claim serves the needs of writing well because it leads naturally into a communicative organization you might call the essay of support. This sort of essay addresses the design questions one by one. You clarify the import of the matter at hand (purpose), state the claim explicitly with whatever elaborations seem needed (structure), and present the pros and cons (argument). You use models wherever needed for clarity.

Besides essays of support, there are essays of explanation. A simple essay of explanation has the same structure as an essay of support — basically, an argument for a claim. But an essay of explanation does not treat its key claim as in doubt. If this seems paradoxical, consider an example. Suppose you want to explain why the sun appears in the sky at a different angle in the winter than in the summer. The fact is not in doubt, but still you argue for it, deducing it as a consequence of the earth's orbit and tilt. To generalize, in an essay of explanation the point is not to support a doubtful claim, but to establish a connection between an accepted claim and other more general principles. We want not just truths, but connected knowledge.

Writing in the design spirit can focus on any design, not just a claim. Moreover, if claims lack palpability for the young writer, concrete designs do not. Anyone who can write can choose and comment on the designs of simple physical objects relatively easily — the designs, for instance, of a fire place, house, kite, or airplane propeller. By the same token, this area of physical designs can get as complex as you want. The designs of Fuller domes, integrated circuits, or cyclotrons also make apt topics for discussion.

Procedures also merit attention, from the elementary procedures of building a kite, playing checkers, or voting to the complex procedures of programming a computer, arguing at trial, or diagnosing a disease. Likewise, systems of various sorts provide reasonable topics, for instance, systems of government, manufacture, trade, or schooling.

If a single design proves too confining, families of designs also offer themes. For instance, you might imagine a little essay called *Wedging Air and Water* that talks about fans, airplane propellers, boat propellers, and perhaps other things, applying the explanatory principle of the wedge to gaseous and fluid media. Or you might take the title *Decision-making Procedures in Government* and review comparatively the designs of the various procedures adopted at various levels of a particular government, or, more expansively, all governments.

These many examples might suggest that the design concept helps mostly by making it easy to think of themes. But that is only half the point. The advice, "write about a design" also fosters concentration. The fact is that many writers, having found a theme, do not know how to treat it in a focused way. They fail to narrow it enough or fail to adopt a particular perspective on it. With a design as your theme comes not just a theme, but a perspective — the design perspective.

For example, suppose you already have a loose theme — student protest movements of the 60's. It is dismayingly easy to proceed in a meandering descriptive way. To guard against that, you can try to decide exactly what design you mean to treat under the general theme. With a little thought, you might arrive at titles and ideas like the following: *Strategies of Protest* focusing on the family of protest strategies and how they evolved as students gained experience; *Leadership in an Antiauthoritarian Context*, examining the design of the leader role in movements that were antiauthoritarian; *Paradoxes of Force*, a claim with argument that the tactics of protesters raised some of the same moral problems that they were protesting against; *Becoming Square*, taking the more conventional lifestyle of former protesters as the design and tracing the causes that led to it—an explanatory argument. Any of these design themes might provide the framework for a tight essay addressing an interesting aspect of the protest movement.

To summarize, the strategy "write about a design" is a design for getting started that helps on three fronts: It (1) provides an easy way to search for interesting topics; (2) encourages focus; and (3) leads toward an organized way of writing about the chosen design that probes it critically and creatively—the design questions. This theme is pursued in the following section.

At this point, some cautionary questions should be asked. First, what if you do not want your essay laden with words like design, structure, and so on? This is a non-problem. Nothing whatsoever in the approach outlined says that any terminology used here has to be used in the writing. You can write in the suggested manner without incorporating the vocabulary at all.

A second cautionary question: By concentrating on design, what are you leaving out? After all, the aim of the design perspective is not to exclude worthwhile topics but to foster connected knowledge. In keeping with this, writing about designs passes up no topic you might want to treat in a discursive way. This follows from the encompassing nature of knowledge as design. The broad applicability of design concepts means that most things can be treated as designs, and those that cannot, such as the weather or the atom, can be treated in terms of claims about them, claims that are themselves designs.

But this breadth notwithstanding, a real limitation exists. Although one can mingle expressive or narrative qualities with the discussion of a design, the approach outlined so far looks toward a relatively discursive piece of writing. Certainly there are occasions where authors seek another emphasis. You may, for example, want to recreate the flavor of the protest movement in a piece of prose, rather than discussing the movement.

What significance does this limitation have? It simply says that we each need to think about the sort of writing we are undertaking and act accordingly. As far as education goes, most people do not write discursive prose very well and would benefit from more practice and guidance in doing so. However, that vote for discursive writing is not a vote against expressive writing on other occasions or even on the same one.

Finally, if writing about a design leads toward discursive writing, does this mean that the design perspective has no relevance to expressive writing? Not at all. Remember, reading by design applies to texts in two ways: You can examine whatever designs the text treats, and you can address the text as itself a design. The same two perspectives appear in writing by design. You can write about a design, which leads to the sort of discursive writing already discussed. Or you can write following various kinds of designs for text, as explored in the section after next. This could lead you to a short story, a sonnet, a riddle, or a joke.

WRITING BY DESIGN: ESSAY ORGANIZATION

You are writing discursively about a design or family of designs. How can you organize your writing? The design questions provide a straightforward answer. At one extreme, you can use the questions as an explicit framework, labeling purpose, structure, models, and argument as you present them. At the other extreme, you can employ the questions only to define the content of what you want to say, say it in whatever order you please, and never mention any words like structure or model.

This book contains examples aplenty of the full range. Almost every section of text one way or another goes through the design questions, often at more than one level. The book itself becomes a reservoir of models showing how the design questions can organize text. But even with so many examples at hand, it is interesting to contrast the same message framed more and less explicitly with the design questions. Consider the following mini-essays on a pet if petty peeve—the misuse of the word "literal."

First of all, a version with the design questions up front:

"Literally" Bungled

Purpose? To urge avoiding a certain misuse of the word "literal."

Structure? In this case a claim: People commonly misuse "literally" to mean "to an extreme degree," when "literally" in fact means "actually."

Model? People say, "The oration literally inflamed the audience." They intend to say that the oration inflamed the audience to an extreme degree. Instead, since "literally" means actually, they end up saying that the oration caused the audience to burst into flames.

Argument? The dictionary defines the meaning of literally as "In a literal or strict sense; really; actually." You might argue that people legitimately use the word "literally" in an extended sense, as commonly happens in informal speech. However, an extended sense should not utterly contradict the basic meaning. Unfortunately, the basic meaning of "literally inflamed" is "caused to burst into flames," which is inconsistent with the intended meaning.

This somewhat stiff presentation reflects in part the blatant organization, in part the fact that so short a piece framed by the explicit design questions leaves little room for the prose to get going, and in part my neglect of literary effects. Nonetheless, even so formal a presentation has its places. For one, wearing its organization on its sleeve, it comes across with great clarity. For another, young writers learning how to handle organization may benefit from making organization absolutely explicit; time enough later to be more subtle and expressive.

A note on models: The model you always need, and the only model given in the above essay, is a model of structure, an illustration of whatever structural description occupies the structure slot. But, as mentioned before, for a complex topic it may be useful to include models in the discussions of purpose and argument, too.

Here is another version of the same essay, one with more literary effects and the design questions implicit rather than explicit.

"Literally" Bungled, II

We all might take more care with the English language. A case in point is a common misapplication of the word "literally." Too often, people use this word to mean "to an extreme degree," whereas "literally" properly speaking means actually.

For example, suppose that you find in the newspaper an account of a recent political rally. You read, "The speech literally inflamed the audience." Of course, you know that the writer means; he wants to say that the speech inflamed the audience, in a metaphorical sense, to an extreme degree. But, if you have an ear for the right use of "literally," you get a bizarre image: The speech caused the audience to burst into flames.

That image surely signals that something is wrong. The dictionary tells us what, offering a clear and unqualified definition of "literally." It means "in a literal or strict sense; really; actually." Accordingly, "literally inflamed" means "actually caused to burst into flames." Someone might try to shrug off this usage of "literally" as an informal extension of the strictly correct one. However, the excuse seems unreasonable considering that contradictory meanings result. That is, "literally inflamed the audience" signifies something not just looser than, but contradictory to, "inflamed the audience." The fact is that "literally inflamed" uses "literally" ineptly and promotes its continued misuse. The moral is: Don't.

This treatment, both less blatantly structured and more expressively worded, simply puts enough flesh on the same bones so that you cannot see them. Even so, the design questions remain in place: First comes statement of purpose—to correct a problem of usage; then structure—the misuse characterized; then model—the example about the political speech; then argument—the evidence of misuse. But this sequence is a rule of thumb, not a law of nature. To explore the possibilities one step further, here is an even more mixed and melded version of the mini-essay.

"Literally" Bungled, III

You are at Sunday breakfast, browsing your newspaper and enjoying the morning's indolence. You wander through an account of yesterday's political rally. And you are assaulted in the midst of your coffee and scrambled eggs by this grotesque event: An audience bursts into flames.

You have become the day's latest victim of inept English. The culprit was this sentence: "The speech literally inflamed the audience." It offers but one example of an irritating trend in speech and writing, the misuse of "literally" to mean "to an extreme degree." In fact, "literally" means actually.

(And so on with the argument.)

What has happened in this example? More flamboyant expression comes coupled with an organizational maneuver. The strongest image in all the versions has been the literal reading of "The speech literally inflamed the audience," the model. The third version puts the model up front for impact, also withholding explanation of the context until the second paragraph to create tension out of the reader's momentary confusion.

Mind you, the third version is not necessarily recommended. It may edge toward melodrama and have a cost in clarity. But whatever your taste and the tradeoffs, the point remains that the design questions allow a range of treatments from formal and explicit to quite loose and re-ordered, all with the same underlying connected knowledge.

WRITING BY DESIGN: OTHER THAN ESSAYS

Knowledge as design applies to writing in numerous ways. As just discussed, the design questions provide an organization well suited to discursive writing. Moreover, design has relevance to discursive writing at other levels. For instance, the designs of paragraphs or sentences merit attention. Apart from discursive writing, poetic and narrative forms have designs that can guide and empower the process of composition, the designs of haiku, quatrain, limerick, or sonnet, for example. Perhaps critical concepts like Ciardi's notion of fulcrum can help too: For some, it may be helpful advice to seek a fulcrum to build a poem around.

What is it like to do non-discursive writing with the help of the design questions? Elephant jokes provide a simple example. Insubstantial though they are, I confess to liking elephant jokes. Also, they have a simple transparent structure, and so make a clear case in point. Remember, *you* do not have to like elephant jokes to find the illustration illuminating.

To write elephant jokes, I need to understand their design. What is the purpose? To be funny. What are some models? Here are several: Why are elephants grey? So you can tell them apart from bluebirds. What is red and white on the outside and grey on the inside? Campbell's Cream of Elephant Soup. Where does the two ton rogue elephant sleep? Anywhere he wants to! How do you fit four elephants into a Volkswagen? Two in the front and two in the back. How do you fit five elephants into a Volkswagen? Two in the front, two in the back, and one in the glove compartment.

After you have recovered from nausea or giggles, as the case may be, we can look at the general structure of elephant jokes. They have a question and answer format. The question typically seems obscure or anomalous. The answer, the punch line, always makes half-sense — not true, but not utter nonsense either. In particular, the answer typically borrows a pattern from another context and applies it, inappropriately, to the elephant situation. For instance, you do fit four *people* in a volkswagen by putting two in front and two in back. The glove compartment is another place where you can put things, although not things like elephants.

As to argument, why should this structure be funny (for some)? The punch line introduces a twist — a surprise fit with the situation set up by the question. But, of course, surprise can take many forms. We can be surprised, for instance, by a scientific insight or an apt metaphor. So surprise does part of the job, but not the whole job. The half-sensible character of the answer seems crucial. If the answer were fully sensible, you would have a case of literal insight or metaphor: The answer would respond to the question with an entirely sound, although unexpected and imaginative, meaning. In contrast, the twist at the end of an elephant joke half fits and half does not. Apparently, this neither here nor there character of the answer pokes our cognitive processes in the ribs.

Try Your Own

Now let me attempt to use this understanding of elephant jokes as a guide to writing some. I will indicate in italics my thoughts about the progress of the enterprise, reserving normal text for the jokes themselves. Here goes.

For an elephant joke, I need a silly question about elephants, followed by a half-sensible answer for a punch line.

I'll try to write some question lines. Why do elephants like aardvarks? Why are elephants afraid of mice? What has two large ears, weighs two tons, and squeeks? Why do elephants need telephones?

Besides questions without answers, can I think of answers without questions? Because it's time to fly south for the winter.

No more answer lines come to mind. Back to questions. Why do elephants like peanuts? Why do peanuts like elephants? How is an elephant like a peanut?

That feels like a sufficient pool of starting points. Now I'll try to write answer lines to go with the question lines that I like best.

Why do elephants like aardvarks? *I can't think of any answer at all.* Why are elephants afraid of mice? *I think of how silly it would be for elephants to fear mice; an elephant could crush a puny mouse. That suggests a line.* Because mice make such a mess when stepped on. *I think of what a mouse could possibly do to an elephant. Maybe tickle.* Because mice tickle terribly when they run up the inside of an elephant's trunk. *I try to think of more. Nothing comes. Time to switch to a new question line.*

Why do elephants need telephones? *Humans use telephones. What silly things would elephants in human guise do?* To call up their hairdressers for an appointment. To trade on the stock exchange. To arrange for body guards. To order pizza. *That could go on forever. For a change of pace, I'll switch to the one answer without a question.*

Because it's time to fly south for the winter. *What would the question be? It has to treat elephants like birds.* Why do elephants feel restless in the fall? *Too vague.* Why do elephants gather in large herds in the fall? *I guess that will do.*

The ones I like best:

Why are elephants afraid of mice? Because mice make such a mess when stepped on.

Why are elephants afraid of mice? Because mice tickle terribly when they run up the inside of an elephant's trunk.

Why do elephants need telephones? To call up their hairdressers for an appointment.

Why do elephants gather in large herds in the fall? Because it's time to fly south for the winter.

The example of elephant jokes shows how an understanding of a genre's design can guide writing in the genre, in this case the genre of elephant jokes. Any genre of jokes lends itself to the same treatment. There are, for example, knock-knock jokes or limericks. Outside the realm of jokes, there are sonnets, short stories, business letters, letters of complaint, recipes, essays as already discussed, journals, write-ups of experiments, and numerous other genres that have some importance and interest.

Steps for Teaching Writing in a Genre

Related here was a personal process of composing elephant jokes. But how does one go about teaching others to write in a genre, within the framework of knowledge as design? If you are in the teacher role, it is useful to think in terms of these five steps.

1. Select a genre — for instance, elephant jokes.
2. Do a design analysis of it yourself, including attention to what makes the genre work well — for instance, what makes an elephant joke funny.
3. Lead the learners to understand the design by:
   a. Straight presentation, using the design questions, or
   b. Socratic questioning, drawing the analysis from them, or
   c. Asking them to figure it out for themselves.
4. Ask them to use their understanding of the structure to compose new model cases (which is also a test of their *operational* understanding).
5. Provide clarification and helping strategies as needed.

For instance, recently in a workshop I taught the participants to write elephant jokes, as a demonstration of writing by design. I had already done steps 1 and 2, selecting the genre and carrying out my own design analysis. I drew a similar design analysis from the participants, using Socratic questioning. Then they attempted elephant jokes themselves, step 4. For step 5, we talked about the strengths and weaknesses of the initial results, quickly reaching a clarification: The main problem turned out to be the half-sensible answer; many people were generating answers that were too sensible and so not funny. Because we had done the design analysis, we could recognize the problems quickly and describe it precisely. The participants went on to attempt answers with more of a twist. Moving toward helping strategies, we began to discuss how to think of such twists.

The rationale for the five steps seems clear, except perhaps for the options under 3: presentation, Socratic questioning, or do-it-yourself. This is a matter of the learners' prior familiarity with the genre and with knowledge as design. For learners acquainted with neither, straight presentation is probably the best recourse. For learners acquainted with the genre to some extent, one can draw a good design analysis from them by Socratic questioning. Learners familiar both with the genre and with knowledge as design may well be able to do good analyses on their own or in small groups. The aim as always is to get learners to do as much of the thinking as they are prepared for.

With all this in mind, what reservations might there be about writing by design? One observes that a design understanding does not guarantee instant good results. The elephant jokes singled out at the end are reasonable examples of the genre, but I threw out several beginning lines and punch lines along the way. A design analysis guides the generation of possibilities, but leaves the job of critical selection to the writer. Also, clearly many genres are much more difficult than elephant jokes, sonnets for example. Design analysis or not, one's first sonnets are likely to be clumsy indeed. Another related reservation points out that the process of writing by design is very different from that of the skilled practitioner. Expert poets or essayists may never have done anything like a design analysis of their genres.

These points acknowledged, writing by design seems all the more worthwhile. A design analysis helps in getting started with a genre, but it would be absurd to expect instant excellence, any more than we expect it from any way of learning anything. Even people who prove to have a strong flair for something are likely to be somewhat halting when they begin. As to experts never having done their own analysis, this is only half true. Your average expert may never have sat down to analyze his or her genre comprehensively, but typically the expert has picked up in the course of experience a number of explicit insights into the genre. It is simply not so that expert understanding is all tacit.

Perhaps because we have the image of the fluent expert in mind, or perhaps because we overestimate how much about a genre is obvious, we typically do not provide enough help when learners attempt a new genre. We tend to say, "Just try it," offering little insight into the structure of the genre and no way for learners to organize their attempts at invention. Writing by design is a way to get a learner started with a genre on a reasonable footing.

WHAT YOU CAN DO

Much of the critical and creative thinking we would like to do focuses on writings, our own or someone else's. Knowledge as design offers a number of ways to approach reading and writing. In your learner or teacher roles, you can put the strategies discussed in this

chapter to work. For a review:
As a learner, you can:

- *Probe what a discursive text says and what you think about what the text says by way of the design questions, "reading by design."* The strategy applies to anything from newspaper articles to philosophical discourses. Remember, several sessions may be needed to develop the skill.

- *Gain insight into different genres, formats, and individual examples of texts by considering them as designs.* Newspaper articles, haiku, short stories, jokes of various sorts, business letters, contracts, and endless other forms of text invite this perspective. You also can think in design terms about others' analytical concepts, such as Ciardi's notion of a fulcrum.

- *Write essays by design, seeking to master the key elements of theme, organization, expression, and mechanics.* In this chapter, we took up finding themes by planning to write about a design, and organization by using the design questions as a tacit organizing principle. Expression and mechanics also invite treatment in terms of design.

- *Approach writing in any genre by way of design.* While not all forms of writing are *about* designs, all *are* designs, and understanding them as designs helps one to write in those forms. The general plan is: (a) come to understand the form in question as a design, and (b) use that understanding as a guide to writing. The plan suits elephant jokes, haiku, business letters, letters of complaint, sonnets, assembly directions, short stories, shaggy dog stories, recipes, and just about any other form you can think of. Naturally, some forms are much harder than others.

In your teacher roles you can:

- *Guide your students' learning with any of the above strategies.* You can lead them through activities using the strategies tacitly. Also, you can teach them the strategies explicitly and engage them in exercises to practice the strategies.

- *For instance, teach writing in any genre by employing five steps.* (1) Select the genre; (2) analyze it yourself, including attention to what makes the genre work well; (3) lead the learners to understand the design; (4) ask them to use their understanding to produce new models; (5) provide clarification and helping strategies.

Throughout all these activities, realism is essential. Reading by design is a much more mindful process than many readers are used to. Understanding the design of a form gets your writing off to a good start but hardly yields instant ease and unimpeachable quality. Reading and writing are still demanding enterprises no matter what strategies you muster.

4 Acts of Design

It's a remarkable thing: Youngsters do works of art. To be sure, most of the works fall short technically and imaginatively, and just as surely we offer youngsters little systematic time for or help in developing their talents. Nonetheless, there they are at their school desks, doing works of art.

Why remarkable? Because we do not ask children young or old to do works of mathematics, physics, history, sociology, geography, or biology. For instance, in school they spend hardly any time trying to devise physical explanations for everyday phenomena. We do not urge them to investigate a local piece of history. They do not undertake to map the geography that surrounds them.

Why does art get special treatment? Do we think that children cannot do works in general, art somehow being a special case? Surely not. Children, after all, tell stories, organize games, fix food, build playhouses. As Piaget has emphasized, they also build tacit theories of the physical world. Do we think that art is easy and so gets attempted while works in other academic disciplines are neglected? Surely not. Technically good art requires considerable skill and practice, and the additional dimensions of expression and imagination pose a further and all the more formidable challenge. Still, we encourage students to do works of art.

Perhaps two other factors lie behind our attitude toward art, factors concerning our understanding of the subject areas. First of all, we think of many other subjects as very hierarchical — learners cannot do works of mathematics, physics, and so on, not even elementary ones, until they have mastered a very large part of those subjects. Second, neither we nor our children have a very good sense of what constitutes a simple work in most other academic areas. We know what minimal thing to do to get a work of art: Fill up this piece of paper with a picture. We do not know what minimal thing to do to get a work of physics or biology or social studies: Fill up this piece of paper with . . . with what? Because neither adults nor children have a good answer to that question, teachers tell students to fill up the blank page with the answers to formal exercises.

Could these attitudes reflect a failure of our understanding? Do modest works of mathematics, history, biology, and so on, stand within reach of learners from the very beginnings of their schooling? Might a mistaken sense of how much skill a simple work requires and our uncertainty about what constitutes a work in various disciplines lead to learners being deprived of important learning experiences, in and out of school? If so, our handling of art, the most neglected of subjects, says something to all the others. This chapter explores the worth of these speculations and argues that teaching and learning based on students' works can be a reality.

INVENTION AND THE DESIGN QUESTIONS

To invent a work you must design it. But what is the activity of designing like? A good reply could serve several purposes. It could guide the novice designer in handling the complex and challenging activity of designing. It could put into perspective the sorts of tasks learners usually undertake and how such assignments differ from design tasks. A good reply might also help teachers, in and out of school, to formulate provocative design tasks for learners. Since an answer seems worth having, let us try out one. *Designing involves answering the design questions as one proceeds, at least tacitly.*

At first, this answer may not seem to make much sense. After all, when we take a work from initial conception to final form we are not particularly conscious of answering such questions. Nonetheless, I want to urge that we do answer the design questions along the way, even if only tacitly. Moreover, being more conscious of the role of the design questions can help us to design better. For instance, let us remember an example already considered: one of the *writing by design* activities from the previous chapter. As discussed there, the person writing an essay does well to write in terms of the design questions, discussing purpose, structure, and argument, and giving models along the way. Although the questions themselves might not be written into the essay explicitly, the answers become parts of the product.

At first, however, nondiscursive writing does not seem to fit as well. For instance, in joke writing, the writer produces a joke, an actual model case of the genre in question, but without including as part of the joke replies to the structure, argument, or purpose questions. Indeed, if the joke calls for an explicit argument, it probably does not work as a joke. Since three of the design questions are not explicitly addressed in the writer's output, it might seem that the joke writer does not answer the design questions during the design of a joke.

But what actually shows up in the joke itself is misleading. The joke writer certainly needs to keep the structure of the joke and the purpose of humor in mind, and, as to argument, needs to think critically while writing—to pay heed to the wit and weakness of a joke-in-draft and accept, edit, or discard it as judgment directs. Accordingly, all the design questions tacitly guide the creative process. If they are not explicitly answered in the text of the joke, they are implicitly answered in the mind of the jokester.

A scientist's work in developing a theory ordinarily yields explicit answers to the design questions. A range of phenomena in need of explanation sets the purpose. The scientist tries to construct general principles that will account for the phenomena— the structure. But even as the theory grows, the scientist must continually attend to its logical coherence and whatever empirical evidence already exists— the argument. Along the way, the scientist considers particular model cases. When the theory has matured, any scientist with a flair for communication tries to make purpose, structure, argument, and models clear in presenting the theory to colleagues.

To use a potato peeler, we only need know how to wield it. A household gadget, unlike a scientific theory, does not ordinarily deal with the four design questions explicitly. Perhaps there is trouble here for the notion that designing involves answering the design questions. But what the consumer needs to know is one question and what the inventor needs to know another. Creating a gadget calls for attention to the four design questions. The inventor of a new potato peeler must consider just what job that potato peeler should do, how to structure the potato peeler to do it, and what arguments recommend for or against the projected design. The inventor does well to build a model of the new peeler and try it out, to guard against the unexpected problems that often arise in the translation from concept to reality.

The logic of all these cases begins to come clear. From the first pages, this book has emphasized that purpose, structure, argument, and models bear relevance to any design and provide a connected way of understanding that design. There is a simple corollary: *A designer has to understand a design to design it; an effective process of design involves attention to the four design questions.* As urged earlier, this view of the act of design can serve several purposes — characterizing the sorts of exercises learners usually do, suggesting other sorts of exercises that they might do, and guiding the novice designer.

DESIGN IN THE SCHOOL OF TODAY

Molehills become mountains, a law of human nature if not geology. Perhaps our concern about designing is misplaced, at least as far as schooling is concerned, because schooling, in various guises, already provides considerable experience with the design process. To understand the potential place of design activities in education, it is important to look at the quantity and kinds of design activities already in the classroom. Perhaps they are there in abundance. On the other hand, perhaps students spend a relatively modest amount of time on design activities of narrow scope.

First of all, plainly, students commit a high percentage of their school and homework time to receiving knowledge. Now nothing is wrong with the activity of receiving knowledge — there is a lot of knowledge worth receiving. Indeed, students could receive that knowledge more efficiently if it were presented as connected knowledge organized by means of the design questions. But students who spend most of their time consuming knowledge, however well served up it may be, are not constructing their own products of mind.

What role does the latter play in education today? For the most part, students' productive work seems to fall into two categories: the solving of problems in mathematics and the sciences, and the writing of essays in various subject matters (the creative writing sometimes done in English is a drop in the bucket). Let us investigate what sort of design such work involves.

A typical math or science problem provides partial answers to the four design questions and asks the student to fill in some more. Consider, for instance, a physics problem where one has to derive a physical constant from some given data. The constant has a certain structure—a number plus units of measure. The structure is already given, since the constant probably occurs in the back of the book if not in the problem statement. The constant has a purpose that the student presumably already knows—whatever the import of the constant is in physics. The part of the design task that falls to the student is producing an argument deriving the constant from the data. This argument uses physical principles, algebra, and arithmetic. As to a model, the text may provide a diagram of the physical situation for the student to use to guide the derivation, or the student may need to generate such a diagram.

Many variants of this scheme occur, of course. In plane geometry, the tasks is to prove a given theorem. Here again the student provides the argument but does not generate the structure— the theorem itself. In math and physics in general, sometimes the student needs to derive a formula rather than a numerical result. The formula—the structure to be produced—may be given in advance, so that the only task is to provide the argument, or may not, so that the student has to generate the formula as a consequence of the argument.

These are important design tasks, because they exercise the students' ability to construct deductive arguments in math and science. However, the genre seems narrow. First of all, the structure to prove or derive—the answer—is completely determined in advance by the problem constraints. Although the problem makes room for invention in developing the argument, it leaves no room for inventing the answer itself. As some prefer to put it, these are convergent rather than divergent problems.

Moreover, most school problems of this sort lack a strong connection to purpose in their disciplines. Although you can calculate the height from which you would have to drop an ice cube to vaporize it or the leverage required to budge the Empire State Building, who cares? Such problems do not address anything in the real world or the world of theory that is likely to be very important. Rather, the problems are mainly pretexts for exercising the machinery of algebraic and scientific deduction. Finally, note the emphasis on deductive rather than inductive inference. There is not much theory testing or explanation generating, but mainly the application of theory to made-up situations to derive or to prove results.

If conventional math and science problems reflect a narrow class of design activities, the problem of writing an essay has far more breadth in principle. Given the assignment to write an essay for your American History course, you could do almost anything touching the subject matter. You might summarize a period, examine a policy, review a military campaign, seek parallels between contemporary and earlier events, and so on. There is ample room here to create purpose, structure, models, and arguments.

The problem is that there is too much room, lacking some framework such as knowledge as design. The previous chapter urged that typical writing assignments leave students at sea. Instead of exercising the breadth of opportunity the essay format provides, they fall into the humdrum practice of writing essays that survey and summarize. This is natural. If you have to write on something and do not have a focus, the easiest thing to do is to tell what you know. But such "knowledge telling," as researchers on writing have called it, is a rather narrow and not very creative style of design.

OPPORTUNITIES FOR DESIGN

So the molehill really is a mountain: We are rightly concerned that schooling does not provide much broad-based experience in creating works of mind. But the mountain stands hollow unless there is hope of doing better. The natural explanation for the limited range of design activities looks to the limited knowledge of students; you cannot start at the top, so the story goes.

Although we can all agree on that, the explanation is deceptive: It mixes up quality of achievement with kind of activity. A learner cannot begin by doing top quality art but certainly can begin by doing art of some sort. Can the same be said for other subject areas? This is the crucial question for the prospects of education centered on works of mind. Let us reach for an answer in terms of types of designs learners can create.

Gadgets

Everyday gadgets are the most familiar kinds of designs — the pencils, erasers, pots, pans, and lampshades that make easier an amazing array of mundane activities. The world of gadgets offers a true playground for beginning design activities. After all, not every gadget has been invented already, and those that have often invite improvement. For example, here are several design tasks that have been employed successfully in classroom instruction.

Design an improvement of an ordinary blackboard eraser.

Design an improvement of the button-button hole system of fastening (it can be a modification or something completely new — but no existing alternatives like zippers).

Design a very light ladder for reaching the roofs of buildings one or two stories tall.

Design a very portable chair you can carry around conveniently to parades and sports events.

Design a table to use for dining in a very small apartment (no card tables please; something different).

These are apt design tasks for a surprisingly wide range of ages, since more sophisticated designers automatically escalate the difficulty of the problem by attempting to make more sophisticated designs. Of course, tasks like these lie far from the normal content of schooling, but they have a place there as well. There is no suggestion here that the design of gadgets should replace the standard curriculum. However, because gadgets are concrete and accessible, they make an excellent focus for practicing strategies of design that later will be applied to more conventional subject matters.

Strategies

A strategy is a procedure designed to help achieve a certain end. Typically, it does not guarantee success. The general's strategy for winning the battle, the investor's strategy for cornering the silver market, or the student's strategy for cramming for the exam may not suffice, even if well thought out.

Life is full of situations where strategies can help. Accordingly, their improvement and invention make good design activities. Especially in an academic context, study strategies invite attention. Here are some design activities chosen to promote self-awareness of study skills and active involvement in shaping them.

> Define whatever strategies you now have for studying for a math (history, physics, etc.) exam. Design three possible improvements in your strategies and try them out informally, keeping a diary in which you evaluate the results.

> Define how you allocate study time. Re-think your strategy and design three possible improvements. Try them out informally, keeping a diary in which you evaluate the results.

> Relevant in and out of school: Do you always plod through nonfiction reading from beginning to end? Reconsider whether working backwards, skipping around, or other tactics might prove better in some situations. Define three strategies and try them out informally, keeping track of your impressions about which works best.

Besides study strategies, problem-solving strategies also invite attention. For example, mathematics provides plentiful opportunities for the design of problem-solving strategies. Here are some examples:

> Design a strategy for mentally estimating the products of numbers of two decimal places. Write your strategy down for comparison with others. Practice it until you gain some fluency with it, debugging it as necessary.

> Select a type of math problem you have trouble with. Analyze the design of this kind of problem and design a strategy for constructing such problems. Construct several and solve them.

> A good mathematical problem solver constructs a representation of the problem — a diagram, for instance. Examine the kinds of representations you use if any. Design three improvements in your strategies of representation-making and try them out.

Of course, projects like these place considerable responsibility on learners. But they need not feel abandoned. Especially early on in discovering how to handle such design activities, learners should receive plentiful support from a skilled peer, teacher, or parent. Learners also can find confidence through working in groups of two or three on a joint design.

Humanistic disciplines present the same richness of opportunities for designing strategies as the mathematical domain. Consider, for instance, history.

Select an historically important battle, studying the circumstances thoroughly. Pick the losing side and design an alternative strategy the side might have followed to win, or, at least, reduce losses. Naturally, as in any design context, you need to develop not only the strategy but an argument for its effectiveness.

Verifying supposed facts about the past naturally poses a troublesome problem for historians, since they cannot go and see or do experiments. List as many strategies as you can that might be used for verifying supposed facts about the past — say the date of a battle or a voyage.

Nations occasionally rewrite their histories when a new political view comes into dominance, amplifying the role of some historical figures, minimizing that of others, and modifying other things. Suppose you wanted to do that in the United States. Identify the difficulties you would have to face and develop a strategy and supporting argument for the task.

Of course, the strategies learners evolve in such situations may not be very sophisticated and may serve their purposes only modestly. However, more important than any single strategy they contrive is the meta-lesson that you can be objective and deliberate about procedures, inspecting them, editing them, and inventing them. This is a powerful perspective for anyone to maintain on his or her own behavior.

Definitions

Definitions are interesting designs in many contexts. A definition has the general purpose of identifying a class of cases important in the situation. The structure of a definition typically involves a statement of the conditions under which something is a such and such. Model cases illustrate. The argument for a definition spans such considerations as clarity, consistency with existing usage, if any, and logical necessity and sufficiency.

There are different kinds of definitions and roles for them. For instance, an effort to define often begins with our intuitive sense of a term's meaning. We try to construct a definition that captures the intuitive sense, in order to sharpen our grasp of the concept and allow us to manipulate it better. We commonly do this in the midst of a conversation: "Let's define terms." Another role for definitions occurs during an investigation, where we invent concepts and terms to name them. We *stipulate* a meaning for a term that overrides any prior associations it may have (although we do well to watch out for stipulating meanings that actually oppose prior associations, since that often leads to confusion.) Definitions play a frequent role in instruction, when students learn the basic concepts in a field. Regretably, instruction perhaps too often is "definition heavy," expecting learners to absorb a sequence of abstract definitions without sufficient model experiences for real understanding.

What opportunities exist for designing definitions? For variety, let us look at two disciplines not already explored, say physics and English. As a well-developed formal science, physics offers few opportunities for devising brand-new definitions until one advances to the cutting edge of the field. However, many old definitions could stand improvement by adding models that illustrate them and convey and intuitive sense of what they address. Here are some design tasks along this line:

> Design several model cases that dramatize the difference between speed and velocity.
>
> Design several model cases that dramatize the difference between weight and mass.
>
> Design several model cases that dramatize the difference between density and mass.
>
> Design several model cases that dramatize the difference between pressure and force.

Such distinctions as these often give learners difficulty. Then how can learners who may not understand the concepts be expected to design models? We can treat that question as presenting an opportunity rather than an objection. Design is not necessarily a quick process where you come up with a good answer the first time. Interacting with the learners, the teacher should help them to refine, revise, or discard their initial designs and generate new ones, until, finally, they are devising correct and vivid examples on their own. When the learners get to the point where they can construct good model cases, surely they have understood the concept.

English, concerned as it is with the handling of a language, makes a natural context for work with definitions. Here are some sample design activities for English.

One approach to defining a genre is to do a design analysis of it. Undertake a design analysis of the short short story, working from a kit of a dozen or so examples.

One sort of definition gives necessary and sufficient conditions for something being a such and such. Learn what "necessary and sufficient conditions" means through some sample definitions. Now try to construct that kind of definition for a noun — the part of speech. Try to find counterexamples for your definition. Then revise your definition to eliminate the counterexamples. How close to necessary and sufficient conditions can you come?

Can you construct necessary and sufficient conditions for an object being a chair? If not, argue why not.

Take a general concept like liberty and generate very different model situations where you would say that people have liberty or do not have liberty. Try to extract a common factor and describe it in general terms. Is your common factor a necessary and sufficient condition? If not, give counterexamples.

Predictions

A prediction is a kind of design basic to many practical contexts and in the sciences, where proving a theory depends on testing predictions. All four design questions apply, as they do to any design. When you make a prediction, you produce an argument concluding that such and such should happen. That answers the argument question. The prediction itself becomes the structure, since it is what the argument supports. The answer to the purpose question concerns the import of the prediction: Why should we care whether such and such happens or not? Is a scientific theory at stake, an investment, a political action? The prediction may be about a particular model case, or a general range of cases where, to test the prediction, you have to pick a particular model case.

Let us shift subject matters again to emphasis that design activities can be found in any subject matter. Here are some prediction activities for biology and for current events.

Read about the relation between tooth structure and life style in wild animals. Make a prediction about the tooth structure of cats and dogs. Take a cautious look and confirm or disconfirm your prediction.

Read about the relation between beak structure and feeding style in birds. Go to a pet store or zoo and examine some birds, getting their names and noting the beak structures. Make predictions about their feeding styles. Then look up the species and see whether you can confirm your predictions.

Read about the leaf structure of plants that live in arid climates. Construct crude models of alternative leaf structures—for instance, fat versus thin—out of tissue paper. What is your prediction for which will lose moisture most quickly? Check it by moistening the tissue and measuring rate of water loss with a sensitive balance. Extend the experiment by building other possible leaf shapes and investigating their rate of water loss.

And in current events:

Wait for an international crisis, hopefully a minor one. Read diverse views about the crisis. Make a prediction about the action some nation will take in the next few days, justifying it with an argument. Monitor the news to see whether your prediction works out; if not, say what went wrong.

The stock market is a natural arena for prediction. Learn about some of the factors said to influence it. Make your own prediction for the movement of the market over a six week period. See what happens and, if you were wrong, try to explain why in terms of economic events during the course of the six weeks.

Pick a current referendum and predict whether it will be approved or not, drawing on media coverage. Wait and see. If you are wrong, try to explain why.

Certainly these exercises in prediction are difficult. Learners should be told straightforwardly that it is no shame to arrive at a wrong prediction in such volatile and uncertain contexts. The educational gain lies in making a careful, thoughtful effort to predict, checking your prediction, and trying to explain why if it goes wrong. Being right is a bonus.

Explanation of Empirical Facts and Phenomena

Whereas prediction concerns forecasting, explanation concerns accounting for what is already known to be so. For a fully connected explanation, all four design questions have to be addressed. You have to answer the argument question, saying why such and such should be so in light of basic principles. You are seeking a deep explanatory argument in the phrase of Chapter 2. The structure is whatever the argument argues for. Often in explanation the structure is a claim we already know is true; but we want to know *why* it is true. Models are examples and the purpose concerns the purpose or import of the structure.

For instance, consider the claim "the sky is blue." For a model, look out the window on a nice day. The purpose concerns the import or relevance of the phenomenon. A blue sky is a very familiar part of life; a physical explanation demonstrates the power of physics to account for ordinary facts. The argument shows how a blue sky follows from the principles governing the scattering and absorption of light.

In a science, the explanatory principles invoked usually are fairly explicit. In a humanistic domain, such as literature or history, or in everyday life, the explanatory principles called upon may be more informal, even commonsensical.

So far this section has touched on several different subject matters. Now cycling back to mathematics, here are some simple facts and phenomena that allow mathematical explanation:

Why do stools have at least three legs? (So they will not fall over, of course, but what principle from geometry is involved?)

If you save your change, what coins do you end up with the most often, next most often, least often, and why? (A matter of different simplest ways of making up amounts of money between 1 cent and 99 cents.)

Why is this betting system not such a good idea: Double your bet every time you lose, so when you finally win you will win all your money back and more.

Here are some exercises in explanation for history:

> Why do some nations end up in a position where they have to import large quantities of food?

> Why is sea power not so important today as it was a century ago?

> Why does the modern world lack great empires like that of Britain or Rome? Is it the luck of the times or is there a reason?

Classification Systems

Systems of classification are designs that occur in virtually all disciplines. In terms of design, the structure of a classification system includes the categories and the rules for classifying something into those categories. The general purpose is making order out of chaos, with additional purposes appropriate to each situation. For instance, the taxonomic system for classifying plants and animals seeks not only to organize but also to capture degree of genetic relatedness.

As to argument, a simple classification system should have at least the following three properties. (1) The categories are exclusive; nothing should fit clearly into more than one of them. (2) The categories are sharp; there are few borderline cases that could fall equally well into one category or another. (3) The categories are exhaustive; anything in the relevant domain can be classified into some category. Other criteria may apply as well, for instance, in the case of plants and animals, genetic relatedness between members of the same category.

A word of warning, though. These criteria cannot be applied blindly. Depending on the situation, it may not be all that important if there are a number of borderline cases. Again depending on the situation, perhaps a few items that do not fit in any other category can be dumped into a "mixed" or "miscellaneous" category with no great harm done. A classification system is a pragmatic tool, not necessarily a perfect vessel.

Here are some classification systems to design for physics:

> Make up a classification system for sources of energy convertible to electrical energy.

> Make up a classification system for principles of locomotion in animals.

Make up a classification system for ways of coping with frictional forces in machinery and biological organisms.

And in English:

Make up a classification system for genres of fiction: historical novels, mystery novels, etc.

Employing a dictionary of contemporary usage, make up a classification system for the sources of slang words and phrases — hip, buzz, grok, totally awesome, etc.

Make up a classification system for your personal most frequent spelling errors.

I have argued by example that manageable design tasks of many kinds can be found in any discipline. There is no need to settle for the rather narrow range of design tasks learners ordinarily undertake. A few general points about the practicality and importance of learners designing round out the argument.

First of all, the kinds of designs mentioned above — classification systems, explanations, predictions, and so on — only sample the many possibilities. Just to mention a few more, there are decisions, experiments, or narratives. With every addition to the list, the opportunities for meaningful design exercises increase.

Second, it should be plain from the examples that doing such exercises in design has a double purpose. On the one hand, learners learn how to handle design tasks that construct and wield connected knowledge in various disciplines. At the same time, they learn how to handle particular "genres" of design, such as classification systems, explanations, and predictions. These genres of design have importance in many disciplines.

Finally, an objection: Might not most learners find at least some of the design tasks mentioned above too difficult? If left solely to their own resources, they certainly would. But learners can be eased into the art of design. The remainder of this chapter explores how that might be done.

MODELS OF MODELING

How can learners come to handle design tasks like those suggested earlier, tasks that ask them to be much more inventive than they are used to? A start on the problem comes from the previous chapter, where, in the case of written works, the following steps were recommended: (1) select a type of design; (2) do a design analysis of it yourself; (3) lead the learners to understand the design by straight presentation, Socratic questioning, or having them figure it out for themselves; (4) ask them to compose new model cases; and (5) provide clarification and helping strategies as needed. The same general strategy applies to any situation, not just essays, poems, and stories. For instance, if you want your learners to compose certain sorts of definitions or classification systems or explanations, you can follow those steps.

But what if you suspect that the learners need extensive guidance under item 5? How does one accomplish this? "Modeling" is a good way to introduce learners to a complex process. The teacher acts out the process for the learners, involving them somewhat, and that way the learners pick up what to do. Modeling is an interesting word to find here. It is a normal word to use, but the usage also suits the design questions well. A pattern of thinking is, of course, a design. In acting out a pattern of thinking for learners, a teacher provides a model case of that pattern of thinking.

What kind of modeling can help when design skills are the aim? The best way to answer that is to offer an example, a model of modeling. Imagine a teacher working with a group of students in late elementary school. The teacher is using a modeling method called *reciprocal teaching*, where the teacher takes turns modeling and asking the students to solo. The design task is to improve buttons, more specifically to improve the button-button hole fastening system. Zippers might be one improvement, but existing improvements do not count. It has to be something new. The students already have analyzed other gadgets and thought about the design of a button as it is (step 3 above). The teacher engages the students in the design task and provides clarification and helping strategies at the same time as follows (fusing steps 4 and 5 above).

The teacher's turn

Teacher: Okay. I want to tackle this design problem. I know in general what I'm supposed to do: I need to answer the design questions. Which one first? Purpose, so I'll know what I'm doing. So the problem gives the purpose—to improve the system of fastening with buttons and button holes. Which design question next? Ralph, what do you think?

Ralph's turn

    Ralph: I'd get some ideas for the improvement. Let's see . . .

    Teacher: Why not try argument first. Criticize a regular button.

    Ralph: Oh yeah. Well, what sorts of things go wrong with buttons? Buttons often pop open when you don't want them to. Sometimes they come off and get lost. (The teacher notes these ideas on the blackboard.) That's all that comes to mind right away.

    Teacher: Try a little more.

    Ralph: I can't think of anything.

    Teacher: Well, you made a couple of good points. Let me take a turn.

Teacher's turn

    Teacher: When you're having trouble thinking of something, it's a good move to consider a model and imagine different parts of it. Let me imagine I was getting dressed in the morning. What happens and what does it tell me about buttons? Well, I see they're a nuisance to button up. I see one's missing too; it came off in the washing machine. One place buttons often get lost is in the wash. There's a couple more troubles with buttons. (The teacher writes these ideas on the blackboard.) Let's say that's enough. Now what? Mary, why don't you take a turn?

Mary's turn

    Mary: I'd pick a problem with buttons to work on. That's a new purpose.

    Teacher: Fine. But why not work on them all?

    Mary: You could, but it would be awfully confusing.

    Teacher: It would indeed. So go ahead and choose.

    Mary: I think I'll pick the nuisance of buttoning and unbuttoning. I think that's pretty important. So I want to improve buttons in a way that makes the whole thing easier. How can I do that?

    Teacher: That's asking for . . ?

    Mary: Structure. Let's see now. I'm thinking of an oval button. It's made of plastic. It slips through the button hole easier because you put it through in its skinny direction. It has four holes in it for thread. That sounds pretty good. I think I'm all done.

    Teacher: It's certainly a good idea. But is Mary really all done? Ralph?

    Ralph: I say you got to have more argument. Evaluate the idea to check it out.

Teacher: Go ahead, Mary.

Mary: Well, I don't know. Maybe . . . Maybe the buttons would slip out easier because they're oval. That might be a problem.

Teacher: Could be. But maybe you can solve it too. Let me make a turn now, because I want to make another point.

Teacher's turn

Teacher: The oval button's an interesting idea. But wait. I don't want to jump to a very specific solution without considering possibilities. Maybe there's a completely different approach to the problem that's much better. Let me think of some general approaches. Let's see. True, I might make the button oval. I could make the button smaller. I could have button holes that somehow open up when you put the button through but then close more. (The teacher notes these ideas on the blackboard.) I seem to be out of ideas. But I'm not satisfied yet. What can I do? Does anyone remember?

Brenda: You could look at a model case, like you did before.

Teacher: Good idea, Brenda. Why don't you try it.

Brenda's turn

Brenda: Well, I'll imagine clothes and how they're fastened. I see lots of buttons, but they all work in about the same way. I see zippers too. Zippers aren't allowed, but maybe something that works like zippers would do. Something else that sticks things together. You know what I think of, I think of that stuff that clings. I think it's called Velcro. Velcro is that kind of cloth that has all the tiny hooks on it, so that it sticks to fuzzy cloth. That's one idea. Or maybe I could use magnets. (The teacher adds "Velcro" and "magnets" to the ideas on the blackboard.)

Mary: But those last two aren't ideas for improving a button. They're ideas for something completely different.

Teacher: Yes and no. That depends on what you mean by improving a button. Does a zipper improve a button? In a way it does. We don't want to be too narrow or we box ourselves in. We could stick strictly to buttons, of course, but let's go ahead and explore the Velcro idea. Brenda, which design question does that start to answer?

Brenda: Structure.

Teacher: Can you fill out the structure a little more?

Brenda: Well, I see a shirt with a strip of Velcro down the front. But right away I see an argument against. The shirt has no buttons. Of course, I don't want buttons, but the shirt looks really strange. I don't know. Should I try to solve the problem or put it off?

Teacher: Ralph, what do you think?

Ralph: I don't know. But it's real crucial problem. If it isn't solved, I wouldn't wear the shirt.

Teacher: Yes, there's no point in putting off tackling a "killing" problem, because you have to solve it to save the idea. So you have a new purpose. Give it a try, Ralph.

Ralph's turn

Ralph: What can I do about the Velcro shirt looking funny? Well, I have one idea right away. Put buttons on the shirt. The buttons don't do anything. They just appear on the front to make the shirt look normal. That sounds like a pretty sneaky solution.

Teacher: And now?

Ralph: Uh . . . argument. Well, it would cost a little more to put buttons on. Besides the Velcro, I mean. But not too much. I don't think that's so bad. I can't think of anything else.

Teacher: Do you know how to try?

Ralph: Oh yeah, a model. Let's see, suppose I'm putting on this shirt that closes with Velcro . . .

Although the example could continue, that much should do to demonstrate the style. One feature of the style deserves special note: *Who does what.* The teacher either models the design process or passes the lead to one of the students. But when one of the students has the lead, the teacher "scaffolds," as it is often called, providing helpful hints to support and clarify the student's effort.

It is fair to ask whether this procedure, which works out so neatly for designing gadgets, can do as well when the teacher and students are trying to design something more abstract, such as a definition. The students already have learned something about purpose, structure, model cases, and arguments concerning definitions of common words in general. Now they are to produce a definition of a common word themselves.

Teacher's turn

Teacher: Okay. This time our purpose is to design a definition.

We want to try to define the word "citizen." So I ask myself, "What do I know about the design of definitions in general?" Well, the purpose is to make the meaning of a word clear. What's the structure like? Ralph?

Ralph: Lots of times it's rules that tell you what the word means. I mean, you can use the word when the rules are satisfied.

Teacher: That's fine. And now argument. In general, we want to be sure the definition fits what people really mean by the word when they use it. Now how can we be sure of that?

(Silence.)

Teacher: Well, we can look for model cases. In particular, we can look for counterexamples, where the way we ordinarily use the words breaks the rule we've proposed. So I've taken the first step. I've reminded us all about the general nature of the design questions for definitions. Now we have a special case to deal with— "citizen." Mary, would you like to start off?

Mary's turn

Mary: Well, if you're a citizen, you can vote. (The teacher notes the idea on the blackboard.)

Teacher: Are you done?

Mary: No, I need to get more ideas at the beginning. I need to search for different possibilities. So, well, there's stuff in the constitution about when you're a citizen. If you're born in the United States, you're automatically a citizen of the United States.

Brenda: People can get to be citizens by passing a test, too.

Teacher: That's several ideas (the teacher writes them on the blackboard). Now what, Mary?

Mary: Well, I guess I need to try to make a definition out of some of them. So, I don't know, how about . . . How about citizens are people who can vote?

Teacher: Okay. Now what, Mary?

(Silence.)

Teacher: No ideas? Let me take a turn.

Teacher's turn

Teacher: So we have a proposed definition. That's structure. Now for argument. Let's check the definition out by looking for counterarguments. Now I don't think of any right away. But when you're having trouble thinking of something, a good thing to do is to think of a model and explore it in various ways for ideas. Imagine a citizen voting, for instance. Imagine people at the polls. Anything special about them? Or imagine all the different kinds of people you know about.

Ralph: Kids can't vote, but they're citizens.

Teacher: Okay, good point. So there's a counterexample to that proposal. Let's see if we can fix the definition or take another approach.

Brenda: Wait a minute. I see another problem.

Teacher: Okay. Let's hear it. Take a turn, Brenda.

Brenda's turn

Brenda: I don't know whether we're defining citizen of the United States or citizen in general. If it's citizen of the United States, there are rules in the constitution. But if it's in general, I don't know.

Teacher: Good point. And which design questions are you worrying about when you raise that point?

(Silence.)

Teacher: It's purpose of the definition—do we want a definition for citizens of the United States or citizens in general? So which would be better?

Brenda: Well, the problem doesn't say, so I guess we have to pick. I guess it's up to me, right? Maybe we can put the problem off. But no, I guess not.

Teacher: It's often a good idea to put a problem of detail off until later, but why not this one?

Brenda: Because we don't know what we're doing. Like what problem we're trying to solve.

Teacher: Sure. In fact it's a general rule: Handle right away problems that are really crucial. Okay, so which problem would be best to take, Brenda?

Again we could continue, but this much suffices to make a couple of points. First, the same sort of thinking that approached a new way of fastening shirts can lead toward a definition of "citizen." Second, here during the teacher's turn the teacher not only modeled thinking for the students but occasionally asked for their help to keep them involved.

STRATEGIES OF DESIGN

Besides modeling how to model, the examples of improving a button and defining "citizen" offered a look at general design strategies. After demonstrating, the teacher can mention these strategies explicitly. Of course, each strategy is itself a design — a design for designing. Consider this list and then the rationale of each principle.

1. Use all the design questions over and over.
2. Possibilities first, commitments later.
3. Ideas first, details later.
4. But face a pivotal problem at once.
5. When stuck for ideas, explore models.
6. Think on paper (blackboard, etc.).

Strategy 1. Use All the Design Questions Over and Over. For instance, in the examples, the teacher saw to it that evaluative arguments and new purposes both received attention. Beginners at design tend to neglect evaluation and establishing new goals for revision, instead accepting the first well-elaborated idea they produce regardless of its problems. This principle works against that tendency.

Strategy 2. Possibilities First, Commitments Later. For example, for both the button and "citizen" designs, alternatives were sought at the outset rather than developing the first reasonable idea that turned up. In general, research shows that creative people explore several possibilities early on in a flexible way, and only gradually move toward commitment. In common sense terms, the approach you take at the beginning of a problem influences greatly the sort of result you will get. Accordingly, an early exploration of options is an especially good investment of effort.

Strategy 3. Ideas First, Details Later. For instance, work on the button began with general design questions. Work on the definition of "citizen" began with a review of the design questions as they would be answered for any definition. People often rush into problems of detail without assessing whether they have a good overall understanding of the problem and a good approach to a solution. This strategy counters that trend.

Strategy 4. But Face a Pivotal Problem at Once. For example, in improving the button, the group addressed the problem of the odd buttonless appearance of the Velcro-fastened shirt right away, because, if that problem could not be resolved, the whole approach would fall through. In doing the "citizen" problem, the group chose to clarify whether the aim was to define citizen of the United States or citizen in general as soon as the matter came up, because the decision would seriously change the nature of the task. In general, the resolution of a pivotal problem may take you off in quite a different direction. Therefore, you had best address it at once.

Strategy 5. When Stuck for Ideas, Explore Models. For instance, when trying to think of more difficulties with buttons, the teacher imagined dressing in the morning. When seeking counterexamples to the proposal that citizens are those who can vote, the teacher imagined people voting to see who was included and who was left out. In general, when you stimulate your mind not only with the questions at hand but with concrete models closely or even remotely relevant to it, you stimulate your mind from two directions at once, so to speak. This often brings to light options you would never think of otherwise.

Strategy 6. Think on Paper (Blackboard, etc.). For example, the teacher noted down options on the blackboard throughout. It is well established that a human being can only keep a few chunks of information in mind at once—a few words, a few sentences, a few ideas. Many problems quickly outstrip what working memory, as it's sometimes called, can manage. Writing and drawing are the standard solutions, meriting mention here only because some people tend to neglect them, thinking of a piece of paper as a place for final products only.

INTRINSIC MOTIVATION

Anyone who has taught, in school or out of it, knows all too well the range of learners' enthusiasm. While one works with gusto, another approaches the same task indifferently. Such contrasts occur not just from learner to learner but from task to task. The same student who puts in extra hours on a science project may make a minimal effort on an English paper. And, of course, the majority of students do not seem very interested in anything academic.

Psychologists have taken an interest in interest and have developed a way of talking about enthusiasm—"intrinsic motivation." When you have intrinsic motivation for an activity, you value the activity for its own sake. You enjoy doing it, find it challenging but not too frustrating, and view it as worthwhile in itself.

You can also have "extrinsic motivation" for engaging in the activity. Perhaps, for example, you will receive high grades or more pay for doing it well. From a logical point of view, intrinsic and extrinsic motivation might simply combine, providing all the more motivation. However, according to research by the Brandeis psychologist Teresa Amabile and others, the presence of blatant extrinsic motives tends to undermine intrinsic motives, leading to competent but less creative work. This bears special relevance to the design perspective on learning because the perspective emphasizes creative tasks, activities where learners analyze and construct designs on their own.

In general, intrinsic motivation turns out to be a rather delicate flower, easily bruised. Research also shows that evaluation, restriction of options, unpleasant surroundings, and various other factors reduce intrinsic motivation and thereby creativity. In fact, intrinsic motivation seems much easier to undermine than to amplify. Accordingly, any approach to teaching and learning, and especially the present one, should avoid so far as possible features that tend to undermine intrinsic motivation. How can we do that? Several factos that foster intrinsic motivation are worth bearing in mind.

Intrinsic Worth.   One contributor to intrinsic motivation is perception of a task or its product as intrinsically worthwhile, worthwhile in itself. For instance, you write a poem for the sake of the writing and the poem; but you run an errand not for the joy of it but to get the errand done. You paint a picture for the sake of the activity and the picture; but you do an assignment to fulfill a course requirement. But what if the assignment is to paint a picture? This mixed case causes trouble. Having an extrinsic motive like meeting course requirements undermines somewhat your perception of the intrinsic worth of the task.

Internal Locus of Control. Another factor fostering intrinsic motivation is an internal locus of control, the sense that you are in control of the task at hand. You are more likely to become invested in a project where you decide how to proceed and what to try for than a project where someone tells you exactly what is wanted and how to achieve it. Blind chance also competes for locus of control. If you feel that fate is pushing you around, the sense of an internal locus of control will falter, and, along with it, your intrinsic motivation.

Feeling of Competence. The feeling that you can handle a task encourages intrinsic motivation; the feeling that the task is beyond you undermines it. Perhaps this amounts to a special case of locus of control—if you cannot handle a task, you are not in control. Special case or not, it is worth a separate mention.

Optimal Challenge. Easy tasks foster an internal locus of control and feelings of competence, but tasks that are too easy bore people. On the other hand, tasks that strain the resources of an individual threaten an internal locus of control and perception of competence. High intrinsic motivation comes with a degree of challenge somewhere between. Of course, the right degree for one person may be the wrong degree for another.

Enjoyment. Anything that makes an activity enjoyable in itself, whether directly related to the activity or not, fosters intrinsic motivation. For instance, pleasant surroundings or a treat after completing the task, *a treat not conditional upon success,* can boost intrinsic motivation and creativity.

The question remains: What to do about fostering intrinsic motivation in learning contexts? As the points above make plain, various features of normal education would tend to undermine intrinsic motivation, for instance, grades, criticism, required work, difficult exercises, and barren classroom environments. There would be no dilemma if one could leave learners alone to do their creative best. But that would be naive. Learners need input, and usually a lot of it. Therefore, feedback and guidance, though they threaten an internal locus of control, must be offered in some form. Leaners do not always want to do what they should do, so probably instruction will always have to be a little coercive in some respects. The question becomes how to preserve and promote intrinsic motivation as much as possible, while doing what has to be done.

Here are several strategies that should help. They have the common purpose of fostering intrinsic motivation. Provided in each case is the strategy, a couple of models, and a brief rationale connecting the strategy to the principles just listed.

Treat the Activities as Intrinsically Interesting. For instance, when teaching math, you can show some enthusiasm for the theorem you are discussing or pick a theorem you feel enthusiastic about. When modeling the process of designing a definition, you can display interest in the evolving explicit understanding of your intuitions about the meaning. In general, not only your actions but your attitudes are models for learners. If you exhibit an attitude of intrinsic interest in things, they will tend to do likewise.

Minimize Evaluative Feedback. It is difficult in formal educational contexts to omit grading. However, on a day to day basis you do not have to emphasize praise or blame. Of course, a word or two of encouragement may be entirely appropriate, but neither the social reward of praise nor the social punishment of blame need dominate your interactions with learners. If they do, the learners may reorient their behavior toward these extrinsic factors and away from the intrinsic interests of the task.

Maximize Informative Feedback. For example, you can try to be very specific about how to make a particular essay better. To put difficulties in a constructive light, you can offer a strategy to help avoid weaknesses the next time around. For trivial computational errors in math, you can suggest checking strategies. In general, if you treat errors as pointers to specific tactics for improving a performance, rather than as sins in themselves, your input may boost rather than reduce the learner's sense of mastery of the task.

Allow Choices. For instance, you can offer a list of designs to undertake, letting each learner select. In giving guidance, you can suggest more than one strategy rather than telling the learners exactly what to do. Choices help learners to experience an internal locus of control.

Avoid Surveillance. You don't have to hang over learners as they work or monitor their efforts on a project constantly. Such actions carry an implicit threat of evaluation and undermine the learners' sense of the intrinsic worth of the task.

Offer Tractable Problems in a Range of Difficulties. You might, for example, list several classification systems to design with difficulty ratings beside them. Leaving to each learner the choice not only fosters an internal locus of control but allows the learner to select an optimal level of challenge, one stimulating rather than boring or frustrating.

Have Learners Work in Groups of Three or Four when they First Attempt a New Kind of Task. By working in a group, learners can pool their resources and diffuse frustration, thus maintaining a sense of competence.

Try to Make the Activity Fun. Perhaps you can maintain an easygoing humorous style. You can keep the physical environment cheerful. You can present unserious instead of serious examples now and then. In general, the more you create an upbeat atmosphere, the more you will highlight the intrinsic value of the activity.

PROBLEM FINDING

When power engineers are planning a thermonuclear power plant, they are problem solving; when the engineers discovered the need for such a plant in light of an impending energy crisis, they were problem finding. When you are figuring out how to fix the broken chain on your bicycle, you are problem solving; when the chain broke and nearly threw you over the handle bars as it jammed in the rear wheel, you were problem finding—and it did not take much finding. When you are writing the lines of a poem, you are problem solving; when you sought the basic idea for the poem, you were problem finding. Of course, this is a little facile. Finding what sort of poem to write could itself be called a problem—the problem that comes before the problem of actually writing it. But the basic contrast should be clear: Behind each problem we usually think of as such, there is the matter of finding the problem in the first place, a widely neglected but pivotal matter.

Problem finding, a term coined by the psychologists Getzels and Csikszentmihalyi to contrast with problem solving, honors the earliest stages of creative activity. Creativity has often been viewed as a matter of insightful problem solving, but these researchers emphasize that there is something wrongheaded about this. Significant creative achievement often involves not just finding a solution, but recognizing a problem not recognized before, or defining a known problem in a new way.

Research on student artists supports this view. Studies have disclosed that those artists rated the most creative also behave differently as they begin to think about a work. They explore more thoroughly and flexibly the opportunities offered by materials they might arrange to form a still life. The most creative artists also remain readier to change direction later if a new idea suggests itself. Their behavior can be summarized in three words: better problem finding. That is, they invest more effort in seeking a basic direction for their work and stay more open to accepting opportunities that suggest themselves along the way. Although the formal evidence for the importance of problem finding behavior comes from studies of artists, it seems likely that problem finding is important for creativity in any field.

We have not paid much attention to problem finding so far. The design tasks suggested earlier for the most part present learners with a problem rather than asking them to find one for themselves. More heed should be paid to problem finding for at least two reasons. First of all, we have evidence of the importance of problem finding in creative pursuits, so we should certainly offer learners some awareness of and practice with it. Second, problem finding should foster intrinsic motivation. To the extent that learners find their own problems, they are likely to select problems that they find more intrinsically motivating.

The question remains how to introduce problem finding. It is easy to say, "Let your learners find their own design opportunities some of the time," but hunting for a design opportunity can be hard. Suppose, for instance, that you send your physics students forth in search of design opportunities. Where do they look? What do they seek? How do they know when they have found it? The general task of finding a problem is too open-ended.

That characteristic suggests a natural solution: Narrow the task a little. Learners can seek design opportunities within certain genres of design that lend themselves to problem finding. For example, suppose that you have been having learners design gadgets. To introduce some problem finding, you might ask them to find an opportunity to improve a gadget. The advantages of this assignment become clear by contrast with a slightly different one: Find an opportunity to design a brand new gadget. It's much harder to discover an opportunity to design something new. To generalize, you can introduce problem finding through genres of designs that offer plentiful design opportunities for the novice.

Here are some appropriate genres in addition to improving gadgets.

Improvements in Policies, Plans, and Laws.   Policies, plans, and laws are important elements in the conduct of governments. They emerge in such subject matters as history or social studies. Each learner can seek a policy, plan, or law of personal interest that presents a design opportunity for improving it. Policies, plans, and laws lend themselves to problem finding for much the same reason that gadgets do — both are accessible to common sense reasoning. To be sure, the improvements learners construct may not be very insightful. But compare the difficulty of finding opportunities for improving principles or laws in science. Novices would hardly know where to begin looking.

Improvements in Problem Solving and Study Strategies. Because learners carry their own problem solving and study strategies with them, and because such strategies often are underdeveloped, they represent a natural domain for problem finding. The algorithms of mathematics provide a good contrasting case. These procedures, already highly refined, are all the more hard for learners to improve because learners usually do not really understand the rationale behind them.

Definitions of Nontechnical Terms in Common Use.   The problem of defining the word "citizen" exemplified this genre. Learners can readily hunt for words they would like to try to define. To tailor the task to a subject matter, you can ask learners to select words relevant to it. The one difficulty is to discourage learners from resolving their definitional problems by immediate recourse to a dictionary. This genre contrasts with the much less tractable one of constructing definitions in technical fields, such as mathematics or law. There, formal definitions already exist, definitions interlocked with a whole structure of other definitions and principles. To tinker with a definition is to tamper with the whole system, a difficult business.

Models for Scientific and Mathematical Terms.   However, as mentioned earlier, scientific terms lend themselves to another kind of attention. Often they come abstractly formulated and insufficiently exemplified. A good model is part of a good definition. There are plenty of opportunities in mathematics and the sciences to improve or invent models designed to make concepts clearer.

Explanation of Tools.   A genre useful for design finding in physics is the explanation of tools. Ordinary tools incorporate various physical principles and invite analysis in terms of them. Remember, for instance, the opening example in this book — the cutting edge. If you are a novice at physics, finding a tool you know enough to say something about is much easier than, for example, finding a natural phenomenon you can explain.

This list could be made much longer, but perhaps these examples will do for the general point. There are many genres of designs appropriate for problem finding by learners in various subject matters. Other genres of designs may serve the needs of instruction well enough if the learners are given a specific assignment, but the learners may not know enough to go problem hunting in these genres with great success. By using the above genres and inventing more to suit other circumstances, we can ensure that learners get some experience in problem finding without being baffled by it.

WHAT YOU CAN DO

As a learner or teacher, in a formal or informal context, you can foster active learning by way of design. In particular, you can:

- *Organize learning around making works of mind.* Works of mind accessible to the beginner can be devised for any discipline. Among the opportunities are gadgets, strategies, definitions, predictions, explanations, classification systems, decisions, experiments, narratives, and more.

- *Guide the making process by the design questions.* Define the purpose of what you are making, seek its structure, think in terms of model cases, and evaluate your product, leading on to new purposes for revision and another cycle. In your teacher roles, you can introduce learners to this process by modeling and scaffolding.

- *Apply the design questions bearing in mind several principles.* (1) Use all the design questions over and over; (2) possibilities first, commitments later; (3) ideas first, details later; (4) but face a pivotal problem at once; (5) when stuck for ideas, explore models; (6) think on paper (blackboard, etc.).

- *Allocate time and thought to problem finding.* Think of the problem formulation as the first product, the product that precedes and shapes the nature of the final product. As a teacher, you can avoid always setting definite problems and sometimes pose tasks of an open-ended nature that allow learners to do some problem finding for themselves.

All this applies broadly to teachers and learners. However, it is particularly the responsibility of a teacher to promote intrinsic motivation in a learning context:

- *Strive for practices that foster intrinsic motivation and avoid practices that undermine it.* You can: (1) treat the activity underway as intrinsically interesting; (2) minimize evaluative feedback; (3) maximize informative feedback; (4) allow choices; (5) avoid surveillance; (6) offer tractable problems in a range of difficulties; (7) arrange group work; (8) try to make the activity fun.

5 Inside Models

We are told that the universe may be finite but unbounded. What sense does this make? Measured by the simplest way of thinking through the idea, it seems to make no sense at all. Imagine yourself riding outward on the crest of a beam of light into this possibly finite universe. Travel long enough and what happens? It seems that if the universe if finite, there must be an end, you and your beam of light running into something that bottles the universe up, makes it finite. But when you imagine that, you have a boundary to what was supposed to be unbounded.

There is a second puzzle too: Running into a boundary seems contrary to the very concept of universe. Having ridden the beam of light to the limit, which feels perhaps rigid like steel or yielding like rubber, you naturally ask, "What's beyond the boundary?" The quick answer "nothing" seems nonsensical. How can there be nothing beyond a boundary? The answer "more space" tells you that you have not really travelled to the end of the universe, because that space should be included in the universe, even if there is nothing in it. So your light beam ride leads you not only to peculiar physical boundaries but peculiar limits of logic as well.

Perhaps standing back a bit from this effort to understand a finite unbounded universe would help. Your ride on the beam of light, the image constructed in an effort to make sense of a finite but unbounded universe, is a model. In conjuring that image, you are trying to render concrete and accessible an abstract notion. Thinking with a model—in our heads, on paper, out of clay, on computer displays, or in innumerable other ways—is one of our basic tactics of understanding.

But the light beam rider model explored so far does not yield an understanding. Well, not all models are good models. Perhaps a model of a different shape can find the sense in the notion of a finite but unbounded universe.

Imagine that you are a two-dimensional being living on the surface of a vast sphere. Suppose that one day you become a light beam rider, setting off on a beam of two-dimensional light, the sort of light your two-dimensional world has. Travel however far you will, you come to no boundary. Rather, you eventually return to your starting point, having circumnavigated the sphere. In short, your universe of the sphere is finite but unbounded.

All that concerns a two-dimensional version of you living on the two-dimensional surface of a sphere. Now suppose that you, in fact a three-dimensional being in a three-dimensional universe, face analogous circumstances. Just as the surface of the sphere contains finite area, our universe might have finite volume. Just as the two-dimensional being who rides a two-dimensional beam of light comes back to where he started without ever encountering a boundary, so might you on such a three-dimensional journey in our universe never encounter a boundary, and for all your ranging eventually simply circle around to where you started. Before getting back, you would not even realize that your path was curved because you were going as straight as you could given that you had to stay on the surface of the sphere. This analogy with a visualizable two-dimensional situation lets us reconcile how space could be finite but lack boundaries.

There is a fair complaint to make, however. While the model shows the possibility of a finite but unbounded universe, the matter of the universe including everything still proves a mystery. Consider again the two-dimensional beings on the surface of the sphere. Although their travels are confined to that surface, there is something outside it—the three-dimensional space in which it sits. Accordingly, what they think of as their finite unbounded universe does not encompass the whole universe at all, but amounts to a mere bubble within the real universe. Likewise, when we contemplate what we take to be our universe, one perhaps finite and unbounded, we might not be contemplating the whole universe but only a bubble within it.

Complaint? Perhaps this is really an insight. The sphere model does good service here in highlighting a circumstance that might be so. Could we not have a status like that of the sphere-dwellers, the universe we can access sitting in a higher dimensional space without our having any way to tell? By capturing this possibility in a model, the analogy of the sphere makes plain the fundamentally limited character of our perceptions. But it also makes plain the reach of our imaginations, which, as we think with models, can carry us to possibilities beyond the reach of our senses.

WHAT IS A MODEL?

It is no accident that models are the focus of one of the four design questions: The finite universe example and others that have gone before show how models are powerful tools of understanding. To wield that power most effectively as a teacher, learner, or thinker, you want to grasp exactly what models are in their full range and potential.

Is "examples" the simple answer? For the most part, the models used in this book have been examples, illustrating, for instance, a theory such as Darwin's theory of natural selection, a method of instruction like reciprocal teaching, or a linguistic form such as elephant jokes. But the notion of models includes more than examples. The sphere with its two-dimensional inhabitants is not an example of a finite unbounded universe since it is a mental image not a physical instance, and also since there is no two-dimensional universe for it to be an example of so far as we know. Nonetheless it provides a model by analogy for how our universe could be finite and unbounded.

The Variety of Models

Then what are models in their full range and color? Since models are designs, the design questions provide a handy way to organize an answer. The purpose of all models remains as surveyed so far — to serve as instruments of understanding. As to structure, the basic tactic of a model is to make something understandable by showing, manifesting, displaying its characteristics.

How can this happen? The case of an example is perhaps the simplest one of all. When you describe an abstraction such as the theory of natural selection, or the Pythagorean theorem, or the notion of knowledge as design itself, the richness and concreteness of the theory commonly escape its articulation in words. The giving of examples that incarnate the abstraction helps us to grasp more concretely what the verbal formulation expresses abstractly.

But there are more ways to do this than by giving examples. Pictures, for instance, often amount to surrogate examples. It is impossible to arrange a visitation by George Washington himself, but certainly one can present a picture of George Washington that displays his appearance. It is inconvenient to provide examples of the Sphinx itself, or the Taj Mahal. But again, pictures offer surrogate examples that will do well enough for many circumstances.

Even the notion of surrogate examples, however, does not stretch nearly far enough to encompass the full range of models. Many models capture perspectives that not only are inconvenient, but impossible, and do not so much picture as present a partially conventional rendering of what they represent. Consider, for example, a Mercator projection map of the world. Now the earth, even as seen from space, does not look like this large rectangle with its oversize Greenland and broad bands for the northern and southern polar regions. Nor are the countries of the real world colored like those on the map. Yet the map conveys information about the world by displaying its layout according to certain conventions.

So a map is a model, but not an example, nor even a surrogate example in the sense that photographs can be. A great diversity of representations stand in essentially the same relationship to what they represent as do maps to their terrains. In much the same way, planetariums "map" the solar system, circuit diagrams "map" electrical circuits, and computer simulations "map" the flow of traffic or the yearly changes in an ecology.

Graphs of mathematical functions provide another case of interest. For example, the graph of the function $y = 5x + 7$ offers what you might loosely call a picture of the function. Yet considering a graph a picture muddles up some important differences between graphs and pictures as usually understood. A picture of the Sphinx pictures the physical layout of the Sphinx, but a graph of a function does not picture any physical layout the function has, because the function has none other than the graph. Nor does the graph picture the equation; on the contrary, the graph and equation alike can be thought of as alternative expressions of the function, so the graph no more pictures the equation than the equation pictures the graph. For essentially the same reasons, the graph does not map the function either. Nonetheless, although neither picturing nor mapping are the right words, the graph shows or manifests the function in a sense that a formula does not. So a graph is yet a third type of model.

As if these complexities were not enough, analogies often serve as models. We have just seen one, as noted earlier—the two-dimensional universe on the surface of a sphere that helped us to understand by analogy how our own three-dimensional universe might be finite and unbounded. In general, analogical models thrive in science. For instance, there is the well-known billiard ball model of a gas, where a gas is treated as a swarm of tiny billiard balls that move about at random and occasionally bounce off one another. With proper mathematics, this model yields accurate predictions about the gross behavior of gases in situations such as changes of temperature, pressure, and volume. Or there is the conception of the atom as a miniature solar system, this analogy quite inaccurate and misleading as it happens. Or there is the analogy that compares the human mind to a computer, an analogy that has been tapped for substantial insights into human thinking over the past twenty years.

The Core of the Concept of Model

These examples convey pretty well the range of models and immediately yield a tip for teachers and learners: Do not take models in the sole sense of examples, but reach further from time to time. However, the very variety of the models mentioned here might raise a doubt. Perhaps the model concept ranges too far, losing whatever central characteristic makes a model a powerful vehicle of understanding. Indeed, one might well ask whether there is anything that does not count as a model.

Then the unity of the concept of model needs to be examined, to see if and how the concept hangs together. First of all, models do not include everything. Many representations do not count as models in the present sense, including ones that are often called models. Newton's laws, expressed as a set of equations for the motion of objects, is sometimes called a model. However, it is not a model in the present sense, because the equations themselves do not display the way objects move, but rather offer formulae characterizing their motions. To put it another way, the equations describe the way things move rather than modeling the way things move. For another instance, you might have a set of equations that capture important features of traffic flow in crowded urban situations. This would commonly be called a model of traffic flow. Yet, again, the example is not a model in the present sense, because the equations do not convey information by showing.

Philosophy offers a concept that can make all of this more precise. In his theory of symbols, Nelson Goodman draws an interesting contrast between two kinds of symbolizing—denotation and exemplification. The prototypical case of denotation is a word, which refers by convention to what it names. Thus, "dog" refers to dogs and "George Washington" refers to George Washington. In contrast, in exemplification, the symbol informs by exemplifying rather than naming. For instance, a tailor's swatch informs us about a fabric that we might use for a piece of clothing by giving us a sample of that fabric; we can read from the sample such features as weave and color. The television set displayed in a department store window informs us about that brand by displaying it; we read the general characteristics of the brand from the given sample. In much the same style, the picture of a zebra in the dictionary informs us of what zebras look like by displaying the look of a zebra.

These cases might suggest that the contrast between denotation and exemplification is simply the contrast between pictures and words. But not so. Words can perfectly well exemplify, as for instance when one quotes Shakespeare to convey the flavor of his style. And pictures occasionally denote without exemplifying the appearance of what they denote, as when, for instance, a rose stands for Christianity without looking like Christianity, a lion for Winston Churchill without looking like Churchill, or an eagle for the United States of America without resembling its geography or government. Pictures also commonly exemplify without denoting; pictures of fictional entities like unicorns or Darth Vader display properties we associate with those entities but do not, strictly speaking, denote anything, since there is no real entity to denote. And, of course, pictures frequently both denote and exemplify. Your portrait on the piano both signifies you and does so by means of exemplifying certain of your features—your hair long or short, brow clear or furrowed, and so on. In summary, denotation versus exemplification simply is not the same distinction as words versus pictures.

The case discussed also might suggest that exemplification always involves something concrete and perceptual. While that is the trend, exemplification occurs in contexts where both the model and what is modeled are quite abstract and nonperceptual. The integers and the operation of addition exemplify—provide a model of—a mathematical structure called an Abelian group. The real numbers with the operations of addition and multiplication exemplify a mathematical structure called a field. Now neither the integers nor the real numbers are dramatically more concrete than what they model, yet thinking of the integers as a special and in some ways characteristic case of an Abelian group or the real numbers as a case of a field helps us to understand these mathematical structures by way of an example.

The Intrinsic Ambiguity of Models

If exemplification captures with precision what models of all sorts have in common, there is another argument against models worth considering, not so much a doubt about the clarity of the model concept as the clarity of individual models. In a sense, models are chronically ambiguous. Take, for example, the case of the tailor's swatch again. The tailor's swatch has a certain weave and color, but it also has a certain shape. Nothing about the tailor's swatch itself tells us that shape does not count. Only through custom and context do we know that we should read the swatch for weave and color, but not shape. What holds for the tailor's swatch holds in general for models. Any example or sample or map or other model will have a multitude of properties that might symbolize; the question becomes which ones count in the circumstances. Nothing about the model itself indicates which properties are important.

Of course, this theoretical problem creates no practical trouble in the case of the tailor's swatch, but it sometimes does in other cases. Here are some mundane examples. In inspecting the floor model of a piece of furniture or an appliance, we often have to ask whether the color of the floor model exemplifies the one and only color available, or whether there are other colors, too. Recognizing this problem, many stores specify on the tag what other colors are available. Or consider people at their first skiing lession, watching the ski instructor demonstrate. It may not be at all clear to them which features of the instructor's actions count, which features he wants the students to notice and emulate. Those skiing instructors who ski well but do not know much about instruction may not even be aware of the ambiguity. Indeed, because their skills are so automatic through years of practice, they themselves may not even be conscious of which of their actions are more or less important to skiing. But experienced instructors will recognize this problem and accompany a demonstration with words that point up the significant features.

The same problem and solution apply to more formal instructional settings. Commonly teachers try to convey a tacit message to students by being good role models, for instance, role models of thoughtful, strategic problem solvers. However, some research argues that many students do not get the message, missing those aspects of the teachers' behavior that count. But, if a teacher explicitly says what counts and what does not, while still modeling the desired behavior, considerable learning occurs.

In summary, arguing against all models is the dilemma of determining which properties of a model are important. But, besides the help from custom and context, this intrinsic flaw in models has a standard solution—labeling. By words or other symbols, we highlight which features of the model count and which do not. In terms of the design questions, adding labels is adding a touch of structure to the unadorned model so that it does not have to do alone all the work of conveying meaning. Two common hazards for teachers and learners are to attend to model only or structure only; the pairing does a better job.

ON THE OMNIPRESENCE OF MODELS

Unveiling the variety of models does little to show how models fill our everyday life and thought, and how much we take them for granted. Their commonality becomes invisibility. But once pointed to they reveal themselves and we discover our deep investment in the tactic of modeling.

The best argument for this proposition comes from our most universal thinking tool, the language we use. We commonly represent abstract concepts by means of concrete actions and objects. For instance, consider our ways of talking about understanding itself. People may say that they *see the point, see what you mean, perceive your intention*. In short, metaphors for perception provide one way of naming the act of understanding. We understand understanding by way of the model experience of seeing. In some locutions, the same model gives us a way to name the act of conveying understanding. We try to *make something plain, clarify it, disclose it, reveal it* — all metaphors of making visible.

However, perception is not our only model for understanding. Other words for understanding have kinesthetic rather than perceptual roots. For instance, to understand something is to *grasp it, penetrate it, comprehend or apprehend it*, the latter two utilizing the Latin root *prehendere*, meaning to grasp. To communicate a point we may *convey it, pass it along, present it, offer it* — again words of physical action. In a somewhat different category but equally metaphoric is the word "understand" itself. To stand under something has become a model for understanding it, perhaps because standing under implies an inside view or direct access to the matter in question.

With both perceptual and kinesthetic models for understanding at hand, you can see that knowledge as design has a bias. To think of knowledge as design is to think of it as an implement one constructs and wields rather than a given one discovers and beholds. The kinesthetic imagery implicit in knowledge as design fosters an active view of understanding worthy of emphasis in teaching and learning. The perceptual model, in contrast, has the passive air of relaxing on a recliner in front of a TV sitcom.

Apart from understanding, our whole way of speaking presents endless examples of one notion riding on another as a model of it. Here are a few examples from diverse contexts. Politicians *run* for election and *occupy seats* in the Senate. Scientists *construct* theories and *challenge* rival theories. Computer programmers make *flow* charts and *debug* programs. Literary critics *interpret* books they read and may *pan* them if unsatisfied. Actors *play* their parts and may even *live* their roles. In all these cases, we understand one notion partly by way of another more familiar or concrete notion that acts as an analogical model for it, especially when we are first learning such words and phrases.

Of course, these are selected examples. For a fairer experiment, let chance choose instead. Consider the first paragraphs of the first article from an arbitrarily chosen issue of the *Boston Globe*. The analogical words and phrases are italicized.

DUKAKIS, INDUSTRY *SPLIT* ON TECH SITE

Jane Meredith Adams, Globe staff

The *fight* to select a location for the $40 million Mass. Microelectronics Center is intensifying, with Gov. Michael S. Dukakis actively *pushing* Taunton over Westborough in a *split* with most leaders of the *high* tech industry.

Meanwhile, some members of the site selection committee are *upset* that the process has been "politicized" by intense *lobbying*.

"It's been politicized and that's where I get *turned off*," said Gerald L. Wilson, dean of the college of engineering at MIT. "I get nauseous."

Dukakis, who has talked with *board* members in person and on the telephone, has argued that the center could serve as a *magnet* to attract industry to the *depressed* Southeastern Massachusetts area, where Taunton is located.

In urging that models are ubiquitous, the emphasis as been on language as a pivotal case, language being the vehicle with which we not only communicate but do much of our thinking. At the same time, casting our attention about, we also find models in evidence almost everywhere outside of language use. Here is a quick survey.

Our world is full of representational pictures, each one a surrogate appearance for something or other. A map of a region denotes it and informs about it by exemplifying its geographical and political layout. Then there are samples—the tailor's swatch, or the model television set, washing machine, fashion, best seller, cadillac, birthday cake, Tiffany-style lamp, racy hubcap, trombone, wheelchair, perfume, Barbie doll, or whatnot in the store window. There are, moreover, demonstrations—the coach's demonstration on how to jump on a trampoline or shoot a foul shot, the fast-talking TV announcer's demonstration of how to cut not only roast beef but old tin cans with a miraculous $9.98 knife, the dance instructor's demonstration of how to execute a split without splitting, the cooking instructor's demonstration of a weightless souffle. There are the examples spelled out in math books, physics books, chemistry books, grammar books, biology books, this book.

The panorama should do a fair job of showing that our thoughts and lives are replete with models. There is one clever objection, though: Perhaps in the case of language these models have mostly a historical rather than a present day significance. Consider, for instance, a word for understanding like "comprehend." Surely most of us ignore the underlying Latin root for grasping that makes this word a physical analogy for an act of mind. Perhaps we ignore the underlying model in most of the words and phrases that have a model in their history. To put it another way, perhaps most of them are dead metaphors rather than live ones. Any live metaphor is a model, because we see the subject of the metaphor through the features exemplified by that to which the subject is likened: When Shakespeare says "Juliet is the sun," we see Juliet as sharing features exemplified by the sun, those features that a human can share at least metaphorically—warmth, luminosity, centrality, and so on. But "the crack of dawn" is a dead metaphor; we hear the words and know the time of day, but usually do not think about the underlying and quite lovely metaphorical meanings. For instance, one reading might be: day breaking out of night, as a chick breaks out of an egg.

Well, some are dead but plenty enough are alive to say that models play an active, not just historical, role in our everyday use of language. For instance, as we sometimes speak of "comprehending" meanings we sometimes speak of "apprehending" them. Apprehend and comprehend share the same Latin root to which we pay little attention. But apprehend, unlike comprehend, has another prominent meaning in today's English, as in apprehending criminals. That sense of apprehend colors our understanding of apprehending a meaning: When we apprehend meaning we are, quite palpably, *capturing* it, as though it were trying to get away. Models are alive in many other usages, too. When we speak of a *split* between Dukakis and industry, or a couple *splitting up,* or *splitting* the atom, the physical enactive meaning of split certainly seems to color our understanding, even though in none of those cases does splitting amount to anything like splitting a log. Similarly, when we speak of a conversation *lifting our spirits,* or ourselves *taking a stand,* or *supporting* someone else's belief, it seems that the underlying physical metaphors energize the language.

Seems? How to test what could be a mere misleading impression? Perhaps by comparing expressions without and with a model basis, to see whether the presence of a model colors our understanding noticeably. Avoiding models, we might say that the conversation improved our mood rather than lifting, elevating, or raising our spirits; that we stated a committed policy or belief rather than took a stand or position; that we provided evidence for someone else's belief rather than supporting it, backing it, underwriting it, buttressing it, or reinforcing it. But clearly phrases like improving moods, stating a policy, or providing evidence lack the vigor of the model-based alternatives. They are even much harder to think of; it took me five times as long to write the present paragraph as the previous one, because I had to struggle to find relatively nonmetaphorical ways to express the ideas. So models are alive and well in our everyday language, doing their work of sharpening understanding.

MENTAL MODELS

There are models in the mind and models in the world. Models in the world include the washing machine or television set in a store window and the demonstration a coach might give. Models in the mind encompass your mental image of the surface of the sphere with its two-dimensional inhabitants and the repertoire of metaphors on which so much of our language rides. These and other mental models do something quite remarkable for us. *Mental models pervade, enable, and sometimes even disable, our understanding and thinking.*

Besides helping us to understand understanding, this proposition has implications for learning and teaching. If mental models are so important, both teachers and learners had better attend to them. And if models are double-edged, usually enabling but sometimes disabling, teachers and learners had better know how to seize the successes and dodge the pitfalls. First, some successes.

Logic and Mental Sketchpads

The case of the *linear syllogism* provides an especially clean contrast between reasoning with rules and reasoning with models. Here is a simple linear syllogism.

> *Alice is taller than Betty.*
> *Betty is taller than Carol.*
> *What can you say about Alice and Carol?*

There are two ways to handle this problem. You can do it with a touch of algebra, using the transitive property of "greater than." If *A* is greater than *B* and *B* greater than *C*, then *A* is greater than *C*. Or you can construct a mental model of the situation, a mental sketch capturing the given information. You picture Alice standing taller than Betty; then you add Carol, who stands shorter than Betty; then you read off your image the relationship between Alice and Carol.

For this linear syllogism, neither the mental sketchpad approach nor the algebra approach seems much easier than the other. But as linear syllogisms depart from the standard form of the transitivity rule, the algebraic approach becomes a lot harder to handle. The mental sketchpad approach gets somewhat harder too, but not as much so. Try, for instance, this example.

> *Alice is no taller than Betty.*
> *Carol is taller than Betty.*
> *What can you conclude about Alice and Carol?*

When the problems get more complicated yet, you may find it hard to maintain a sufficiently elaborate mental model. But you can easily supplement your mental model with a physical one — marks drawn on a real sketchpad to represent the heights of the girls, for instance. Try this problem, in your head or with paper and pencil.

> *Alice is shorter than Betty.*
> *Carol is taller than Deborah.*
> *Emma is taller than Deborah and no taller than Alice.*
> *Which girl is shortest?*

Problems like this show that our mental sketchpads have limited capacity to hold information. But they permit remarkably flexible manipulations. Consider this problem, which, if you have good mental imagery, you can do without paper and pencil.

Imagine a wooden cube painted red. Now imagine that you take a saw and cut the cube into three equal-sized slabs with two vertical cuts. Now, keeping the slabs together, make two more vertical cuts at right angles to the first two. At this point, you have cut the cube into nine columns of equal size. Now turn the cube on one side and make two more vertical cuts. The net result is twenty-seven little cubes. Now for the question: How many cubes have no painted sides, how many one painted side, how many two, how many three?

Many people can answer this question simply by doing the suggested actions on their mental sketchpad and counting up how many little cubes of each kind result. Perhaps mental cinema makes a better metaphor than mental sketchpad in this case, considering how easily you can animate scenes.

Stored Environments

The sketchpad has a relatively low capacity; when problems get complicated, they require the aid of paper and pencil. However, people have much more elaborate mental models for circumstances that they have had time to become familiar with. Environments are a simple example, as this mental experiment shows. Count all the windows in your home by doing a mental tour of all of its rooms. Probably you can do this with little difficulty, and you go about it in much the same way as everyone else. One by one, you go through the rooms in your house and create a mental image of each, keeping it on your mental sketchpad while you count the windows.

This simple experiment shows that mental models take at least two different forms in the mind. There is what appears on your mental sketchpad, which holds a model of a room for immediate inspection. But also there is the source of your sketchpad images: Somewhere your mind maintains a mental model of your home with all its rooms in place. This mental model is not necessarily stored in the form of images, but it must be available in some sense, because you can pull any part of it onto your sketchpad.

Of course, none of this is limited to the visual domain. For instance, consider our sense of hearing. We have stored mental models of complicated sounds and sound sequences and can pull them onto our mental sounding board to examine them. For an auditory analog of the window counting task, take a song whose lyrics you know by heart and run through it mentally to count the number of times the word "the" occurs.

Returning again to the home environment, probe a little more the full mental model in your memory that you never see all at once. Suppose you are standing in your living room. Now point upward, through the ceiling, and think what you would find there. Is it an attic, the roof, a bedroom, a bathroom, the apartment of an upstairs neighbor? Whatever it is, you almost certainly know, and can probably even visualize yourself floating through the ceiling to encounter whatever exists there, although this vertical route is one you never have nor ever could readily travel.

Your understanding of your home might have been much simpler than this exercise shows. You might only have a mental model of your home as a kind of maze, where one room connects to another that in turn connects to others. If this were your level of understanding, you could not do the above task, because the maze representation does not give any information about what is directly above your living room, only information about what connects to what. Instead, you possess something more sophisticated: a three-dimensional layout exhibiting relationships among parts you have never directly experienced in juxtaposition.

Models of Action

Static layouts are not the only sort of mental model, of course. We understand action and its significance in large part by having or constructing a mental model of it. One good example appeared in the first paragraphs of this chapter—the surface of the sphere with its two-dimensional dwellers, whose travels on that surface helped us to grasp what a finite unbounded universe would be like.

In everyday situations, one of our most powerful resources is the ability to create mental simulations of what might happen. For instance, you are preparing for a job interview and naturally concerned about it. So very likely you run through the possible events of the interview mentally, imagining what your prospective employer might say and how you might answer. Or, for instance, you are going to try to persuade a friend to join you in a business enterprise, so you imagine what your friend's reservations might be and how you might answer them. Both you and your friend, in talking the matter over, try to imagine what might go wrong with the enterprise. Could supplies become scarce? Could there be a strike? What if inflation escalates? Such simulations seem much more mundane than exploring potential universes by means of mental imagery, but they involve essentially the same tactic of thought — modeling.

How important constructing a mental model is in understanding action becomes plain when we encounter situations that challenge our capacity to do so. Here, for example, is a little narrative designed by psychologists John Bransford and Nancy McCarrell to produce befuddlement. As you read this, consider how well you understand what is going on and how well you might remember it later.

> The procedure is actually quite simple. First you arrange things into different groups. Of course one pile may be sufficient depending on how much there is to do. If you have to go somewhere else due to lack of facilities that is the next step, otherwise you are pretty well set. It is important not to overdo things. That is, it is better to do too few things at once than too many. In the short run this may not seem important but complications can easily arise. A mistake can be expensive as well. At first the whole procedure will seem complicated. Soon, however, it will become just another facet of life. It is difficult to foresee any end to the necessity for this task in the immediate future, but then one never can tell. After the procedure is completed one arranges the materials into different groups again. Then they can be put into their appropriate places. Eventually they will be used once more and the whole cycle will then have to be repeated. However, that is a part of life.

Chances are that you found all this quite abstract and vague. Indeed, research shows that if you were given a memory test on it, you would have trouble recalling many of the details, because they do not hang together as part of a concrete sequence of events. Well, the paragraph describes washing clothes. Now go back and reread it again with that context in mind. As you read along, you will find yourself interpreting the sentences in laundry terms and constructing, sentence by sentence, a mental model of the narrative, something you could not do during your first pass because you lacked the context that made the sentences meaningful — that is, modelable. The text will seem much clearer and, in fact, you would score much higher on any test of memory.

The Power of Repertoire

Imagine you are giving a simple test to a famous grandmaster level chess player. He has ten seconds to look at the board. Then he turns away to face a blank board along with a full set of pieces. Can he do what chess masters are so commonly reputed to be able to do? He certainly can. It takes him only moments to reproduce the arrangement of the pieces on the board just as he saw it a few seconds before. He does far better than a novice attempting the same task.

Now you repeat the test in a slightly different fashion. This time the chess master sees not an arrangement of pieces that arose during an actual chess game, but a random placement of the same number of pieces. Again, he looks for ten seconds, turns away, and faces the blank board. This time, however, he can only place a few of the pieces in their correct positions, in fact no more than a novice. Why?

Mental models of a certain sort provide an answer. It seems that the chess master has a repertoire of patterns built up over years of play, configurations of pieces that he knows by heart. These patterns do not include every possible arrangement of all the pieces that can arise in play, for the number of such patterns is far too large for the capacity of the mind. Rather, the patterns are of medium size, involving a few pieces in configurations that often recur from game to game. Estimates made by indirect means suggest that the chess master has accumulated an enormous repertoire of these medium-sized patterns, something of the order of 50,000. He cannot tell you about them, because most of them function unconsciously. But function they do, mediating his perception of the board.

These patterns in effect are mental models—models of various configurations of pieces that might occur on the board. The chess master's repertoire of models mediates his remarkable feat of replicating a board arrangement that occurs during normal play. While you or I, looking at a chess board, see a somewhat haphazard array of pieces, that same layout for the chess master is full of meaning. He sees it as composed of perhaps half a dozen models from his repertoire of models. Grasping the entire layout that way, he can easily remember the few patterns involved and reproduce the whole a few seconds later. However, since his repertoire of models includes only those that arise in the normal course of play, he is no better prepared to replicate a randomly arranged board than we are.

The sheer size of the chess master's repertoire seems overwhelming, and it may be that most other areas of great skill do not require so extremely extensive a repertoire. But studies of a number of other areas of skilled performance suggest that skilled performance in general depends on having a suitable collection of mental models that function perceptually to encode problem situations. The expert encountering a problem understands it, often quite spontaneously, by seeing in it one or more of these familiar patterns. Such results have been obtained for computer programming, problem solving in physics, and problem solving in mathematics, to mention but three areas of skill that have been investigated.

This reliance on a repertoire of models seems surprising, since we usually think of performances like chess play or mathematical problem solving as a matter of superior logic. And, indeed, an important role for logical and imaginative exploration of possibilities cannot be gainsaid. After all, the patterns in terms of which the expert can operate will not yield maximum leverage unless they are used in a flexible, combinatorial way. Nonetheless, the patterns clearly enable the expert to work in much larger chunks than a novice could, and with the fluency of perception rather than the tedium of belabored analysis.

Perhaps the role of repertoire will seem more plausible in light of some examples closer to home than chess or mathematical problem solving. We are all experts, for example, in the language we speak. We all have very sizable repertoires of words that we use in combination to express a remarkable variety of things. Above the level of the word, we all have also mastered large repertoires of model phrases that stand us in good stead in a wide range of conventional situations.

For instance, there is the repertoire of greetings—good morning, how are you, how are you today, how are you feeling today, how are things going, what's new, haven't seen you for a long time. There is the repertoire of apologies—excuse me, I beg your pardon, forgive me, pardon me. There is a repertoire of farewells—goodbye now, see you later, see you soon, don't do anything I wouldn't. Now if we, in our everyday lives, have such repertoires, imagine what elocutionary riches a diplomat must have to navigate international waters of sensitive discourse. Rather like the chess master, he or she will possess standard phrases and standard ideas for situations we never encounter. To be sure, the diplomat often will have to invent by combining or modifying models from that repertoire. But the diplomat's skill will depend in large part on the stock of templates.

MENTAL MUDDLES

The several sorts of mental models looked over so far show what a flexible and powerful resource mental modeling can be. However, as warned earlier, sometimes mental models disable our thinking. This paradox is worth appreciating, among other reasons because it puts us on the alert for problems with mental models in teaching and learning.

For instance, try this puzzle. If Alice sits to the left of Betty and Betty to the left of Cathy, does Alice necessarily sit to the left of Cathy? (More formally, is the relation "to the left of" transitive?) The impulsive answer is yes, buttressed by a mental image of Alice, Betty, and Cathy seated along one side of a table. But that mental model can be challenged with another: What if the trio are seated around a round table? Then Alice is on Cathy's right, not her left. Misrepresentations also arise in ordinary discourse, buoyed by commonplace metaphors. For example, consider the nation as a family, which therefore must share according to the politics of some, or not get into debt according to the politics of others. On second thought, consider that a nation is different enough from a family that neither of these arguments by analogy carry much weight.

People often reason out political and other situations by constructing mental models of possible scenarios. To do this properly, you may have to construct several scenarios in order to explore what different chains of events might occur. Unfortunately, many novice reasoners seem to stop at the first plausible model they create. For instance, facing the question, "Would a five cent deposit on bottles and cans reduce litter," some reasoners say, "Yes, because people would return the bottles for five cents" and stop. Others say, "No, because five cents isn't enough" and stop. Such one-shot modeling treats the first plausible model arrived at as inevitable. All these risks can be seen as instances of a general human trend toward rigid behavior, a trend that sometimes clearly involves mental models and sometimes may involve only rules or principles without any mental models in the sense of mental exemplificational symbols. So inflexibility should not be blamed on mental models specifically. However, mental models are one among other sorts of mental codes that carry this hazard.

Besides mental models we construct on the spot to examine a problem, there are those mental models that sit more or less permanently in our minds, like the models we maintain for our homes or environments. These long-term mental models serve us well so long as they are right, or right enough to guide whatever we need to do. Occasionally, however, the guidance we require diverges from the model.

Therapists sometimes try to deal with such situations by "reframing"—helping a person to see the situation in a new way, according to a new model. For a particularly nice example, my colleague Dr. Abigail Lipson was treating a college student who had entered a spiral of frustration because there did not seem to be enough time in the day both to complete studies and to fit in some distracting and relaxing activities. The problem was not so much the sheer quantity of time available as the crowding and jostling of many different things. Therapist and student successfully reframed the situation with a new mental model, the 48 hour day: Think of every two days as one and plan your activities within that more generous space. Simple as it sounds, this proved a liberating reconceptualization for the student.

Semipermanent mental models of a very different sort cause trouble for nearly every student of physics in high school and college. As mentioned in chapter one, most students initially have a "naive physics," a physics based on their practical experience of the world but not well aligned with Newtonian physics. This naive physics shows up in intuitions students have about forces, velocities, and accelerations, for example. Moreover, naive physics is not only mistaken but stubborn. Even after substantial instruction—for instance after a first year college course in mechanics—most students still have not revised their underlying mental models, and, although they may be able to solve conventional problems mechanically by using the correct equations, they fail on certain novel problems because their intuitions about what forces are at work lead them astray.

For example, imagine a ball thrown into the air. In Figure 5.1, you see a simple drawing of the trajectory of the ball. Three points are labeled — A, where the ball is on the way up, B, when the ball reaches the top, and C, when the ball is part way down. Your task is to indicate what force or forces are at work on the ball at point A, at point B, and at point C.

People usually answer as follows. At A, they report two forces at work — gravity, which points downward, and the force of the ball's velocity, which points upward, exceeds the force of gravity, and so keeps carrying the ball aloft. This is, of course, a verbal statement about the forces that operate, but perhaps it reflects a kinesthetic mental model in which people imagine the circumstances and feel the forces. They feel gravity pulling down and a greater force, the force of the ball's velocity, pulling up. The upward force gradually wears out. By the time the ball reaches point B, the upward force has worn out to the point that it just balances gravity, so the ball is stationary. What happens at C? Here, the upward force of the ball's motion at A has either completely worn out or at least has dwindled to much less than the force of gravity, which carries the ball downward.

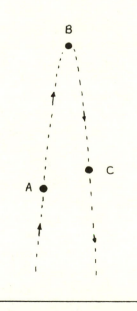

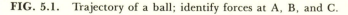

FIG. 5.1. Trajectory of a ball; identify forces at A, B, and C.

This typical account of the forces at work is very wrong indeed. According to Newton's laws, only one force operates at *A*, *B*, and *C*, the force of gravity. Furthermore, the force always has exactly the same effect—to accelerate the ball in the downward direction. On the upward trajectory, the ball has a considerable upward motion, so this acceleration downward takes the form of deceleration. At *B*, the ball has accelerated enough in the downward direction to be still for an instant. It continues to accelerate downward, moving more and more quickly until it passes *C* and ultimately hits the ground.

The contrast between the Newtonian and the typical student's account of the forces at work can be put quite succinctly: For Newton, a constant velocity (assuming no friction) involves no sustaining force; only *changes* in velocity involve force. This is the relationship captured in Newton's famous $F = ma$, which shows that when acceleration is zero, force is zero. All the changes in the velocity of the ball require only one force, the force of gravity that is constantly pulling the ball downward and eventually wins. For the student, however, velocity itself carries a force that maintains motion. When the ball travels upward, as at point *A*, it possesses some sort of push that carries it upward despite the force of gravity that pulls it downward.

From the standpoint of mental models, especially striking is the vividness of the illusory force that we feel through our kinesthetic intuitions. Imagine a truck, its motor turned off, coasting slowly toward you. Feeling bold, you try to stop the truck by pushing on its hood. What does the truck do? It pushes back! It pushes back so strongly that you will hardly slow the truck down at all. The velocity of the truck certainly seems to have a force behind it.

From a Newtonian standpoint, everything but the last sentence is sound. When you try to slow the truck down, you do indeed feel a force. But, according to Newton, you feel the force because you are decelerating the truck a little bit, *not* because the velocity of the truck carries a force. However, merely asserting this does little to undermine the strong kinesthetic intuition that the truck's motion carries with it a push. After all, if you touch the truck you can feel the push; it is immediately perceptually *there*.

Where does the typical but mistaken model come from? The usual answer is that we induce it from our experience with a frictionful world. In high friction situations, such as pushing a book along a table top, you have to sustain a force to sustain motion. So people come to think that any velocity, even the velocity of something rolling where friction is slight, must have a sustaining force behind it. Very likely that is part of the story behind our mental muddle. It is also likely that a natural preference for conceptual simplicity favors the naive view. There is something simpler about viewing velocity as sustained by a force—simpler until one starts scrutinizing the model to see whether it really hangs together.

Whatever the cause, what is the cure? Well, we know what it is not—teaching physics in the conventional manner, which demonstrably does little to revise the naive model. One current proposal, as noted in the first chapter, is to provide a new range of experience through computer simulations that highlight the properties of Newtonian motion. From such computer models, students can internalize revised mental models. Recent research suggests that this tactic has some effectiveness. My own student experience suggest another not so elegant cure. When I took physics, I somehow learned which forces suggested by my intuitions really counted and which did not. When I think about the ball problem, my kinesthetic intuitions tell me about the upward force of the velocity, but I know to discount it. So rather than revising my kinesthetic mental model, I have added a censor to it. With the censor in place, I use my mental model to good effect.

My guess is that the minority of students who treat the ball problem correctly have by and large added a censor, just as I did. Perhaps if physics instruction included explicit recognition of the sorts of difficulties that arise from naive physics, students could rather easily learn to add censors to their mental models. One would prefer a corrected model, of course, but a censor may be a much more efficient solution.

Whatever the cause and cure of misleading mental models in physics, the case of physics symbolizes the problem of mistaken mental models in whatever domain they arise. It shows that mental models can be erroneous, and that acquiring theoretical knowledge that should revise those models or add a censor does not necessarily do so. Through the example of physics and other examples reviewed here, we all in our roles as teachers and learners can understand how mental models may disable as well as enable—or even both at the same time, since the naive mental model of physics is quite enabling for practical everyday affairs—and can keep alert for such mental muddles when they arise.

TEACHING AND LEARNING WITH MODELS

Be wary of misleading models, of course. But that is a side issue compared to the principal problem with models in learning contexts: not enough of them. To be sure, example-giving is a frequent instructional tactic. But common as it is, much of education clings too stubbornly to abstraction, without enough models to illustrate and enliven them. The cure for this on the learner's side is to call for more models. Learners need to recognize that they need models and can seek them out. Learners can press teachers or experts for models or thumb through the pages of a source in search of models, when the author does not place those models conveniently close to the generalizations they illustrate, as often happens. And—this tactic should not be slighted—learners can make models up for themselves, in an effort to clarify whatever generalizations are not illustrated by model cases. The effort to do so may prove difficult if the generalization is vague, but the very act of trying does a service, disclosing in just what ways the generalization lacks specificity.

On the teacher's side, this whole book illustrates how models aid thinking and learning, so here only a few principles need be mentioned.

When Should the Model Come? Instruction can always be organized in terms of design, since the design concept fits virtually anything you might want to teach. In presenting a design, the principal model typically comes either after a statement of the purpose of the design, or after a brief sketch of its structure. A rule of thumb was mentioned in an earlier chapter: If the structure can be stated in a sentence or two, give the structure and then one or more models, because the structure helps to organize the understanding of the model. On the other hand, if the structure takes a paragraph or more to state, it is hard to hold in mind without the concrete model to help. So give the model before the structure. Another reasonable tactic is to present a sketchy structure, one or more models, and then full structure. Yet another is to present structure and a model simultaneously, illustrating each point of structure with a model. As these options make plain, no rigid formula is intended.

Why not give a model first, before purpose? Simply because the purpose of a design is such a key piece of information about it and usually so compact to state that there is not much point in delay. Why not hold back on a model until after the argument? Simply because the argument typically gains from having a model to refer to. Of course, these reasons yield a rule of thumb about the placement of models, not a law of nature. But unless some special circumstances intrude, the rule of thumb serves well.

Use Models Freely in Purpose and Argument.   The principal model in discussing a design is a model of structure, but there is no reason to feel that other models have to be kept out. It is often useful to give a model case or two for the purpose of a design. Likewise, working through an argument in the context of a model is often helpful—either the model given for structure or another one introduced especially for the argument. Models are like salt; they lend a bit more presence to almost anything.

Use Countermodels.   Countermodels as well as models often serve clarity in teaching and learning. Countermodels are models that exemplify an opposite or contrasting case to the case in question. For instance, one might attain a sharper sense of justice through examples of injustice or of democracy through examples of tyranny. When a subtle distinction needs to be drawn, the countermodels can reflect this: Examples of *subtle* injustice or tyranny illustrate how the superficial trappings can mislead as to the core.

Ask Learners to Produce New Models.   Because a teacher teaching a group always risks a somewhat passive audience, two questions have to be faced. What can learners do to exercise the ideas they are learning? How does the teacher know that the learners really are grasping what is being said? Both questions get answered if the teacher routinely asks learners to produce new models, either in the midst of a presentation or as homework. For instance, a teacher who has discussed Darwin's theory of natural selection might ask the learners to make up an account of how a seal's flipper or an elephant's trunk could have developed. A teacher who has outlined Ciardi's concept of fulcrum in a poem might ask learners to take a poem at random from a book and try to find and discuss a fulcrum in it. A teacher who has introduced the four design questions themselves as an analytical tool might ask learners to analyze an everyday design using the four questions. In all these cases, the teacher might call for one or several models, depending on pedagogical judgment.

What are some of the advantages of this tactic? In producing models, the learners have to apply the ideas provided by the teacher. Furthermore, since the teacher has asked for something new, the learners cannot just feed back rote knowledge; instead they have to invent, offering fresh incarnations of whatever concepts the teacher has described and illustrated. Not only does this lead the learners to apply the concepts in an active way, but it is hard for the learners to think up models for something they do not understand. Consequently, the teacher can tell whether most of the learners grasp the topic from the answers that come back.

Provide Clarification and Helping Strategies. Asking for new models is a strong test of understanding. Often a teacher will discover that, however clear the explanation seems, many of the learners cannot produce new models. When that occurs, the teacher needs to provide further clarification and strategies to help the learners to generate models.

Ask for New Analogs if New Examples cannot be Found. If the content of instruction is a particular rather than a generality, it makes no sense to ask students to produce new *examples* of the particular: The particular is its own one and only example. A teacher can ask for new instances of government charters, but not of the U.S. constitution specifically, or of sonnet form, but not of Yeats' "Leda and the Swan" specifically. But a model need not be an example. In such cases the teacher can ask for learners to find and discuss an analogous case in the same style—another government charter or another sonnet, comparing and contrasting the new case with the given one. Such a tactic exercises and gauges the leaners' understanding and also escalates the level of generality: The learners start to think in terms of a family of designs rather than just particular instances. Indeed, if time allows, one might want to ask for analogies too, even when new instances can be found.

EVIDENCE FOR THE EFFECTIVENESS OF MODELS

Some arguments for the proposed strategies have been offered along the way. But it is fair to ask after evidence for the effectiveness of teaching with models. The best evidence comes from conventional practice. Imagine mathematics taught without worked-out examples, geography taught without maps, physics taught without diagrams or laboratory exercises, and — the ultimate absurdity — literary theory taught without examples of literature. Even though instruction often should include more models, models already play so important a role that our actual practice makes the best case for their relevance.

For experimental evidence on the same point, a look is needed at situations where models do not see routine use, where instead it is in question whether models would help. Here are four such cases.

Naive Physics.   As mentioned earlier, there has been a successful experiment in helping students to understand physics better by means of computer models. In a study carried out by Barbara White, a number of students took a pretest composed of various questions about how to direct the motion of a spaceship by pointing it in various directions and firing its rockets. Then the students played a series of computer games in which they guided a spaceship through a frictionless, gravity-free space to achieve various objectives, such as turning a corner or hitting a target. The students could control the spaceship only by blasting its rockets briefly in certain directions. As the students started to play, they soon discovered that the spaceship did not behave as their naive physics would lead them to expect. Gradually, they begin to revise their expectations. After playing the games, the students repeated the test, disclosing substantial improvements in their grasp of the physical principles involved. Control group students, who received the test twice but did not experience the game, showed no improvement the second time.

Memory.   A substantial body of research has demonstrated the power of visual mnemonics in enhancing rote memory. Suppose, for example, that you want to remember a shopping list of one dozen eggs, two cartons of milk, a bunch of celery, and sausages. You might form the following mental image to aid your memory: the celery standing upright, a dozen small eggs set in its leafy top, the sausages making a circle around its base, and you "watering" the whole from a milk carton. The extensive research on mnemonic uses of imagery shows that such visual mental models powerfully abet memory.

This has been applied to foreign language vocabulary learning through the "keyword method" reported by Richard Atkinson and Michael Raugh. The method recommends associating a foreign word with its English equivalent in two steps, as follows. Taking the foreign word, say "hombre," which is Spanish for man, you think of an English word that sounds like all or part of it, say "home." Then you form a visual image connecting the English word with the meaning you want, say a giant man sitting in a home with his legs sticking out the door and his arms out windows on the sides of the house. Research on the keyword method has shown that it yields substantially greater retention of vocabulary than students' usual practices. The research also revealed that, after a few retrievals, learners spontaneously begin to recover the English equivalents directly, without using the mnemonic. Thus, the keyword method provides an initial scaffolding that holds the vocabulary in place until it "sets" and then gets out of the way.

Plane Geometry. The Geometric Supposer, a computer program developed by Judah Schwartz and Michael Yerushalmy, engages students in problem finding in plane geometry by providing them with a model world in which they can easily formulate and test conjectures. Conventional geometry instruction provides theorems and their proofs and asks students to demonstrate simple theorems, but gives virtually no attention to discovering mathematical results. The Geometric Supposer offers a remedy. The program allows a student to ask for constructions that the program then displays. For example, a student might request a triangle with all three medians drawn to observe whether they really intersect in a point. Moreover, at the user's request, the computer will repeat the same construction with new triangles, making them up so that the student can check whether the common intersection of the medians appears on several arbitrarily chosen examples.

In this way, the Supposer provides a world in which learners can try out geometrical constructions, make conjectures about rules they obey, and test those conjectures efficiently. (To be sure, students could make the same constructions with compass and straightedge in principle, but in practice the manual process demands so much care and time that it defeats fluent exploration of possibilities.) Students can then go on to try to prove the conjectures they formulate. The Supposer can be used instructionally in various ways, for instance as a supplement to conventional geometry instruction or as a course in itself. Initial results suggest that the geometry world provided by the Supposer can restore meaningful mathematical inquiry to plane geometry. For instance, students commonly rediscover important theorems without the help of texts. Moreover, on a couple of occasions students have discovered entirely new theorems.

Computer Programming. Richard Mayer conducted a series of experiments on the benefits of including in programming instruction a model of how the computer works. The experiments involved brief instruction in a simplified version of the programming language BASIC and in a file management language. The students in one group learned at the outset a simple model of how the computer worked, not at the hardware level but at a level appropriate for understanding the language concerned. The students in another group received only the language instruction with no model.

Mayer tested all of the students both on problems very like those they had studied and on other problems that called for the students to transfer their knowledge to fresh programming situations. The results showed that the students without the model often outperformed the others on the problems that mimicked the training problems, apparently because those students had learned the training problems in a very literal and rote way. However, the students who had received the model did much better on the transfer problems than the other students; the model had helped them to gain a substantially more flexible and general understanding.

Of course, these four experiments do not prove that models always powerfully enhance instruction. Nor is that even true, as you can see just by thinking about it. Knowledge as design recognizes that models themselves, mental or physical, are designs. Designs can be good or bad. If a good model very likely will help in instruction, a bad one very likely will hinder. Accordingly, the research evidence reads best not as votes for some sweeping claim about the inevitable efficacy of models, but as clear demonstrations that models can enhance instruction. How often and how well they do so depends on the art of the designer, whether teacher, psychologist, curriculum expert, or you sitting with a son or a daughter and groping for a model that will make clear why the people who live on the other side of the earth do not fall off, or, if they stay put, why we do not fall off.

WHAT YOU CAN DO

In your roles of teacher or learner, you can call upon models in the broadest sense, not only examples but also diagrams, analogies, maps, graphs — anything that makes something more accessible by exemplifying features of it. In particular, you can:

- *Introduce models of designs anytime as needed.* You can employ models for structure, where a model almost always helps, but also for purpose and argument, where models often sharpen understanding.

- *Use countermodels as well as models.* Countermodels present contrasting cases that can help a learner grasp a concept. Subtle countermodels, that differ only in nuance from the notion being learned, can help to convey the notion with precision.

- *Take pains always to identify what features of the model (or countermodel) are significant.* Remember, a model leaves ambiguous which features count, so you need to single them out.

- *Use mental models much as you would use physical models.* As a teacher, learner, or thinker, you can play out a chain of events in your mind, solve a problem by mental imagery, do a "Gedanken experiment" — German for a thought experiment that you run in your mind alone.

- *But be wary of mental models, which sometimes carry assumptions that need to be challenged.* To understand why a sound concept does not seem right to someone or why it is not taken to heart, often one must look to the person's tacit mental model. As a teacher or learner, you may have to address that model directly, describing and discussing its assumptions and comparing them with other options.

- *Use the task of finding or devising new models as a creative activity.* One common problem with teaching or learning something through direct instruction is that the learner has no opportunity to exercise the knowledge in fresh ways. A good creative challenge here is to construct a new model, one that reaches beyond those models that figured in explaining the knowledge as a design in the first place. (Remember, when the design under discussion is a relatively specific one, with only a single natural choice for a model, you will need to seek models by way of analogy.)

- *Use the task of finding or devising new models as a gauge of understanding.* If you as a learner can produce new models that truly reflect the features of the design in question, you both understand the design reasonably well and have some power to apply that understanding. If you as a teacher find that your learners can devise new models of an important design you have taught, you can be sure they are at least somewhat enlightened and empowered.

6 Inside Argument

"Argument" is a word with a bad reputation. On the one hand it reminds us of siblings' squabbles or of battles conducted across a courtroom. On the other, it recalls mathematical arguments, which many of us find more fearsome than any personal fray. Arguments, it seems, are something to avoid.

But such a reading is clearly reading in. "Argument" need not mean anything contentious or mathematical either. Really, the term refers broadly and neutrally to reasoning in order to make decisions or test the truth of claims. We neglect such reasoning only at our hazard.

Consider the life situations that call for reasoning. You explore the pros and cons of buying this car or that, taking this course or that, marrying this partner or that. You ponder who to vote for, whether or not smoking should be banned in public places, what sort of vacation to take this year. You write an essay or a letter of complaint or a political speech, in each case giving reasons for your position.

Just as important as your personal handling of argument are the ways it underpins civilization. Law, for instance, finds application through argument, and, if those applications sometimes seem convoluted, they do better by us than lawless anarchy. Science, for example, rests on empirical and mathematical arguments and serves up electric lights, refrigerators, and medicines.

Finally, argument plays a key role in understanding, hence its role as the fourth of the four design questions. So we do well to comprehend an art that does well by us in so many ways. This is the topic of the present chapter. And we do well to learn how to reason better, the topic of the next chapter.

ARGUMENT AS DESIGN

An argument, of course, is a design—a structure shaped to a purpose. One can hardly find a better snapshot of that structure than this classic child's question and flip answer:

Why?
Because.

As a design, every argument has the purpose of specifying "why"—what is the justification, what is the explanation, how do we know? At issue might be the truth of a scientific theory, the identity of a culprit, the desireability of a candidate, the folly of a plan. No matter which the case, every argument addresses some such claim or theme.

The "why" and "because" together give the basic structure of any argument: Why such and such? Because so and so. For example, why Newton's laws? Because of certain experimental evidence. Why call Jason the culprit? Because his fingerprints were on the doorknob. Any argument brings reasons to bear on the claim in question. The claim stands or falls *because* of the reasons.

This reasons-conclusion structure serves so well in our discourse that we have many other ways besides "because" to signal it. Consider the following patterns for instance: conclusion *since* reasons, conclusion *on account of* reasons, reasons *therefore* conclusion, reasons *so* conclusion, reasons *consequently* conclusion, reasons *thus* conclusion. The simplest arguments add only a few words to these patterns, as in offhand dialogues like "Why do you think it will rain today?" "Because the weather report said so." Or, "Why should I take out the trash?" "Because you promised to."

But of course arguments get much more complicated than this in both everyday and academic contexts. Sometimes an argument exhibits a long chain of reasons with intermediate conclusions leading to a final conclusion. Mathematical proofs usually have this structure. Here is a more colloquial example:

> *Fenster usually goes to the horse races on Saturday.*
> *That's today, so he's probably at the races.*
> *When he goes, he usually bets a lot.*
> *When he bets, he usually loses.*
> *So he'll probably lose a lot today.*
> *Therefore, Fenster won't have much cash tomorrow.*
> *Fenster doesn't like to go to races unless he can bet.*
> *So he probably won't want to go with us to the dog races tomorrow.*

You might say that series of statements has one *line of argument*, one string of reasons that hang together and build toward a conclusion. But many arguments have quite a different structure—several lines of argument, each a separate reason or chain of reasons bearing on the case pro or con. For example, consider the following argument about the likelihood of life on Mars:

> *The low temperature is inimical to life.*
> *Also, life might not survive in the thin atmosphere.*
> *The Mars lander did find some signs that indicate life.*
> *But certain of its tests failed, too.*
> *There are arctic environments on earth with characteristics similar to Mars, environments that support primitive life.*
> *Therefore, all in all, primitive life at least seems possible on Mars, but we can't say for sure at the present.*

In this example, each sentence offers a different line of argument. Note the contrast with the argument about Fenster. If you show that one point in the Fenster argument is wrong, that spoils the whole argument, because the reasons hang together like a chain and every link must hold. If you show that a point in the Mars argument is wrong, this just removes the one point from consideration, leaving the other points still relevant.

The fourth design question calls for an argument about argument itself: How does the structure of argument serve well the purpose of justifying claims? This question gets harder when in the next section we consider what makes a *sound* argument. But quality of argument aside, responses come easily. First, why do arguments need both reasons and a conclusion? Because without a conclusion there would be nothing to be justified, and without at least one reason, nothing to justify the conclusion. Why do arguments usually contain terms like "therefore" or "because?" Because such terms signal clearly the reason-conclusion relationship.

Why do arguments often have chains of reasons rather than one reason alone? Because a chain can connect to the conclusion evidence that stands more than one step away from it; so a chain lets us bring more evidence to bear. Why do arguments often have several lines of argument? Because it is often the case that several sorts of evidence bear on a conclusion, so the structure of arguments must reflect this reality. All this finds the structure of argument straightforwardly adapted to its job of giving evidence for claims.

SOUND ARGUMENTS

What is a sound argument? The question is crucial, since the arguments we make or accept often determine our decisions about what to do and what to risk. Then how do we know when an informal everyday argument truly justifies its conclusion? (Formal arguments like syllogisms and mathematical proofs are taken up later.)

To a first approximation, we know through intuition and common sense. Nearly anyone has some practical feel for when an argument suffices and when it does not. Suppose, for instance, there are dark clouds on the horizon and different people offer the following conclusions:

Maybe it will rain later today.
Probably it will rain later today.
For sure it will rain later today.
Maybe it will hail later today.
Maybe it will rain frogs later today.

Most of us feel much the same way about these conclusions. "Maybe it will rain later today" seems justified, because it is carefully hedged. "Probably it will rain later today" appears a little bold and "For sure" entirely unwarranted. The "Maybe it will hail later today" seems less justified than a prediction of rain because hail occurs much more rarely than rain. Although it has, supposedly, rained frogs (that were earlier sucked up from a swamp by a tornado), certainly the mere presence of dark clouds does not make such a wonder likely.

These examples reveal our reservoirs of common sense about everyday arguments. But arguments about contentious matters, such as who will make the best president or whether capital punishment is an effective deterrent, involve reasons not so readily appraised. After all, were such matters straightforwardly arguable to a conclusion they would not be persistent dilemmas. To help us in thinking clearly about hard cases, here are three standards designed to guarantee a sound informal argument.

1. *True reasons, or reasons assumed true.*
2. *Rightly weighted reasons—reasons giving appropriate weight to the conclusion, neither too much nor too little*
3. *Complete reasons—reasons bringing to bear whatever knowledge you have or might readily obtain that could influence the conclusion.*

One can test whether these standards make sense with a series of model cases. To start off with, this argument meets all the standards:

Avocets are birds.
Most birds can fly.
So probably avocets can fly.

Avocets are indeed birds and most birds can indeed fly, so the reasons are true. They also carry weight; taken together they give good grounds to think that probably avocets can fly. What about counterarguments? The argument given includes all we know about avocets (suppose), so the argument as given is complete. So it is a sound informal argument, and the conclusion "probably avocets can fly" is justified.

Notice that the conclusion may turn out to be false. There are birds that do not fly, penguins and ostriches for example, so avocets too might lack the equipment for flight. But the information available gives no hint of this. We have to fall back on the statistical point that the overwhelming majority of birds can fly, and so *probably* avocets can. The argument and conclusion are sound until data to the contrary force us to revise both.

Now what happens when one of the conditions goes wrong? Here is a model case that violates the "true reasons" condition.

> *Alligators are birds.*
> *Most birds can fly.*
> *So probably alligators can fly.*

We would never call this a sound argument. The logic is the same as with the avocets, but we know that alligators are not birds so the conclusion is not sound even though the logic is. Of course, this model case is extreme. In everyday arguments, violations of the truth condition occur commonly but more subtly. Here are three you might hear.

> *Whales are fish. (Misconception)*
> *So I suppose they can stay under water as long as they want.*

> *Italians have fiery tempers. (Cultural stereotype)*
> *So watch out for dealing with this Italian fellow.*

> *I'll get my homework done anyway. (Past experience says no.)*
> *So you should let me go to the movies.*

Besides the truth condition, there is the weight condition, which the following example blatantly violates.

> *Alligators are reptiles.*
> *Most birds can fly.*
> *So probably alligators can fly.*

All the reasons are true; alligators indeed are reptiles and most birds indeed can fly. But being a reptile has nothing to do with flying. That reason, even together with "Most birds can fly," carries no weight at all. Of course, as with the truth condition, the violations are more subtle in normal argument. Here are some that you might actually hear.

Darwin's view of man evolving from the animals is demeaning.
It can't be true. (Supposing the view is really demeaning, being
demeaning has nothing to do with the truth of a theory.)

I keep coming back to the fact that the defendant has served
time twice before for this sort of crime.
So I don't see how, but he must have done it.
(A bad record overweighted relative to other evidence.)

The stock market has gone up three days straight.
I think it's time to get aboard in a big way.
(Overestimating the persistence of a trend.)

Finally, the following model case blatantly violates the completeness condition.

Penguins are birds.
Most birds can fly.
So probably penguins can fly.

Both of the reasons are true, and this argument has just the same
logic as the argument about avocets. But we certainly do not want
to conclude that probably penguins can fly, because we know they
cannot. What has gone wrong? The difficulty is quite straightforward: We have more information about penguins than about avocets. In particular, we have counterarguments such as the following:

I've read in books that penguins can't fly.
I've seen penguins in zoos and they didn't fly.
Penguin's wings don't seem to be for flying; they are short and
stubby, not at all like the wings of a normal bird.

In other words, the penguin argument without these counterarguments is incomplete. It leaves out relevant knowledge we have,
knowledge that in this instance overwhelmingly makes the opposite
case. Here are some more realistic examples of incomplete arguments.

The snow is a ready source of water if you're lost in winter.
So eat snow until you get out.
(Snow is indeed a source of water, but eating snow when you're
lost in the cold is deadly—it drains the body of heat.)

My dummy baby brother made the mess.
So I shouldn't have to help clean up the blocks.
(Responsibility isn't the only issue; family cooperation and baby
brother's inability to pick up the mess by himself are parts of the
picture.

All this environmentalism costs us tax dollars.
It prevents our exploiting natural resources.
It destroys jobs, since some companies move away.
So it's really a bad idea just to save a few trees.
(A one-sided argument, perhaps the most common kind of
incompleteness.)

JUSTIFYING THE STANDARDS

Do the three standards accomplish their design objective of guaranteeing sound arguments? This calls for an argument about the standards themselves. In fact, one can prove that the standards are logically both sufficient and necessary for a sound argument, one that yields a sound conclusion based on available knowledge.

First of all, *if* an argument meets all three standards, *then* it justifies its conclusion. Why? Well, in what respect might the conclusion be unsound? Perhaps the argument omits some crucial information; but that cannot be, because the argument satisfies the completeness standard. Perhaps the evidence does not sufficiently weight in favor of the conclusion; but that cannot be because the reasons are properly weighted according to the second standard. Or perhaps we have our facts wrong; but the first standard says no, all the reasons are true. Could anything else be wrong? No. Any reservation you think of will have to be a reservation about the truth of reasons, the weight attached to reasons, or the completeness of the argument because that is all there *is* in an argument to question—the reasons themselves, their bearing on the conclusion, and the completeness of the whole ensemble.

Now the proof in the other direction: *If* an argument justifies its conclusion, *then* it meets the three standards. Suppose we have an argument that in our view justifies its conclusion. Does it meet the truth standard? Certainly we would not feel the argument was sound if it included false reasons. Does it meet the weighting standard? Certainly if the argument overweights reasons we would not consider the conclusion sufficiently justified. If the argument underweights reasons we would consider the conclusion too weak. So the argument must meet the weighting standard. As to completeness, if the argument omitted information that had the potential of changing the conclusion, we certainly would not view the argument as it stood as justifying the conclusion, so the completeness standard must be met as well. In summary, the three standards capture logically what we mean intuitively when we think of an argument that justifies its conclusion.

Despite all this, there is a natural objection to the three standards: They cannot be applied mechanically. All three require good judgment or further argument. For instance, you have to judge accurately whether a reason is true or not, or argue it out to check its truth. You may make a bad judgment without knowing it, or argue it out badly, and be misled. Likewise, the weight of a particular line of argument and the completeness of the argument as it stands call for good judgment or further argument, either of which might go awry.

These are indeed unfortunate features of the standards. But complaining about them is a little like complaining about a stove because it is hot and you might burn yourself. The stove *has* to be hot to do its job and the standards *have* to call for good judgment or further argument to do their job. In the formal logic of mathematics, which is discussed later, the truth of the premises is a matter of assumption, but in informal argument about real-world matters, the truth of premises is bound to be in question from time to time. Consider also the weight standard. In the formal logic of mathematics, an argument either does or does not prove its conclusion. But in formal reasoning, an argument may suggest its conclusion, make its conclusion probable, prove its conclusion almost beyond doubt, or many of numerous other shades. The shade to suit the case at hand has to be judged or argued out. Likewise with completeness. We can never be sure we have polled our memories for all information that might bear on the issue. We have to judge or argue that we have done enough.

In summary, the standards do not provide a mechanical approach to checking informal arguments. No standards could, because informal arguments are messy and uncertain in ways that formal arguments are not. But the standards offer an organized way of hunting for weaknesses in an informal argument.

FORMAL PATTERNS OF ARGUMENT

This chapter puts formal and informal argument in an unusual pecking order. It is standard to introduce formal arguments such as syllogisms, examine what gives the force, and treat informal arguments as loose or hedged cases of formal ones. An informal argument becomes a formal argument in casual dress. It wears terms like "probably" or "usually" or "for the most part" that leave the skeleton of the formal argument intact while warning everyone that the argument carries less than mathematical force.

Here, however, formal argument is treated as a variant of informal argument. Nothing in the proof about the soundness of the standards depends on whether the argument in question is formal or informal, so the three standards apply to formal arguments too. But they apply in a simplified way, making formal argument a special case. In particular, the completeness standard turns out to be satisfied trivially, while the weight standard proves purely a matter of logical form. Often, although not always, the truth standard also is satisfied trivially, since the premises are assumed true, as in the axioms of Euclidean geometry. To see how all this works, consider these designs for formal argument.

Patterns of Logic

Purpose? To achieve the greatest possible weight, not merely suggesting or favoring a conclusion but *proving* it beyond doubt (assuming the truth of the reasons).

Models and Structure? Here is a model case of formal logical argument. To the right appears the general form of this inference.

Some soldiers are gardeners.	*Some A are B.*
All gardeners are sun-lovers.	*All B are C.*
Therefore, some soldiers are sun-lovers.	*So some A are C.*

We all can feel the inevitability of the conclusion. If indeed some soldiers are gardeners, every one of those very soldiers must also be sun-lovers, since all gardeners are sun-lovers. No other line of argument could undermine the inference. To be sure, we could discover that some gardeners are not sun-lovers after all — but this challenges one of the reasons, not the argument proper.

Characterizing all patterns of logic that guarantee their conclusions goes beyond the scope of this sketch. Indeed, it is no mean task. For instance, three-line arguments with alls and somes, usually called syllogisms, come in 27 different correct forms by one way of reckoning. There are other varieties of formal argument, too. A few more examples will have to stand in for thoroughness. The following syllogism is just as valid as the one above, but much harder to grasp.

Some gardeners are soldiers.	*Some B are A.*
No sun-lovers are gardeners.	*No C are B.*
So some soldiers are not sun-lovers.	*So some A are not C.*

People have a great deal of trouble judging whether syllogisms with forms like this are correct. Fortunately, we only encounter such patterns in logic texts and psychological experiments, virtually never in real-life situations.

Mentioned in the chapter on models was another sort of formal argument with a perfect guarantee — the linear syllogism. Instead of alls and somes, it concerns relations like greater than and smaller than.

Ann is older than Mary.	*A is greater than B.*
Mary is older than Joyce.	*B is greater than C.*
So Ann is older than Joyce.	*So A is greater than C.*

Here is yet another pattern of formal logic:

If it's noon, the clock chimes.	*If A, then B.*
The clock is not chiming.	*Not B.*
So it's not noon.	*Therefore, not A.*

Of course, you can object to this argument. Maybe the clock is not reliable, so it will not necessarily chime exactly at noon. Or maybe the clock is chiming but you have a hearing problem. However, these objections challenge the reasons, not the logic. Granting the reasons, the conclusion follows absolutely.

Argument?   How do we know that these designs for formal argument guarantee their conclusions? As noted earlier, the three standards for argument apply.

Truth of Reasons.   Formal argument often finesses this point. In many contexts, the premises of a formal argument are stated at the outset and *assumed true*. In the first example, for instance, "some soldiers are gardeners" is a given, not part of the argument. Likewise, mathematical argument treats the axioms as givens.   Any objections to the givens are not counted as objections to the argument itself. Only one thing can go wrong: inconsistency. Sometimes you may start off with a logically inconsistent set of premises. Only in that rare and special sense does truth of reasons become at issue for formal mathematical argument.

Of course, one does find formal arguments with premises that are not simply assumed to be true. Such an argument is sound only if its premises are in fact true as well as its logic sound. An argument with sound logic is said to be *valid*, regardless of the truth of its premises. Valid logic guarantees a sound argument when the premises are assumed true, as in Euclidean geometry, but not when the premises may be questioned.

Weight of Reasons.   The crux of formal argument is the weight standard: Why do formal arguments lend perfect weight to their conclusions, no matter what the subject-matter of those conclusions? Broadly speaking, because the weight of a formal argument depends only on the abstract form of the argument, as given on the right side of the arguments listed above. It is the shape the argument takes that counts, not what the argument concerns.

We find these logical forms compelling because we perceive their general validity in any particular model we construct.   To take the first example again, if *Some A are B* and *All B are C* then those very *A* that are *B* must also fall among the *C*'s. We can model it diagrammatically, with mental images, or any way you want, and still the same inevitability appears. It seems part of the meaning of *some* and *all* that such consequences follow. As noted above, arguments with this logically inevitable character are called *valid*.

In philosophy it is controversial whether the reliability of logic is just a very well confirmed generalization about the way *some* and *all* behave or whether the reliability has an ultimate justification. There is a dilemma about what further justification to offer; certainly not a formal logical one since the soundness of formal logic is what is at issue. This technical issue cannot be explored here; models will have to suffice to convey at least an appreciation if not a proof of the security that formal logic supplies.

Completeness of Reasons. This is never a problem with formal logic. If you have one valid formal argument for a conclusion, the argument is complete. Since that on argument guarantees the conclusion, you do not need to add other arguments on the same or the opposite side of the case. The only thing that could go wrong is untruth or inconsistency in the premises; however, this violates the truth standard, not the completeness standard.

Patterns of Mathematical Proof

Purpose? The same iron-clad guarantee offered by formal logic is also sought in mathematics.

Models and Structure? Mathematical logic takes a variety of forms, algebraic argument being one of the most familiar. For example:

$3x + 5 = 11$
Therefore, subtracting 5 from both sides, $3x = 6$
Therefore, dividing both sides by 3, $x = 2$

The rule applies here says that the same thing done to both sides of an equation preserves the equality.

In one situation, this principle seems to falter. Here is a simple example:

$5x = 3x$
Dividing both sides by x, $5 = 3$

The problem, of course, is that $x = 0$ in this case, and you are not allowed to divide by zero. The trap occurs because you may not have determined yet that $x = 0$. This does not reveal a flaw in the logic of mathematics, because the rules for manipulating equations specifically exclude division by zero, including division by expressions that eventually turn out to be zero. When such an expression shows up later, you have to backtrack and count as unacceptable a step that previously seemed solid.

Argument? Mathematical arguments are formal logical arguments employed in the discipline of mathematics. The truth of premises usually is assumed. Mathematical arguments aspire to perfect weight and pose no problems of completeness as discussed before. The further question is *why* must mathematical demonstration draw only on formal argument? The answer is that in principle mathematics could be looser; we could, for instance, accept measurements of a wide range of right triangles as a mathematical justification of the Pythagorean theorem that the sum of the squares of the two legs equal the square of the hypotenuse. But by convention we do not view this justification as a *mathematical* one.

Accordingly, it misses the point to ask why mathematical patterns of reasoning turn out to be so reliable. They do not "turn out to be," but are *selected* to be perfectly reliable, a matter of design. Behind all of mathematics is, and has been since the days of Euclid, an aesthetic ideal demanding absolute logic.

SOME PATTERNS OF INFORMAL ARGUMENT

Informal argument follows many patterns adapted to diverse kinds of evidence and the varied ways that evidence can support claims. A few examples will give a better sense of the range and reliability of informal argument.

The Pattern of Estimating Probabilities

Purpose? To reach a probabilistic conclusion based on a sample.

Models and Structure? One example will have to represent a complex and many-sided topic:

> *Out of a sample of 100 people chosen at random, 60 said that they planned to vote in favor of a certain referendum.*
>
> *So probably about 60% of the votes will vote this way.*

This example stands for any case where you forecast the disposition of a large set of elements by examining a random subset. That is only one sort of statistical forecasting; there are many others.

Argument?   Truth of reasons is always at issue, of course. If the observations prove inaccurate, the inferences from them can hardly be sound. This point applies to all subsequent examples too, but no need to repeat it over and over.

What about weight and completeness? This probabilistic pattern of argument provides no absolute guarantees about either. As to weight, there is some possibility that by chance alone the sample of 100 people does not reflect the general trend; perhaps only 40% of the population really favor the referendum, despite the 60% in the random sample. As to completeness, perhaps you know some news about to break that will change public sentiment, so you have a line of argument against the 60% prediction.

However, there is one sort of guarantee. Completeness problems aside, probability theory proves that the 60% is a best bet estimate. That is, 60% stands a better chance of being close to the actual figure than any other estimate based on the same data would. Moreover, with further calculations, you can determine how likely it is that the estimate will be wrong by more than a certain amount. For instance, you can compute the probability that the actual percentage will turn out to be more than 10 percentage points away from 60%. So, if a prediction within 10 percent is close enough for your needs, you can figure out your chances of committing a serious error relative to those needs.

These points show that probabilistic argument does carry a certain weight. Nonetheless, it is dismaying to see how shaky probabilistic argument is compared to formal argument. But we get spoiled by dwelling on strict logical argument. Some uncertainty is the typical situation for most reasoning.

The Pattern of Induction

Purpose?   To establish a generalization based on experience.

Models and Structure.   Inductive generalizations are the stock in trade of science and also commonplace in daily life. Here are some samples:

Tony made many mistakes on his last 20 addition problems.
So probably Tony's addition is unreliable in general.

Every one of the many times I've come to this traffic circle at
rush-hour, there's a traffic jam.
So probably there's always a traffic jam then.

Christine has spoken enthusiastically about the last several movies
she saw.
So Christine probably enjoys movies in general.

Argument? Although all of these inferences seem reasonable, none provides an absolute guarantee. They suffice only for saying "probably." One limitation on weight is the risk of bad luck in sampling. For instance, perhaps two percent of the time there is not a jam at the traffic circle at rush-hour, but I have never been there during the two percent. There are potential completeness problems, too. Perhaps, for instance, you know that Christine has been under pressure at work. So you might add the counterargument that her recent enthusiasm for movies reflects escapism rather than genuine love for the cinema.

But there is a deeper dilemma than that. The justification for simple inductive generalizations is one of philosophy's classic problems. The difficulty boils down to this: Nothing guarantees that the future will repeat the past. Furthermore, it is easy to construct cases where induction mechanically applied yields absurd conclusions. For instance:

Every number I have ever seen written is no bigger than
1,000,000,000,000,000,000,000,000,000,000,000,000,000,000,000.
Therefore, probably all numbers are not bigger than that one.

To be sure, we immediately see the flaw in this conclusion because we know something else about numbers that tells us bigger numbers exist. But there are many matters in the world that we do not know much about already. How can we trust our generalizations when we might be fooled as above, but in a case where we do not know enough to catch the error? In fact, how have we managed to make as much sense of the world as we have, relying constantly on induction? Perhaps we have just been lucky.

Again, this deep and vexed issue can hardly be engaged here. There is, however, a straightforward answer to a slightly different question: What protects our use of induction from the kinds of cases that quickly lead to trouble? The answer is the completeness standard. We should never expect patterns of argument short of formal logic to do by themselves the work of yielding sound conclusions. We need complete arguments too — arguments that take into account whatever else we know that might bear on the conclusion. The argument about big numbers, for instance, has a completeness problem: We know something else about numbers that shows us our inference is mistaken.

The Hypothetico-Deductive Pattern

Purpose? To test the validity of a scientific or everyday hypothesis.

Model and Structure? Einstein's theory of relatively predicts that gravity affects light. For instance, when a beam of light from one star passes close to another, the gravity of the second star will bend the beam off its normally straight course. We can check this prediction by observing whether our own sun distorts the perceived positions of stars appearing just outside its edge. We can make such observations only during a solar eclipse, because otherwise the glare of the sun prevents our seeing the stars. In fact, observations made during eclipses have shown that the distortion in position does occur and to the predicted degree.

The pattern of argument is simple enough:

Einstein's theory predicts a displacement of a star's image.
The displacement is indeed observed.
This lends some more support to Einstein's theory.

Such a pattern of reasoning is called *hypothetico-deductive* argument. The structure of the argument motivates the name. You begin with an hypothesis (the hypothetico part) and deduce a consequence that you can observe (the deductive part). Then you make the observation. If the observation agrees with the prediction, this evidence lends weight to the hypothesis. (Some authors reserve the term hypothetico-deductive for slightly more elaborate forms of argument that, for instance, include the consideration of alternative hypotheses.)

The hypothetico-deductive pattern can provide evidence against as well as for theories. For example, the Einstein experiment might have gone as follows:

> *Einstein's theory predicts displacement of a star's image.*
> *The expected displacement is not observed.*
> *So Einstein's theory is probably wrong.*

Note that we still say only *probably* wrong. Perhaps, for example, we made a mistake in the calculations leading to the prediction. Nonetheless, in general, negative evidence, "disconfirming evidence" as it is called, counts more heavily than positive or confirming evidence. This is because usually theories claim great generality: "Always everywhere such-and-such." So you only have to find one clear case where the theory fails in order to disprove it, but you have to find many varied cases of success to develop confidence in it.

Hypothetico-deductive argument appears not only in science but in everyday life. Many commonplace situations involve casual versions of hypothetico-deductive reasoning. Here is an example of disconfirmation:

> *I hypothesize that, using a certain system, I can detect trends in the stock market.*
> *I go through several rounds of predicting trends and investing.*
> *After some months, I have lost several thousand dollars.*
> *I conclude that my hypothesis is false.*

Here is a case of confirmation:

> *The desk and ceiling lamps suddenly go out.*
> *I hypothesize that the problem is a fuse rather than a general power failure.*
> *I predict that the lights in the next room, which are on a different circuit, will work.*
> *The lights in the next room do work.*
> *So probably my hypothesis is correct.*

Notice, though, that I still might be wrong. Perhaps the desk and ceiling lamps blew out simultaneously, unlikely though that is.

Argument?   The deductive part of hypothetico-deductive reasoning, the inference from theory to prediction, may or may not employ formal logic or mathematics. To the extent that it does and that no special assumptions or approximations have to be made (but in science they often do), the deductive part will have the usual guarantee strict logic provides.

The evidential part of hypothetico-deductive reasoning involves a special case of inductive generalization, reviewed above. We test an hypothesis, perhaps many times in many circumstances, and finally conclude that the hypothesis holds true in general. Accordingly, hypothetico-deductive reasoning faces the same hazards of weight and completeness as inductive argument in general, and whatever partial justification for inductive argument we have applies to hypothetico-deductive argument as well.

The Evaluative Pattern

Purpose?   To justify an evaluation, such as "X is good," "X is bad," or "X is mediocre."

Model and Structure?   A typical evaluative argument includes a number of reasons weighing for or against the value of something, culminating in a summary statement. For example, this might be said about a movie:

> *The characterizations were weak.*
> *There was lively and engaging action throughout.*
> *The sound track was too loud.*
> *The suspense kept the audience's attention throughout.*
> *The plot was a bit corny.*
> *Therefore, all in all, it was good entertainment but not a great movie.*

As in this example, evaluative arguments typically have several lines of argument on both sides of the case. This is even more so for evaluative than for other sorts of informal arguments, since almost always many different considerations apply when you are evaluating something, and each consideration yields a line of argument.

Argument? Evaluative arguments present a classic problem of weight. How does descriptive evidence come to have evaluative bearing? For example, given the descriptive point that "the suspense kept the audience's attention throughout," who says that keeping attention is *good*? The answer is that there has to be an unstated premise, in this case something like "Holding an audience's attention is good in a work of art."

We need to seek a hidden premise for a simple reason. If the logic is sound, an evaluative term like "good" cannot appear for the first time in the conclusion; otherwise the conclusion would add information that did not appear in the premises. In fact, philosophy has a name for this blunder. The notion that you can reason from descriptive premises to an evaluative conclusion is called the *naturalistic fallacy*. So, when an argument seems to do this, we presume that there is a tacit premise that fills in the missing step.

This solution leads to another concern about the weight of evaluative arguments. It is often taken for granted that the (usually tacit) premises connecting description to evaluation are general rules holding for a range of cases, in other words, standards for the object in question. But, the complaint goes, what *are* the general rules in such areas as painting or music? Efforts to state such rules have led to endless debate. Yet, lacking such rules, it seems our arguments carry no weight.

This objection is answered by recognizing that general standards are not always necessary after all. Many time, *particular* judgments carry weight. For example, the above argument included "The sound track was too loud." Too loud by what standard? No general standard was given; moreover it would clearly be very artificial to specify a standard in, say, decibels. Rather, the perceptual experience and accompanying judgment of the movie goer justifies the "too loud."

In general, statements of the form "too X," where X is some characteristic, have as their backing the supposed good judgment of the maker, not any statable but unstated general standard. Much mischief comes of supposing that all evaluative arguments depend somehow on general standards. Such a belief sends us off on a quest for standards that prove as elusive as the Holy Grail. We do better to recognize that often good judgment—whether of paintings, shoes, or steamships—underwrites evaluative arguments.

This does not mean that such arguments are haphazard. Principles there are, but their application often requires case-by-case judgment. For example, we all understand that volume, like many other attributes, can be excessive in principle; but to peg the level at which the volume becomes "too loud" requires judgment. We all understand that as a principle action tends to be engaging, but deciding whether this movie's action was really engaging rather than, say, just busy or artificial, requires judgment.

This explanation of how evaluative arguments carry weight certainly does not leave them problem-free. Indeed, the frequent lack of general standards opens the door to divergent judgment. I say the sound track was too loud. You say it was okay. So what can we do? Little more than listen again to check our impressions.

Not only weight but completeness poses a problem for evaluative argument. It is very easy for one person to overlook a feature another sees, and hence not count that feature in his or her appraisal. In fact, some research of mine suggests that two people often attend to quite different things in works of art. It is almost as though they perceive different works. Here more so than in the case of divergent judgments there is a natural solution. Both parties can alert each other to overlooked features; if both parties share values and perceptions, their appraisals may then converge somewhat.

In general, sound evaluative argument comes easiest when there are common perceptual tendencies and tastes in the community. Lacking that, we rely on individuals considered connoisseurs for one reason or another, individuals whose judgment we credit as better than our own. When even the connoisseurs disagree, especially after trying on one another's viewpoints, then the basis for evaluative argument falls apart.

The Causal Pattern

Purpose? To use our common sense knowledge of the world to determine causes and consequences of events.

Models and Structure? Much of informal reasoning depends on weaving together causal stories, stories based on knowledge of causes and intentions we have picked up from living a normal life. For example:

Frank is late getting home from work tonight.
There is no special crush at the office.

> *So there's probably another one of those traffic jams that occur at the traffic circle from time to time.*

Or, for another example:

> *Unemployment is a serious problem in our community.*
> *Candidate Simmons has a definite plan to bring in new industry.*
> *His opponent, vague on this point, is stressing human rights and better education.*
> *Therefore, people are likely to vote for Simmons.*

Behind these arguments lies a rich repertoire of knowledge about what causes what in the world. For instance, you follow the first argument because you know that pressure at the office sometimes can keep employees working late, and that traffic jams also make people late. You appreciate the second argument in part because you know that new industry will create new jobs and that people tend to vote for whomever best serves their wallet, human rights and education aside.

Argument? Of course, such causal arguments can run afoul of difficulties with either the weight or completeness conditions. On completeness, for instance, you might know that Simmons has mob connections the newspaper will soon disclose. So you forecast that the bad publicity will undermine his support. This objection relies on the same resources of mind as the original argument — it invokes yet more of your causal understanding of the world.

As to weight, causal predictions inherit their bearing from the constituent causal principles we know of, which we assemble to predict the particular case. Notice the risk here. If we make up a complex causal account out of several principles, each one of which is only 90% certain, then we may end up with a whole story that is very uncertain indeed because it depends on a series of 90% sure gambles, at least one of which is likely to go wrong. So causal arguments are strong only to the extent that the constituent causal principles are strong and the "probabilities" do not concatenate too much.

Neither deep nor exhaustive, this survey at least should show that informal patterns of reasoning are designs of many kinds, each trading away the strength of formal logic for applicability to situations formal logic cannot treat. The question remains: How do people learn to use them?

Most of these patterns of argument we learn intuitively. They occur routinely in everyday discourse. If we want to give ourselves advice, far more important than distinguishing various patterns of argument is to heed the three general standards of truth, weight, and completeness. These are our first line of defense against careless conclusions, whatever the form of argument.

However, it also has to be said that some difficulties in reasoning evade both our intuitive grasp of patterns of argument and any deliberate care we take with the standards. Certain inferences involve pitfalls of a psychological or technical nature, pitfalls invisible to the uninitiated. For example, vivid models exert a pull on the mind that can bias objective reasoning. If you learn that your friend Ralph bought a Volvo that turned out to be a lemon, this single example will undermine your good option of Volvos much more than it should.

Compounding the vividness effect is a small sample effect. People commonly believe that a small sample from a population will be quite representative of the whole population, when by chance it can easily be quite nonrepresentative; so people generalize from small samples more boldly than they should. Paradoxically, people distrust the predictiveness of large samples drawn from very large populations—say one-thousand people from a population of two million—because the sample does not constitute a sizable percentage of the parent population. In fact, statistical reliability in such cases depends almost entirely on the size of the sample and hardly at all on the fraction of the parent population that the sample represents.

These sample pitfalls give warning that the three standards plus common sense do not equip one fully for everyday reasoning. But it is my belief that the standards and their serious practice, as explored in the following chapter, make a better start on building reasoning skill than attention to particular pitfalls, each one of which occurs only from time to time.

KINDS OF ARGUMENT

So far the focus has been on justificatory argument, argument designed to test a claim. However, not all arguments aim at justification. Some instead attempt explanation, others persuasion, and still others other things. Some comparisons among such types will round out this look inside argument. For a start, it is worth reviewing the role justificatory argument plays in answering the design questions.

Justificatory Argument. Such arguments appeared in this book long before the present chapter. Remember that to understand many designs you need a reasoned evaluation. Does the symphony, salmon mousse, or chair do its job well and why, whether that job is to delight your ear, palate, or bottom? A reasoned evaluation is a justificatory argument for an evaluative conclusion about the design in question, a conclusion that expresses how well the design serves it purpose. For instance, you might argue that the salmon mousse was, all in all, very good, mediocre, or awful, depending on such factors such as taste, texture, and appearance.

Justificatory arguments also appear when you are treating claims as designs, for example claims like "Columbus discovered America in 1492," or, from economics, "good money drives out bad money," or, from science, "no object can attain the speed of light," or, from literature, "Bacon wrote the plays normally attributed to Shakespeare." As sketched in Chapter 2, you need to ask the design questions of such claims, including the argument question. The resulting arguments normally are justificatory.

Explanatory Argument. Just as important as justificatory argument, explanatory argument cuts in a different direction. Explanatory argument aims not particularly to establish truth, but to explain. It seeks to show not *that* such and such but *why* such and such. For example, why does a pencil have an eraser? So you can correct mistakes. Why do most pencils have six sides? So that they provide a better grip and will not roll off tables. Certainly these arguments do not seek to prove what we already know—that pencils have erasers and six sides. Rather, such arguments address the "why" of a design in terms of motives.

Chapter 2 contrasted "surface" and "deep" explanatory arguments, the latter explaining something by means of deep principles. Recall, for instance, the discussion of the cutting edge in terms of the wedge and other principles. Remember that the discussion did not try to prove that cutting edges really cut, which we all know, but rather explained why they cut.

Here is a fresh example of deep explanation. Why are the days longer in summer than in winter? Remember that the earth's axis has a tilt relative to the plane of the earth's orbit around the sun. Consequently, in the summer, when the earth travels in the part of its orbit where the north pole tilts toward the sun, the rotation of the earth leaves a place on the northern hemisphere in the sun more than 12 hours. The further north the place, the longer the day; far enough north and the sun stays in the sky all day. This purely geometrical phenomenon can easily be demonstrated with a globe for the earth and a lamp for the sun.

This explanation, like all explanation, takes the form of an argument. You begin with certain information, such as the fact that the earth's axis is tilted. From that you derive logically the phenomenon to be explained—the long summer days. But notice again: You are not trying to establish that summer days are indeed long. We already know that. Rather, your argument has a different aim, to show *why* they are long.

Hypothetical Argument.   Hypothetical argument is the first step in hypothetico-deductive argument. Recall that hypothetico-deductive argument starts by deducing a prediction from an hypothesis and continues by testing the prediction. For instance, commencing with the hypothesis of Einstein's theory of relativity, one can predict apparent shifts in positions of stars close to the disk of the sun during a lunar eclipse. This deduction does not seek to prove the prediction. After all, the prediction is in question; we proceed to test the prediction as a way of confirming or disconfirming the theory. Rather, the purpose of hypothetical argument is to produce a prediction to test.

Persuasive Argument.   As its names suggests, persuasive argument aims to persuade. Its goal is not to establish a sound conclusion, but to create belief in a conclusion that may or may not be sound. An effective persuasive argument might, but need not, be a sound justificatory argument. Sad to say, many audiences find selected anecdotes and appeals to sentiment and self-image much more persuasive than a sound justificatory argument.

With these kinds of argument in mind, it is interesting to lay out some features of a sound justificatory argument and tally whether effective arguments of the other types require such features.

Types of Argument

Characteristic of sound argument:	Justificatory	Explanatory	Hypothetical	Persuasive
True reasons	yes	yes	not all	no
Correct weights	yes	yes	yes	no
Completeness	yes	no	no	no
Sound conclusion	yes	no	no	no

What lies behind the contrasts apparent in the table? The first column simply reminds us that all three standards for a justificatory argument apply and guarantee a sound conclusion. The second column concerns explanatory argument. There, true reasons and correct strengths are needed, else the conclusion would not follow from the principles invoked to explain it. However, neither completeness nor a sound conclusion are required, because the conclusion may be in question on other grounds. For instance, someone reports sighting a flying saucer. You try to explain this sighting by ascribing it to unusual meteorological phenomena, or even invaders from Mars. But, at the same time, you doubt whether a sighting occurred at all; perhaps the supposed witnesses were just seeking publicity. In general, it is commonplace to consider explanatory arguments for conclusions that are in doubt and might have counterarguments.

For similar reasons, hypothetical arguments need not be complete nor have sound conclusions. Indeed, the whole point of an hypothetical argument is to generate a conclusion and then to check its soundness. So one cannot require in advance that it is indeed sound. Nor can one assume in advance that the argument is complete, because that would mean by definition that there was no more evidence to bring to bear on the truth of the conclusion. In addition, not all the reasons in an hypothetical argument are true: The theory under test is in question and might turn out to be false, yet it functions as one of the reasons from which deductions are made. Of course, the other reasons should be true.

Finally, persuasive argument, as the table indicates, need show none of the characteristics. To be sure, a persuasive argument may sometimes benefit from true reasons, correct strengths, or completeness, but only when such features increase its persuasiveness. To put this more cynically, a facade of true reasons, correct strengths, and completeness will do just as well as the real thing. Persuasive argument in the "no holds barred" sense is no partner of the other kinds of argument, but their adversary.

These contrasting types of argument have import not only for our understanding but for our practice of argument. In particular, there is a tendency to confuse explanatory and justificatory arguments. You ponder X. You, or someone else, explain how X might be true. Now X makes sense. So you come to think that probably X is true, because it is so plausible. But *making sense is a weak test of truth*. We can even see why it is only a weak test. An explanatory argument shows how something makes sense relative to some of our other beliefs. But the conclusion need not be sound; we may already have the knowledge with which we could challenge it. To fail to make such challenges is to treat a sound explanatory argument as though it were a sound justificatory argument.

A confusion between justificatory and persuasive argument also can cause trouble. Certainly, in many situations, people have motives to persuade others of something. Such circumstances promote a blurring, occasionally deliberate, between persuasive and justificatory argument. So it is a *caveat emptor* world, where receivers of arguments must strive to apply the standards of a sound justificatory argument, despite the distractions of persuasive wrappings.

Persuasive argument poses an even more subtle threat: We very often persuade ourselves. It is in our own best interest, when arguing with ourselves, always to use justificatory arguments. After all, we want to sort out the soundest course of action for ourselves, all things considered. However, the soundest course of action is not always the most appealing; so we fall into the trap of persuading ourselves, practicing deception on the one person for whom we have the most reason to avoid it.

The next chapter treats the art of argument specifically, but here it is worth viewing the problems of argument on a broad scale. You might say there are two pitfalls writ large in our practice of argument. There is the tendency to treat what makes sense as true, confusing explanatory argument with justificatory argument and settling for coherence, which explanation provides, but neglecting completeness, which it does not. And there is the tendency to treat what appeals as true, confusing persuasive argument with justificatory argument and settling for superficial satisfaction of the standards or neglecting them altogether.

WHAT YOU CAN DO

As a teacher, learner, or thinker, you need to reason about all sorts of things, academic and practical. The nature of argument as a design for truth-testing offers some straightforward advice about reasoning well.

- *When reasoning with others or by yourself, separate out your conclusion from your reasons; signal the onset of conclusions with "because," "therefore," or a similar word.* Remember: Very often people find themselves debating in a general way without declaring specifically what the claim at issue is. In fact, people often slide from claim to claim, unaware of shifting ground. Reasoning begins by separating out the claim and holding it constant (if it turns out not to be quite the claim you want to investigate, then revise the claim, of course).

- *In building an argument, try for truth of reasons, rightly weighted reasons, and complete reasons.* After thinking out the pros and cons in a situation, make a deliberate effort to check each of these three conditions. Ask of each reason, "Can I challenge it?" "Have I weighted it rightly, considering its reliability and bearing on the conclusion?" Ask of the whole situation, "Can I think of any more arguments of a different sort that might apply?"

- *In reasoning about something, distinguish different sorts of argument.* Are you evaluating the truth or appropriateness of something? That is justificatory argument, to which the three standards apply. Are you just explaining? Try for true reasons and correct weights, but completeness is not so important unless you want your explanation to stand up as the only explanation.

- *Beware of persuasive argument.* Watch out for it in others. Guard against persuading yourself.

7 The Art of Argument

Both everyday and academic life require us to reach sound conclusions. Informal argument provides our principal means of doing so. At one extreme, we face questions so easily resolved that we hardly have to think about them, such as whether alligators can fly. At the other, life poses vexing questions about human rights or destinies that may take decades of pondering for their resolution, if they ever yield. Neither of these extremes puts pressure on our day-to-day reasoning abilities, since the one is trivial and the other intractable. In between, however, lies a range of medium-difficulty questions that we handle better or worse to our own immediate profit or loss.

But perhaps there is no real problem. It is often felt that people handle this midrange well. They rarely reason badly about what counts. However, both common experience and experimental evidence urge that this simply is not so. Common experience tells us that students perform poorly on essay writing and other tasks that call for constructing informal arguments, even though their efforts count toward grades they view as precious. Newspaper editorials and other public expressions of argument often violate the three standards discussed in Chapter 6 with blatantly one-sided and simplistic positions. Also, it seems that people often do not reason carefully enough about matters of immediate personal relevance, such as which house or car to buy or whether or not to start a certain business.

As to experimental evidence, a brief overview of some research on informal reasoning will clarify how well people do, what sorts of difficulties they have, and how much education helps.

A STUDY OF INFORMAL REASONING

Concerned about informal reasoning abilities and their relation to education, two colleagues and I collected samples of arguments from 320 individuals in eight groups: high school freshmen, high school seniors, college freshmen, college seniors, first year graduate students, fourth year graduate students, people out of school several years without a bachelor's degree, and people out of school several years with at least a bachelor's degree. The arguments we gathered addressed some vexing social issues current at the time of the research, issues of a common-sense character that anyone might think through. For example, one issue was "Would a law requiring a five cent deposit on bottles and cans reduce litter?" Another was "Would restoring the military draft significantly increase America's ability to influence world events?"

We evaluated the arguments people produced in a number of ways. One especially illuminating measure was number of lines of argument. For instance, on the deposit law questions, the argument "People would return the bottles for the five cents instead of littering them" was one possible line of argument, while "They tried such a law in another state and it worked well" was another. Even when more details were given, each of these only counted as one line of argument. Accordingly, number of lines of argument measured how wide a net a reasoner cast.

Simply in terms of number of lines of argument, what picture did our data paint? The average score for high school students was about 2, for college students 2.9, and for graduate students 3.5. People out of school without a bachelor's degree scored about 2.3, and with a bachelor's degree about 3.1. The numbers are disappointing; the issues were chosen to be arguable in a number of ways, but most individuals considered only two or three arguments on an issue.

Furthermore, education has only a modest effect on number of lines of argument, much less of an effect than the figures above suggest. Our data analysis showed that the differences between high school, college, and graduate school scores reflected not learning to reason better, but selective admissions policies in college and graduate school, which tend to favor those more facile at skills like argument. We isolated learning effects by comparing first year with fourth year students in high school, college, and graduate school. The results showed a gain with education of about *one tenth of a line of argument per year.* This means that on the average it would take ten years of education to enable a person to discover one more line of argument.

Number of lines of argument was not our only measure. Others included number of sentences, number of points mentioned on the side of the case opposite the one the person had adopted, degree to which the person stuck to the topic, and a simple rating of overall quality of argument on a five point scale. In all cases, two judges working separately made the evaluations; we found good agreement between the judges. All the measures showed the same disappointing pattern as did lines of argument: mediocre performance, more so in the less educated groups, and a very slow rate of gain with education.

It is also interesting to ask what sorts of weaknesses appeared in the arguments. Problems of completeness, weighting, and truth of reasons were all apparent. Perhaps the single most obvious weakness was one-sidedness. People did not give due attention to the side of the case opposite their own, often mentioning no reasons at all on the other side. For one example of such a completeness problem, someone might argue, "Suppose we had a military draft; this would strengthen the army; we'd look like we had more clout, so other nations would respect us more." But the same person would miss the equally sensible counterargument "A draft would cause protest as it did during the Vietnam war; protests make the U.S. look disunified; so other nations, seeing us divided among ourselves, would respect us less."

Problems of weight were just as common. Some of the time, people would treat as relevant reasons that bore no connection to the conclusion. For instance, one participant remarked, "The U.S. can't get more influence because the U.S. already has a lot of influence." This argument sounds odd because, in general, having a lot of something does not mean that you cannot get more of it. People also would often use generalizations that did not apply to the particular case for special reasons. For instance, someone might argue "More manpower will make our army stronger and therefore increase our influence." But perhaps this does not carry so much weight, because someone might object, "Nowadays it's missiles and technical expertise that count, not manpower." Other sorts of weighting problems occurred as well.

Finally, of course, there were cases where the reasons given in themselves were simply false or debatable. On a question about art (the exact issue does not matter here), people would often support their position by saying "Art is creative. Therefore such and such." Now it is true that we think of art as creative, but this is a stereotype. A great deal of art is extremely conventional.

To summarize broadly, informal reasoning appears poor, improves little with education, and displays difficulties with each of the three standards completeness, weight, and truth. All this urges us in our teacher and learner roles to pay direct attention to strengthening skills of informal argument. Partly for this reason, argument appears explicitly as one of the four design questions: not only because it helps us to understand a design, but because it is a part of understanding that needs particular attention and exercise.

IMPROVING INFORMAL ARGUMENT

How should we go about improving the practice of argument? Whatever skills are taught, any such effort should not neglect values. Those values are better conveyed by actions that make them real than by lip service to precepts in fact neglected. Opportunities arise in any setting from the school room to the dinner table, where discourse can respect or neglect reason-giving and the taking seriously of objections. It is characteristic both of lower class family life and, shockingly, of much of schooling, that reason-giving plays little role, especially balanced reason-giving where both sides of the case get serious attention.

Always presuming attention to values, explicit strategies can be taught. There are many possibilities. Here is a strategic approach to informal reasoning that lends itself to instruction in school or out of it. The approach builds on the three standards, which should be introduced first, and offers several reasoning strategies, each one escalating in care and thoroughness.

Metastrategy: Option-finding versus Decision-making.   Our discussion of argument has focused on deciding upon the truth of a claim or among courses of action. In either case, a decision has to be taken among specified options—true or false, this plan or that. However, we have to remember that in realistic circumstances the claims or courses of action themselves are not given but thought up. One can waste a great deal of time, suffer from illusory dilemmas, and even adopt unfortunate courses of action through failure to explore the options among which to take a decision.

For instance, suppose you are examining the truth of a claim. Is it the right claim to ponder? Instead, perhaps it is too extreme to warrant serious exploration; a hedged claim would be better. Or perhaps it is not the precise claim advanced by another person whose position you want to criticize; you had best examine carefully what the other person actually said. Or suppose you are choosing a course of action. Are you confronting an unnecessary dilemma posed by extreme options? Is there no middle way? What are you taking for granted about the situation that you need not? How many very different approaches to the situation can you conceive?

These questions should make plain why alternating between *option-finding* and *decision-making* is a "metastrategy" that rides above the process of decision-making itself. Even in the midst of pondering the options at hand, one does well always to remain aware that the best resolution may lie in other options yet undiscovered and to remain ready to search them out.

With this metastrategy in mind, let us turn to the problem of argument per se: appraising the relative merits of the options at hand. How might one examine their merits with heed to the standards of truth, weight, and completeness that provide for well-grounded decisions?

Strategy 1: Snap Judgment.   Snap judgment is about the simplest style of argument one can have. It is hardly argument at all, except in the limited sense that your decision stems from the one reason of the snap judgment itself. Suppose, for instance, I live in the midst of a city and have no car. I hold only a modest job, but I have the chance to buy a used car at a good price. How do I decide whether to accept the deal or not? Maybe I just make a snap judgment—yes or no! Whichever the case, the snap judgment may suit the circumstances perfectly well. Perhaps I have such a full sense of my life situation that I can settle the matter in an instant, and further thinking would do little to unsettle it.

Strategy 2: Quick Argument. However, the car costs a good deal, good deal though it may be, and brings various responsibilities. Where will I park it, for example? So perhaps I should think more carefully. "Quick argument" gives a recipe for the occasion. In quick argument, I list the reasons that occur to me readily. I take care to list pros *and* cons, since I know that, if I feel an impulse pro, I may unfairly neglect the cons or vice versa. Perhaps I get something like this:

Pro	*Con*
Convenience says yes.	Expense says no.
Shopping easier.	I can go on a holiday instead.
Weekend country drives.	Hard to park.

Sometimes this may be enough—the reasons might pile up on one or the other side of the case overwhelmingly. But if no preponderance emerges, what is my recourse?

One good move, here or earlier, would be to take the metastrategy about options seriously and explore thoroughly what my transportation options are. Suppose I do this and it still seems that the right choice to make at the moment is whether or not to buy the car. How can I pursue the decision further?

Strategy 3: Complete Argument. In *quick argument,* I took a step toward completeness by looking at both sides. But now I treat the issue of completeness very seriously, making a vigorous effort to list all the factors I can that bear on the issue one way or the other. I set myself a quota of at least five reasons on each side, to keep myself from getting lazy. I elaborate reasons, adding some in response to others. I think through in my mind what it would be like to have a car or to proceed as now. Perhaps I add items like the following to my pro-con list.

Pro	*Con*
Easy trips to visit parents.	Costly to rent parking space.
Public transportation costs too.	Plenty of public transportation.

Public transportation slow.	Driving in city pretty slow, too.
Public transportation crowded.	Repair costs occasionally.
I deserve a little luxury.	How do I find a good garage?
Flexibility, e.g. late at night.	Gas and upkeep, too.
Essential outside city.	Keeping car clean a nuisance.

Extending the list like that might yield a clear decision. But not this time, so what is my last recourse?

Strategy 4: Careful Argument. I guess I have to get serious about this. I must consider carefully whether each reason is true (the truth standard) and what weight it should carry (the weight standard). This can become complicated, because I may find myself generating subarguments about the soundness or weight of particular reasons, and may have to take care that those subarguments too are complete, with true and soundly weighted reasons.

For example, going over each reason, I come to "essential outside city." How much weight do I initially see this as carrying? My first impulse is "moderate." But let me think seriously about the reason's truth and weight. Is it really true that a car is essential outside the city? Well, what about buses? They don't go where I want to. What about a borrowed car? No, I don't really have anyone I could ask routinely. What about rental? That's interesting if I only took a few trips a year. But no, I'd like to go nearly every weekend, I think. Any other ideas? None come to mind. So I'll say it's true that I need a car for out of city travel. Since the arguments seem to be all on one side, I don't have to pursue this issue further — I can treat it with *quick argument.* On the other hand, if my offhand reasons had come out more evenly, and I thought the issue was pivotal, I'd have to make the subargument about the issue a complete one, maybe even a careful one.

Now what about weighting? Before I said that out-of-city travel was moderately important. But perhaps that's too weak, since I decided I'd like to travel outside the city nearly every weekend. Is that realistic? What about the winter? Well, I enjoy winter and like to ski cross-country, so that makes sense. Do I really have the time? Yes, I rarely work on weekends. Also, I have friends that would be fun to take trips with. Other sides to the story? Perhaps I could get bored. I might, after a while. Probably I would; I've become bored with other pastimes. So perhaps, realistically speaking, I'd take a trip only every three weeks or so after the first couple of months. So let's leave it at a hair less than moderately important.

A QUICK ARGUMENT FOR THIS APPROACH

This strategic approach to informal argument calls for at least a *quick argument* to evaluate it. Here then are some pros, some cons, and some reasons for not taking the cons seriously.

What makes this escalating strategy of snap judgment, quick argument, complete argument, and careful argument, with attention to the metastrategy of exploring options, a reasonable approach to reasoning better? Partly, it inherits its worth from the three standards built into it; the standards were justified earlier. The escalating sequence has another advantage. It reflects the reality that many questions of truth or decision simply do not require full attention to all three standards nor even careful exploration of options. To present reasoning as though it always demanded *careful argument* is both mistaken and daunting.

This may seem sound for everyday arguments such as the car purchase problem, but perhaps in academic and scientific contexts you always need careful argument. However, such contexts differ in their demands just as do everyday situations. For instance, the strategies suit questions of whether you have a sound interpretation of a poem or whether there is life on Mars just as well as purchase decisions. But in such cases are you making a casual personal investigation, priming yourself for an exploratory conversation, preparing a lecture, or planning a professional article? And how readily does the issue yield? A transparently affirmative or negative case in casual academic circumstances invites no more than an intuitive snap judgment. At the other extreme, academic writing calls for (although not so often receives) the rigorous attention of careful argument.

Other Approaches

Rival approaches to improving informal reasoning also deserve comment. One such approach is to teach formal reasoning as a way of enhancing informal. However, both in the last chapter and later in this one, some fundamental differences between formal and informal argument are examined. These differences show that informal reasoning poses distinctive challenges calling for a frontal attack, not treatment by proxy.

There is another established approach to improving reasoning: learning about informal and formal fallacies in reasoning. In this approach, people become acquainted with such pitfalls as ad hominem arguments or affirming the consequent, to mention just two classic slips in argument. Ad hominem argument means impugning another's argument unfairly by directing criticisms against the person rather than the logic: "Jones may say all this neatly enough, but he doesn't even have a college education." Affirming the consequence refers to taking an "A implies B" statement to mean that "B implies A" too: "Jones has red hair; oh, there's someone with read hair so it must be Jones." The list of fallacies is long; these skeletons in the closet of human reasoning can provide a skeleton around which to organize instruction.

It certainly makes sense to know about a few persistent troublemakers. But several problems plague the fallacy approach. First of all, many pitfalls in informal reasoning are not on the classic list because they are not fallacies in the normal sense. For instance, one-sided argument is a major problem but not a fallacy in the usual sense of a logically unfounded step in reasoning. Second, the fallacies commonly listed derive from a theoretical rather than an empirical tradition and give a distorted sense of the sorts of fallacies that occur most often in everyday arguments. For instance, ad hominem argument, on everyone's list, never appeared at all in our sample of six-hundred-plus everyday arguments, although it does happen sometimes, of course.

Both these problems could be solved by a revised list of fallacies, or, perhaps more broadly, pitfalls, that prominently included one-sided argument, gave proportional treatment to ad hominem argument, and generally retailored the classic list. But there is a third worry not so easily worked around. The list of pitfalls still will be quite long. It is not easy for learners to acquire such a diverse list, take it to heart, and police their own reasoning carefully. In contrast, the standards and few strategies sketched above have a much simpler structure and, if carefully practiced, guard against a wide range of pitfalls in any case.

Direct Instruction

Another possible reservation about the approach outlined here concerns instructional tactics. Learning explicit rules and principles has been suggested. Some educators find more natural and attractive the notion of learning from models and through immersion and practice, without explicit identification of strategies. Plausible though this sounds, there is good evidence that it is not effective, as noted at the end of Chapter 1. Apparently, in viewing models alone, many learners do not pick up the crucial aspects of the performance.

The last several points do not argue specifically for the strategies presented in the previous section. They argue generally for a strategic approach involving a small set of strategies designed to cover a wide range of pitfalls and learned explicitly as designs, in particular with structure made explicit rather than through models alone. Any approach with these properties should help to build better skills of informal reasoning. It is also crucial to remember the primary importance of conveying values about sound reasoning, not just tactics.

All this granted, the strategies sketched do slight something about making hard decisions. What do you do when you have a tie, especially one that seems intractable? It will come as no surprise that there are strategies for this, too.

TIE BREAKERS

Here are some decision-making principles of wide applicability. Commonplace though they seem, they are often ignored. Together with the reasoning strategies reviewed earlier, these principles can help to decide upon a path of action or the truth of a claim in everyday and academic contexts.

Semi-landslides. If you think about arguments pro and con, one possible outcome is a landslide—almost all reasons on one side. Such issues often do not require much thought, since you can detect the overwhelming "vote" of the evidence by an intuitive snap judgment. But there is another quite common and more subtle outcome, a semi-landslide. In a semi-landslide, there are many more reasons pro and con or con than pro, and enough more of about equal weight to yield a clear decision.

But not enough more so you can forecast the outcome without a list. That is the point. By never making a list laying out the pros and cons, you can miss a semi-landslide. If you just mull over reasons mentally, an issue often seems more vexed than in fact it is because of a "can't see the forest for the trees" effect: You never regard the reasons fully arrayed against one another. A list exposes the shape of the forest, hence the role of explicit listing in strategies 2-4.

From Counting to Weighting.   A pro list and a con list that seem to weigh equally create a decision problem. Sometimes it helps to weight each individual reason. You can do this by labeling each reason with a number or with a label like "very important." You can appraise the overall picture by summing the weights on both sides or pairing up equally weighted reasons on either side to see whether one side has considerable unmatched weight. Sometimes weighting every reason yields a clear decision when the list alone does not. (This does not mean that you have neglected weighting before and only now take it into account at all; rather, you have been treating it informally and intuitively but now actually spell out what you take the weights of each reason to be.)

Weight to the Issue.   Proper weighting of pros and cons often involves more than just considering how important the reasons are in a general sense; it requires considering *exactly* what the claim at issue is and how strong an assertion it makes. Suppose, for example, the claim is "TV violence rarely leads viewers to serious crime." The data show only a few cases where TV inspires real crime, so you decide the data support the conclusion: The counterexamples do not carry enough weight. Now suppose the claim is the very similar, "TV violence has little significant role in inspiring real crime." You might disagree with this, because those few counterexamples now carry considerable weight; although rare, such cases cause enough grief to count as a significant threat to society in your view. In other words, "rarely" is one thing, "significant threat" another; you have to argue to the details of the claim.

For another example, consider a scientific claim like Newton's laws. It is not enough that Newton's laws explain almost all the dynamic phenomena we observe. They fail in some critical special cases and a physical law should hold up *all* the time. Even though the "vote" of the evidence overwhelmingly favors Newton's laws, a modicum of clear counterevidence upsets them in favor of quantum mechanics and relativity theory.

People often neglect weighting to the issue and tacitly or explicitly weight reasons by some vague sense of general relevance or importance. So weighting to the issue needs attention. Moreover, sometimes weighting to the issue helps to resolve what looked like a tie, because the seemingly balanced pros and cons, considering the exact issue, become decisive evidence one way or the other.

Go for the Core. When arguments appear roughly equal, another helpful tactic is to try to see the core of the matter. This goes beyond weighting because you challenge your prior perception that most of the reasons you have written down have at least some bearing. You might conclude, for instance, that "basically this is a moral problem, so the non-moral reasons don't count for much." Or "basically, this is a financial bind, so the nonfinancial reasons are secondary." Or "basically I need hard evidence; these common-sense reasons won't cut much mustard with my client." When *going for the core* works, it often yields not only a decision but a feeling of insight, because many reasons that seemed important before get discarded as noise or secondary factors, yielding a clear and firm decision. Unfortunately, not all issues have a core to go for, but the way to find out is to try.

Avoid Severe Downside Risk. When deciding among possible courses of action, you can often clarify the dilemma by asking, "Which path minimizes the chance of a really bad outcome?" For instance, suppose you are a manager vacillating between hiring A, who could work out superbly but also very badly, or B, who would almost certainly work out pretty well but not superbly. You might resolve the dilemma by preferring B: If you hire A and it went wrong, there would be a terrible mess.

Avoiding options with a risk of great loss is not always a good strategy. All depends on the relative value you attach to the potential gains or losses in the situation. However, we usually value a certain gain less than a numerically equivalent loss: An extra year's worth of income won would benefit most people much less than a year of income lost would hurt them, for instance. We do well to remember this assymetry between gains and losses and to consider eliminating options that have a severe downside risk.

Defer the Decision, Search for Evidence. Quite frequently the best decision for a hard-to-decide issue is not to decide it. In reasoning about an issue, you may discover a number of open questions that you can investigate. Or you may realize that, in the natural course of events, your own experience will put you in a better position to assess an issue later. Often the circumstances do not really require you to decide now, but only seem to. You can ask for an extension, or make a provisional commitment, or keep options open in some other way. People often worry too much about decisions they do not really have to make now and could make better later.

Find New Options. As emphasized earlier, the metastrategy of option finding is a recourse at any point. One particularly apt occasion for seeking new options occurs when the options at hand pose a dilemma: After careful argument, each turns out to have some advantageous but serious drawbacks. In such circumstances, one does well to transform the dilemma from a *which* into a *how* problem. For instance, recalling the car purchase example, suppose I find that, despite careful argument, I cannot decide between those at hand—buy the car or live as before. Perhaps I would do better to consider again *how* I might solve my transportation problem. A number of options might serve. I could buy a car, rent a car, take taxis, buy a bicycle or motorcycle or motorscooter, or perhaps purchase a car jointly with a friend. By broadening the field of options, perhaps I can find one that has most of the advantages and few of the disadvantages posed by the options at hand.

All the strategies described here are common-sense ones suited to everyday and academic situations alike. Although everyday examples have been emphasized so far, in academic arguments many tradeoffs also occur and tie-breaker strategies may help. Perhaps you want an evenhanded assessment of Nixon's performance as a president. Perhaps you are evaluating the pros and cons of deficit financing. Perhaps you are analyzing the adaptive tradeoffs of size in birds, from the hummingbird to the ostrich. Perhaps you want to examine the contemporary acceptability of *The Taming of the Shrew* with its demeaning treatment of women. The apparatus of arguing and decision making given above suits all these cases. This does not mean that it can settle them all, since room for disagreement always exists. But at least the strategies can help you toward a fully developed position.

More can be said about informal argument, of course. To mention one direction that has hardly been touched upon, for certain situations there are powerful mathematical tools of decision making — expected utility, Bayes' theorem, and payoff matrices, for example.

THE CHALLENGE OF FORMAL ARGUMENT

Formal argument also deserves attention here. People in scientific and technical programs or professions often have to construct such arguments, usually mathematical ones. Others encounter formal problems in school and often find them daunting. Finally, although not so importantly, a number of popular puzzles and games have a formal character. All this gives good reason to equip people to handle formal as well as informal arguments.

But perhaps it is the same endeavor. Do the strategies surveyed in the last two sections empower the formal reasoner as much as the informal reasoner?

The answer is an emphatic "No!" The distinctions between formal and informal argumentation mentioned in the previous chapter make an important difference in the practice of formal versus informal argument. To be sure, the two share broad structural features such as reasons, conclusions, and lines of argument. But beyond that, structural differences between them challenge the reasoner in fundamentally different ways. Consider these three contrasts, for example.

Long Chain versus Fork Structure. A proof of a mathematical theorem usually contains many individual steps, each leading to the next. Only one line of argument appears, since the one deductive chain proves the theorem absolutely. In contrast, you rarely find a well-developed informal argument in the form of a long chain of reasons each leading to the next. Since each informal step has some uncertainty, a long chain accumulates uncertainty that makes it very weak. Moreover, since no line of argument offers a perfect proof, multiple lines of argument usually are needed to make the best possible case.

In summary, formal arguments typically have a long chain structure, one line of argument leading to the conclusion. Informal arguments typically have a fork structure, several short lines of argument, the "tines," converging on the conclusion.

One Side versus both Sides.   A logical proof only offers an argument on one side of the case. After all, if you have proved the conclusion absolutely, there is no point in looking for an argument on the other side since one cannot exist (providing your premises are consistent, as discussed in the previous chapter; in practice, inconsistent premises rarely appear so the qualification is minor.) In contrast, a line of informal argument never proves the conclusion absolutely, so arguments on the other side of the case might exist and usually do. A sound informal argument with reasons only on one side is rare.

A Closed versus an Open World   Formal logic occurs in a closed world; it flows only from the terms and premises given at the outset. These are not subject to challenge, except on grounds of inconsistency. In contrast, an informal argument travels in an open world. It may challenge the premises it starts with, ultimately dismissing them. It may introduce data or principles from any source.

These differences in the typical structure of formal and informal arguments alter the challenge they pose to reasoners. Broadly speaking, formal argument presents a challenge of path-finding: The reasoner must discover one logical path from the givens to the proposition in question, either proving the proposition or disproving it. The path is usually long, since easily proveable propositions are not considered interesting. Often it is hard to see such a path or even to set a likely direction. On the other hand, formal reasoners need not worry about whether the premises are sound, whether a counterargument exists once they have found one path, or whether some information outside the world of the problem might upset the conclusion. Protection against those hazards comes with the formal territory.

In contrast, reasoners in an informal situation have little trouble finding at least one path. Lines of argument are short and often plentiful. The hazards are different here, matters of neglecting the other side of the case, missing important lines of argument on either side, failing to critique the premises, and so on.

As these differences show, the strategies of the last two sections were fine-tuned to the hazards of informal argument and not to the path-finding challenge of formal argument. For the latter we also need strategies tailored to fit. A look at mathematical argument, the kind of formal reasoning people encounter most often, is in order.

THE ART OF MATHEMATICAL ARGUMENT

The mathematician and educator Alan Schoenfeld has developed and tested an effective approach to constructing mathematical arguments. Schoenfeld works in a tradition begun by the mathematician George Polya, who in his classic *How to Solve It* and other books examined a side of mathematical problem solving called *heuristics*. A heuristic is really just another term for a strategy. A heuristic, or a strategy, is a rule that often helps one to find a solution even though it does not guarantee finding a solution. I use the term heuristic rather than strategy here to reflect the tradition in the discussion of the mathematical problem solving. Heuristics or strategies contrast with *algorithms* such as our procedures for adding or subtracting. Algorithms guarantee solutions: If properly carried out, they always yield the correct answer. Polya argued that mathematicians arrived at proofs by exploring the problem with a number of heuristics, heuristics that often left no trace in the final proof.

Ever since Polya's work, mathematicians and psychologists have tried to improve students' mathematical problem solving by teaching heuristics. Schoenfeld's approach addresses several pitfalls in mathematical problem solving discovered through his own and others' research. On the one hand, Schoenfeld found that college students do not manage the overall problem-solving process well. For instance, students often persist in an unfruitful approach for too long, fail to check their solutions and so let errors pass, or get off to a bad start by not thinking carefully at the outset about the nature of the problem. To combat such malpractices, Schoenfeld designed a top level *managerial strategy* for students, a strategy to help them pay attention to the right things at the right time.

Students display difficulty at another level as well, not knowing or not thinking to use particular heuristics that can help to crack the nut of difficult problems. Students commonly omit so simple a move as making a diagram, which often helps immensely. Students miss such opportunities as "without loss of generality" arguments, where you substitute a simpler problem for the given problem by showing that the solution to the simpler problem in fact entails a solution to the original one.

Accordingly, Schoenfeld designed his strategy to help students at the level of heuristics as well as at the general managerial level. But what form does the strategy take? Briefly described, the managerial level involves five phases as follows.

- *Analysis.* Represent, understand, and get the feel of the problem. Go to design next.

- *Design.* Maintain an overview, check your progress, and design your general attack. If you have an approach underway, is it proving fruitful or should you switch? What other approach could you take? You can go to *exploration* to explore new approaches or *implementation* to carry out an approach.

- *Exploration.* Do this when you do not know what to try, which may be much of the time. Explore the problem in ways that may yield particular approaches. When you have some approaches, go back to *design* to choose a direction. But if your approach is a newly formulated subproblem or related problem, go to *analysis* to make a proper start on the new problem.

- *Implementation.* In this phase, you try to implement a likely approach. *Implementation* should be semi-routine, a matter of algebraic manipulation for instance. If *implementation* moves along well and reaches a result, go on to *verification*. If no solution results or the process drags, go back to *design*.

- *Verification.* You arrive here with a seeming success. But is the solution really valid? You can check your solution several ways. If it does not pass the tests, go back to *design*.

Now let me offer a model case. I consider a simple but subtle problem in geometry and relate my actual effort to solve it by following Schoenfeld's strategies. Later, all the heuristics will be listed.

The problem. Four beetles begin at the four corners of a square of side one. Each beetle starts to crawl directly toward the beetle clockwise from him. Since the beetle he is following also moves, he must shift his course clockwise bit by bit. So, as in Figure 7.1, all four beetles, each pursuing the next, spiral inward until they meet at the center. The question is: How long a path does each beetle trace? Finding the answer does not require calculus.

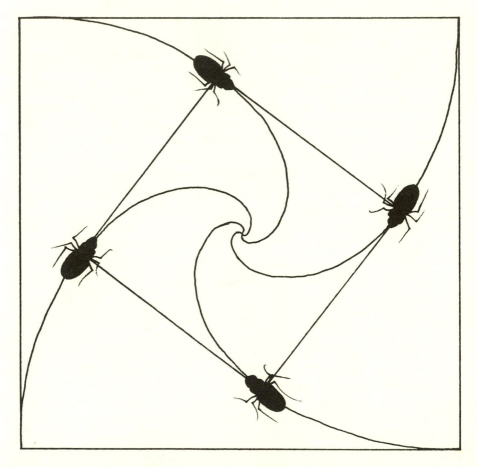

FIG. 7.1.   The four beetles problem

Analysis. Schoenfeld recommends "draw a diagram" as a first step, so we have Figure 7.1. The path traced by the beetles forms a rotating, shrinking square. Perhaps that will help somehow. Under *analysis,* Schoenfeld also recommends considering special cases if possible, but this already is a special case—a unit square—so I can't make it more special. I do note that at each stage it's as though the beetles are starting over again with a smaller square. That is, at any point, as they continue to crawl, they repeat what they did at the outset, starting from the corners of a square and pursuing the next clockwise beetle, although the square has become smaller now. Maybe the way the task recurs within itself will help somehow.

Design. Should I go to *explore?* I have one idea already: The way the beetles' task repeats within itself might lead to an equation relating the starting situation and later situations. Maybe that would allow me to solve for the length somehow. I'll try a brief *Implementation.*

Implementation. I try to set up an equation that takes advantage of the repetition, but nothing comes of it. Back to *Exploration.*

Exploration. Schoenfeld lists a number of heuristics under *exploration,* graded from less to more drastic. Let me try some. The first suggests "replace conditions by equivalent ones." How could I do that? Perhaps I could replace the beetles by a mechanical system with strings and pulleys, a system that makes the length of the path plain. Right now, I don't see how to do that.

Another heuristic recommends introducing auxiliary elements, for instance, construction lines in geometry. I play with this idea for a minute, but nothing interesting emerges.

Another heuristic suggests reformulating the constraint somehow. I toy with the idea of an elastic band stretched around four corners, each corner pulling toward the other, but this analogy fails immediately.

Another heuristic proposes assuming a solution and determining its properties. That's interesting. Perhaps I can guess the solution. The solution doesn't require calculus, so it must be simple. I wonder if the solution simply is 1, the side of the initial square. I imagine the side curling around to spiral into the center. Certainly the side is long enough to reach. I bet the solution is 1. Working on that conjecture, now I have to understand why it *should* be 1.

I make no progress on this, so I move to another heuristic:

changing perspective or notation. I sketch the paths the beetles would take if I folded the square horizontally or along a diagonal. No insight results.

So I go back to exploring why the solution might be 1, assuming it is. I imagine how the square defined by the four beetles shrinks. It's as though the square were consumed as the beetles spiraled inward. The idea of the square being consumed is interesting. What if each beetle ate a string attached to the next beetle? That sounds promising, because the string to start with would be 1 unit long and, when the beetles met at the center, each beetle would have eaten that 1 unit's worth of string. I switch to *design*, asking myself if I should try to push through an analogical proof using the "string eater" view of the problem. I decide "yes."

Implementation. I need to show that a string-eater prescription for the beetles' behavior would yield the same path as the original prescription, where each beetle simply follows the clockwise beetle. If both lead to the beetles walking the same path, then the answer becomes transparent. As just mentioned, obviously the string-eater model predicts that, when the beetles meet, they have eaten exactly the unit string and hence have travelled exactly one unit.

So do following and string-eating yield the same path? I imagine the starting situation. Each beetle holds in its jaws a string one unit long running taut to the tail of the next beetle. To take a tiny bite, a beetle must take a step the same size as the bite directly toward the next beetle, to create slack for the bite. So taking a bite requires taking the same size step toward the clockwise beetle. Therefore, string-eating leads to the same itinerary as following. The length of the curve must be one unit.

Of course, I might want a more formal proof than that; moreover, the string-eating notion could serve as the basis for a formal proof. However, in this context let's settle for the analogy and check the proof.

Verification. Schoenfeld suggests several heuristics for verifying answers. Does the solution use all the pertinent data? This one appears to, yes. Does the solution conform to reasonable estimates or predictions? I noted earlier that a side of the square certainly had enough length to reach the center. Can the solution be obtained differently? I could explore that, although I'm not sure what other approach to take. Does the solution withstand tests of symmetry, dimension analysis, and scaling? That general question leads me to ask whether the proof makes sense for other sorts of figures.

Immediately I detect a possible problem. Imagine a 12-sided figure, with 12 beetles eating string. Each piece of string does *not* have enough length to reach the center. Yet, if the beetles each simply follow the next, they clearly will spiral into the center. Therefore, in a 12-sided figure, following does not seem to be the same thing as string eating. Perhaps I've made a mistake in equating following and string eating for the square figure.

I draw a diagram (Figure 7.2) to try to understand what happens in the 12-sided case. I see a crucial difference between that situation and the square case. As the beetle starting at the corner of a 12-sided figure takes a step closer to the clockwise beetle, the clockwise beetle takes his own step and pulls away somewhat. In the square case, the clockwise beetle takes a step at right angles to the direction of the first beetle and so doesn't pull away.

This has implications for the equivalence of the *string-eating* and *following* prescriptions. In the 12-sided figure, if a beetle lunges one step forward to get a bite, because the next beetle pulls away the first beetle doesn't get a bite of the same length as his step, but a much shorter bite. So bite size and step size match in the square, but not in the 12-sided figure. Now I see what's crucial about my argument and the square: Because each beetle steps at right angles to the path of the next, bite size equals step size and string eating amounts to following. But the same argument does not generalize to figures with more, or in fact fewer, sides.

This better understanding of the essence of the proof seems to be a sufficient check, so I stop here.

FIG. 7.2. What happens in a twelve-sided polygon

HEURISTIC POWER

How did Schoenfeld's design help me to attack this particular problem? There were three crucial junctures. (1) I guessed the solution in direct response to one of the suggestions under *exploration*. (2) I arrived at the string-eating notion primed by previous thoughts. In particular, during *analysis*, I recognized the presence of a rotating shrinking square, which very likely prepared me to think later of the full square as being consumed, this leading in turn to the notion of the string-eating beetles. My pondering of mechanical systems perhaps also helped here, since I had mental images of strings and pulleys. (3) The heuristics of verification led me to discover a possible objection and resolve it, arriving at a deeper understanding of my proof.

Of course, Schoenfeld's design might help different people in different ways on different occasions. Space does not allow giving a fuller account here; those seriously interested should consult Schoenfeld's writings. However, provided here in outline form are the lists of heuristics accompanying the *analysis, exploration,* and *verification* stages. (*Design* and *implementation* have no heuristics, *design* being very general and *implementation* specific to the mechanics suiting the particular approach.)

Analysis
1. Draw a diagram if at all possible.
2. Examine special cases:
    a. Choose special values to exemplify the problem and get a "feel" for it.
    b. Examine limiting cases to explore the range of possibilities.
    c. Set any integer parameters equal to 1, 2, 3, . . . in sequence and look for an inductive pattern.
3. Try to simplify the problem by:
    a. Exploiting symmetry, or
    b. "Without loss of generality" arguments (including scaling).

Exploration
1. Consider essentially equivalent problems.
    a. Replace conditions by equivalent ones.

b. recombine the elements of the problem in different ways.
c. Introduce auxiliary elements.
d. Reformulate the problem by:
   i. changing perspective or notation.
   ii. considering argument by contradiction or contrapositive.
   iii. assuming a solution and determining its properties.
2. Consider slightly modified problems.
   a. Choose subgoals (obtain partial fulfillment of the conditions.)
   b. Relax a condition and then try to re-impose it.
   c. Decompose the domain of the problem and work on it case by case.
3. Consider broadly modified problems.
   a. Construct an analogous problem with fewer variables.
   b. Hold all but one variable fixed to determine that variable's impact.
   c. Try to exploit any related problems that have similar form, givens, or conclusions (you might be able to use either the solution method or the solution itself to help with the original problem.)

Verification
1. Does your solution pass these specific tests?
   a. Does it use all the pertinent data?
   b. Does it conform to reasonable estimates or predictions?
   c. Does it withstand tests of symmetry, dimension analysis, and scaling?
2. Does it pass these general tests?
   a. Can it be obtained differently?
   b. Can it be substantiated by special cases?
   c. Can it be reduced to known results?
   d. Can it be used to generate something you know?

Finally, what evidence argues that Schoenfeld's design in fact helps students to solve mathematical problems? Schoenfeld conducted several experiments examining whether and how heuristics plus a managerial strategy work. In one teaching experiment, the students were eleven freshmen and sophomores in a small liberal arts college. They participated in an intensive seminar in mathematical problem solving, attending a two and one half hour class for eighteen days and doing an average of four to five hours of homework per day. The students learned the approach just illustrated through a number of explicit examples and extensive practice.

A control group took both pretest and posttest, showing no improvement; so a practice effect from the pretest did not in itself improve posttest performance. Prior experiments by Schoenfeld gave evidence that explicit heuristic instruction was necessary. Demonstrations of how to solve problems without explicit identification and explanation of the heuristics did not lead students to discover the heuristics on their own. Nor did practice alone improve performance very much. Accordingly, the question became what gains would the students show when explicitly taught a managerial strategy and heuristics and given plenty of practice in their application.

Schoenfeld measured gains in several ways. One was a 0–100 point rating scale summarizing how many approaches the students explored and how far they carried each approach. A score of 100 indicated completely solving all the problems. The students scored an average of 20.8 on their pretests, but an average of 72.2 on their posttests. Another test asked the students to sort 32 problems into piles that lent themselves to similar approaches, without actually solving the problems. The data showed that, as a result of the instruction, the students came to classify the problems more as professional mathematicians did. A test of transfer revealed that the students also carried over what they had learned to mathematical problems of quite a different character. Finally, although the reported results concerned only one group, Schoenfeld mentions obtaining essentially similar results for a group of twenty students tested the year before.

What about the other side of the case? It is worth noting that the students in Schoenfeld's experiments have been fairly able college-level students taught in small groups. Students in trouble or larger groups of students might show weaker gains. For another concern, an abbreviated or revised set of heuristics might better serve students studying a narrower range of mathematical problems. For instance, high school students studying plane geometry would find a few of the heuristics inapplicable. However, in the balance, Schoenfeld's results seem quite encouraging, especially arrayed against the generally dismal record of schools in improving mathematical problem solving.

Another more general reservation concerns the enterprise of mathematical problem solving itself. Certainly we would like students to develop mathematical arguments better than they do. But, at the same time, it is important to remember that problem *finding* plays an important and neglected role in mathematical and other forms of thinking. Helping students to become better problem solvers very likely does not help them to become better problem finders.

Assistance can be found, however. A book by Stephen Brown and Marion Walters, *The Art of Problem Posing*, addresses this neglected side of mathematics, exploring a number of ways to make problem finding part of classroom practice in mathematics. The *Geometric Supposer*, a computer program that facilitates the discovery and testing of conjectures in plane geometry, was discussed at the end of Chapter 5. In general, instruction in problem solving should go hand in hand with instruction in problem finding to give learners a fuller and more inventive experience of mathematics.

WHAT YOU CAN DO

As a thinker and learner in any context that invites reasoning, you can foster your own reasoning in a number of ways:

- *Maintain the completeness, weight, and truth standards for sound argument.* Remember how easy it is to let one or another of the standards slip; keep alert.

- *Put into practice the simple strategies for informal argument offered here.* Pay heed to option-finding, not just decision-making. Escalate through (1) snap judgment; (2) quick argument (with attention to both sides); (3) complete argument (with a serious effort at thoroughness); and (4) careful argument (with truth and weight checked, expanding subarguments as necessary to resolve uncertainties insofar as possible).

- *Resolve near ties in arguments through a number of strategies. For instance, (1) Look for semi-landslides; (2) weight to resolve a tie in simple counts of reasons; (3) weight exactly to the issue; (4) set aside those reasons that do not concern the core of the matter; (5) choose so as to eliminate options with a severe downside risk; (6) defer the decision and seek further evidence; (7) find new options.*

- *Treat formal argument as a separate challenge and learn means to handle it.* Recall the contrasts between formal and informal argument; handling one well does not necessarily help you to handle the other well.

- *Improve performance on problems of mathematical proof and derivation by putting into practice Schoenfeld's strategies.* Use the phases of analysis, design, exploration, implementation, and verification, with associated heuristics.

- *Be your own strategist.* Different sorts of problems call for different approaches to reasoning. For instance, take seriously Schoenfeld's effort, because he has thought carefully about what is needed, but, if you are facing distinctive types of mathematical problems, make your own adaptation.

- *Look for opportunities to engage in problem finding.* Remember that problem finding has as much importance as problem solving.

As a teacher, you can:

- *Raise learners' awareness of completeness, weight, and truth standards and their constant slippage.* In nearly any subject-matter, opportunities to do so arise.

- *Teach the strategies listed above explicitly.* Remember, research evidence suggests that explicit instruction does more good than simply being a model reasoner for those who learn from you.

- *Do not teach formal argument expecting that it will enhance informal argument dramatically, nor vice versa.* Remember that the two pose somewhat different challenges.

- *Encourage students to be their own strategists.* The overarching lesson, more important than any particular strategy for reasoning, is to be strategic, to self-consciously reflect upon and design one's ways of thinking.

- *Make room in your instruction for problem finding as well as problem solving.* Remember that problem finding constitutes a crucial aspect of thinking characteristically neglected in instruction.

8 Schooling Minds

I have tried hard not to write a book about schools and schooling, because learning is something that happens in many contexts besides schools, and often at the direction of the learner rather than any teacher. Hopefully I have succeeded to some extent. But I can't seem to escape schools for long. Elementary school was just a stepping stone to high school, that to college, that to graduate school, and that to a position at the Graduate School of Education at Harvard, a school in large part *about* schools. I seem to be getting in deeper rather than out further.

So maybe there is nothing for it but to plunge headlong. Musing on my own early schooling, I'm struck by what now seem arbitrary reactions. I hated, for instance, pasting words onto forms to complete sentences—not because the task was trivial but because the paste was repulsive. The reservoir of paste was a large glass jar in one corner of the room. I remember feeling the cool glutinous weight of a gob through the piece of scrap paper on which one would procure it. There were in the class those creatures from another planet who could use the stuff neatly, but I never got the hang of that. Strive as I would to apply the paste with paper dabs, it always made its way to my fingers, dried there, and left me compulsively trying to rub it off.

On the other hand, I liked diagramming sentences. Nifty the way one could break down a sentence into units, as you might pry the back off a watch, apply a jeweler's screwdriver, and one by one lay out upon your table all the gleaming gears. Perhaps there is something to be said for diagramming sentences as a process of analytical inquiry; but I doubt if it helped my grammar much. I just liked it.

I also liked fractions. Regular numbers were a bit boring because they lacked complexity. Fractions, on the other hand, did somersaults — invert and multiply. They were tricky enough to provoke some interest.

I hated Latin because I hated French. If it had not been for French, I would not have taken Latin and therefore would not have hated it. In the seventh or eighth grade — I can't remember which — we had a special course in French, the main feature of which was making up scrapbooks out of magazine pictures of cars, vacuum cleaners and, whatnot, under each one writing its French translation. This so soured me on the language that, when I got to high school, I could not abide the thought of taking it, so I took Latin. A big mistake in terms both of natural affinity and practicality. (No, I do not think Latin improved my understanding of English words.)

I liked my teachers, even in subjects that were far from favorites. With few exceptions, they seemed to me then and now to be able, committed, and kind. All in all, the likable outweighed the onerous in my early education. However, my experience was dominated by that great neutral ground of things neither loved nor despised, but simply there with a middleweight thereness that required slight attention and provoked no passion.

Now schools wear a different guise for me. They are so *meaningful*. It's no longer their scrambled impact on a boy's raw perceptions that counts, but their calculated leverage on learning. Most learning before adulthood occurs in schools, and so what happens in them deserves the most cogent thought we can give it. So with honor and regret to my less studied sensations of the years gone by, let us go back to school . . .

WHAT HOLDS SCHOOLS BACK?

"What is not a zebra?" Well, nails, novels, noodles, napalm, and the game of Nim are none of them zebras, for a start. The question, "What holds schools back?" is not as open ended as "What is not a zebra?" but it almost seems to be, so many reasonable answers come forth from beleaguered teachers and principals, commissions on education, dismayed parents, and other constituencies.

Acknowledging the complex social factors that deepen the malaise of schools, here in this context of knowledge as design we do best to focus on the tacit hypotheses behind educational practice — hypotheses that, while meant to promote success, instead interfere with it. Four of those hypotheses seem especially mischievous. Consider them one by one.

Knowledge is Information.   Much already has been said about this one, and the alternative of knowledge as design has been presented.

Technical Knowledge First, Application Later.   Some special cases of this tacit hypothesis are as follows. You cannot think scientifically or do science until you already know a lot of science. You cannot do any worthwhile writing until your spelling and grammar are in good shape. You cannot do anything like real mathematics until you can perform all the basic arithmetic operations fluently and accurately. You cannot make sense of modern society without studying the details of American and European History.

People Learn Skills mostly through Practice that Builds on Talent.   Corollaries of this hypothesis run along these lines: No one can teach you how to write. No one can teach you how to solve word problems in math. No one can teach you how to understand something hard to understand, to invent a gadget, to think up an experiment in physics, to write a poem. Teachers can only give you lots of exercises relevant to such accomplishments. And, if you happen to have the talent, you may eventually develop some skill.

Standard Problems and Exercises Capture the Skills of a Discipline.   Special cases of this tacit hypothesis are as follows. When you read a chapter of history and answer the factual and interpretive questions at the end, you are doing a large part of what historical thinking involves, albeit on a small scale.   When you solve a textbook chemistry problem, you are doing a large part of what being a chemist involves, albeit at an elementary level. When you prove a theorem in mathematics, you are doing a large part of what a mathematician does, only on beginner's material.

Merely to state these tacit hypotheses is to make them look frail. No teacher, principal, or curriculum designer would admit to holding them as such. They are not explicitly espoused but implicit in the practice of education. They survive not because of evidence, but because they are the simplest ones to act upon.

Simplest in this sense: They are all reductive. The first reduces knowledge and know-how in general to received and passive knowledge. The second reduces skill to a matter of knowing the particulars and building on them. The third reduces skill acquisition to a matter of practice. The fourth reduces the scope of skill in a discipline to the scope of the skills that conventional problems and exercises require. The result is a dramatically simplified formula for education: Teach the facts and technical procedures, such as the algorithms of arithmetic, and provide plenty of practice with problems. The rest will take care of itself—for those students that have the knack.

The most misleading thing about this simplified formula is that it works pretty well for smart students—because the smart students develop for themselves the skills they need. Contemporary research shows that able students accumulate a large repertoire of general "metacognitive" knowledge about how to handle academic tasks. But the same research shows that the simplified formula fails for less able students, who do not spontaneously evolve these strategies. Furthermore, perhaps the simplified formula is wrong even for the best students, who would do better yet with more explicit attention to developing metacognitive knowledge.

BRIDGING FROM INFORMATION TO DESIGN

What can be done? Perhaps it is better to ask what might be done. The caution in that subtle shift of auxiliary verbs nods to the realities of schools—teacher burnout, student apathy, lack of community support, and, perhaps more than anything else, the enormous inertia of educational institutions public and private, from primary school to graduate school. Despite these caveats, a dedicated effort from within school systems to introduce a new style of instruction might help to turn them around.

The cornerstone for this new style of instruction is knowledge as design. You will remember that for a long time too much of teaching has suffered the thrall of "knowledge as information," with the passive view of knowledge that this formula projects. In light of the emphasis in Chapter 5 on mental models and the warning in Chapter 6 about persuasive images, the problem can be put this way: "Knowledge as information" describes a seductively simple but misleading mental model of the nature of knowledge. The aim should be to displace this model with the more accurate and provocative "knowledge as design." The trick is to handle instruction so that this enlivening mental model pervades the imparting of knowledge.

What steps might be taken in that direction? Here are some particulars.

Make the Theory of Knowledge Plain to Students. There is no need for education to keep its theory of knowledge a secret, especially when that theory is accessible and action-oriented. So let us make plain to students our posture toward knowledge. Let us teach them the notion of knowledge as design and the four design questions that expand on that theme. Let us do that quite as explicitly as it has been done in this book, with plenty of examples to make the concepts clear. No hidden curriculum.

We need not worry about young children being able to grasp the notion of knowledge as design and the design questions. After all, it is really rather simple, building as it does on ordinary experience of everyday designs. Even first-graders can have a basic appreciation of the sense behind the designs of tricycles and pencils and how the design questions abet understanding those designs. Of course, the sophistication with which one would address the design questions would vary with the sophistication of the learners.

Present Knowledge from the Perspective of Design. Having made the epistemology plain, let us put it into practice, routinely presenting knowledge from the perspective of design. This means using the design questions as a guide, whenever we need to convey some knowledge about long division, the agricultural industry of the United States, the history of Africa, the effects of sunlight on plant growth, or the rate of fall of objects in a vacuum. It means in each case deciding what design or designs to focus on. It means getting explicit about the purpose, structure, model cases, and arguments concerning each design. The preceding chapters have illustrated how that can be done with a wide array of academic and not so academic topics. It is reasonably easy. We always have the recourse of taking a claim as a design, if no other suggests itself, and since the claim can be about most anything, that allows us to treat any topic.

Treat Knowledge as Functional.   Knowledge should be seen and treated as functional, as something that gets put to use much as a screwdriver or a hammer. To do justice to knowledge and to the learner, we have to keep the learner doing something with the knowledge gained.

In some subject areas, this poses little immediate problem. Exercises in math or physics or English provide a context for putting knowledge to work. (But, some reservations about "short answer" exercises appear below.) In other subject areas, however, putting knowledge to work requires more effort. How might you lead students to use the fact that blood circulates? Well, perhaps by asking students to draw implications beyond the delivery of oxygen to the cells of the body. There are, for instance, implications concerning the transfer of heat in the body, the loss of heat, as when your face and head are unprotected in cold weather, the carrying of leukocytes to sites of infection, and no doubt others. How do you lead students to use the fact that President Nixon had to withdraw from office because of Watergate? Well, what generalization might it illustrate? What new law if any might it suggest? What historical analogies does it provoke? In general, calling for further claims, arguments, and models, including analogical models, are all handy ways to put knowledge to work.

Target Performances, not Target Information.   A corollary of this concerns the setting of instructional objectives: Select target performances rather than target information. For example, how should we formulate our instructional objective for a lesson on circulation of the blood? According to a knowledge as information perspective, a reasonable formula would be "The students should know that the blood circulates." A somewhat more sophisticated approach highlights understanding rather than just knowing: "The students should understand that and why the blood circulates." This is a little better, but there are at least two problems with it. First of all, how are the students supposed to manifest this understanding? Just because they regurgitate on a test the fact that the blood circulates does not mean that they understand it. Second, the "understanding" formula does not press toward any active use of the knowledge in question.

A better approach makes the instructional objective, "The students will be able to execute such and such performances beginning from the fact that the blood circulates," with some specifics about the "such and such." These performances might involve making new arguments or drawing inferences and supporting them, as suggested above. They might involve thinking of other model cases of circulation and making comparisons and contrasts among them. For example, what analogies exist between the circulation of the blood and a delivery system like water or electricity in a city?

Add Strategic Knowledge. Knowledge as design holds that all knowledge has a tool-like character. However, some knowledge is explicitly tool-like, designed to manipulate other knowledge and facilitate thinking and problem-solving activities of various sorts. The four design questions themselves are examples of such strategic knowledge. Another example is the writing principle urged in Chapter 3: Pick a design to write about. Another is a principle discussed in Chapter 4: When you are stuck, you often can get an idea by thinking of a model case and imagining it from various perspectives. Another is the escalating series of strategies for informal argument in Chapter 7: snap judgment, quick argument, complete argument, and careful argument. The recommendations closing each chapter under the heading "What You can Do" summarize the strategic content of the chapter.

In addition, the contemporary literature on metacognition and the teaching of thinking skills offers strategies in plenty that might be taught. Nickerson, Perkins, and Smith's *The Teaching of Thinking* reviews the state of the art in teaching thinking skills, discussing the evidence that this can be done and mentioning along the way a number of strategies that such efforts have sought to teach. The two-volume set *Thinking and Learning Skills*, edited by Segal, Chipman, and Glaser, includes articles discussing both a number of contemporary programs to develop thinking skills and also important theoretical issues in the area. Several other sources are listed in the references. From these we can harvest a range of metacognitive skills worth imparting. Furthermore, we can present them as designs, each one a tool for thinking with its special purpose, structure, model cases, and explanatory and evaluative arguments.

While often thinking skills are taught in courses separate from the normal curriculum, knowledge as design argues for teaching them integrated with the subject matters, at least in considerable part. Thinking skills might be taught separately at the same time, of course, just as one uses and even learns some math in physics or chemistry but also studies it as such in math classes. But without some integration into the subject matters, thinking skills are not as likely to empower the active use of knowledge for critical and creative thinking.

Products rather than Short Answers.   A focus on design naturally favors products rather than short answers as the outcome of student activities. Several points recommend such an emphasis, as was argued in Chapter 4. First, outside of school almost all worthwhile activities involve products rather than short answers, whether the product is a plan for an advertising campaign, a poem, or a well-crafted chair. Second, knowledge as design reveals designing to be the paradigmatic human activity, and designing anything invariably involves producing some sort of extended product rather than a brief answer. Third, although some might think that students do not know enough to deal with products, Chapter 4 showed how appropriate assignments can be found and offered numerous examples for a range of subject areas.

BRIDGING FROM TEACHER TO STUDENTS

The "knowledge as information" formula makes the teacher's role clear: The teacher should have information and impart it to the students. But knowledge as design makes the problem of instruction much more subtle. Put it this way. If I give you a dime, and you can hold on to it, you have it; likewise, if I give you a datum and you can remember it, you have it. However, if I give you a design like a screwdriver, really having it means a lot more than holding on to it. I have to give you some idea about how to use it. Moreover, even an explanation may not suffice. You may have to see me model its use and you will probably need to practice its use before getting the hang of applying the tool. Likewise, simply imparting a piece of knowledge by no means guarantees its right and ready application. In knowledge as design, teaching involves a lot more than transmitting in a memorable way.

Here are some suggestions:

Stated Target Performance.   Students are likely to learn better if they know explicitly what the target performances are. This is more of a problem and more of an opportunity for the knowledge as design perspective than the knowledge as information perspective. In the latter, students already know they are supposed to remember the information, although they may not be very excited by the prospect. But knowledge as design risks leaving students at sea because of the many possible target performances a teacher might have in mind. So, in our teacher roles, we should explain what the target performances are.

Closed Loop Teaching.   Much of teaching is open loop, meaning that the teacher gets no immediate feedback about whether or not the students are learning. Straight lecture format suffers from this ill. You might think that a more interactive teaching style, where the teacher frequently questions the students, guards against open loop teaching. Unfortunately, unless the teacher takes care, it often simply fosters the illusion of closed loop teaching without the reality. Commonly, only a third or a quarter of the class raise their hands in response to questions, but answer more or less correctly. These alert and forward students suffice to keep the class lively and the teacher happy; but the rest of the class may not be learning much.

Open loop teaching takes a risk even when you are teaching knowledge as information, but at least there what the students are supposed to learn is clear cut; perhaps they can make up for knowledge not memorized in class by studying their notebooks or textbooks later. Knowledge as design brings with it greater risks, because the teacher seeks not just to transmit information but to impart skill and understanding, which are both more difficult for students to attain and harder for the teacher to test with simple questions. The danger of an illusion of efficacy without the reality becomes greater.

Closed loop teaching, then, asks us all in our teacher roles to probe the productive abilities of a whole range of students frequently. This can be done, for instance, by posing questions to the class, but asking people not to raise their hands. Instead, you call on anyone. Apart from its information yield, this tactic presses all students to keep thinking, always a problem in large classes where many students can lapse into the passivity of mechanical note taking or daydreaming.

Another approach with the same double advantage of providing feedback and encouraging all the students to keep thinking goes like this. Pose a question, wait for several seconds, and then ask who has an answer. If not many do, you can wait several more seconds and ask for a show of hands again, hopefully then taking answers. But if there are still not many hands raised, that in itself indicates the need for making the point or posing the question or modeling the skill more clearly. You can ask the students why they are having trouble generating answers, treating the difficulty as an interesting problem to be dealt with rather than any failure of the students.

The Teacher as a Model. It is a commonplace that teachers function not just as sources of knowledge but as models for students — models of attitudes toward knowledge and of ways of handling knowledge. In particular, in our teacher roles, let us try to be exemplars of knowledge as design. This means we should sometimes model our own thinking processes, to display clearly the designs for the process of thought that usually stay hidden. It means that we should try to maintain an open, inquiring, and inventive attitude, even if only by acting, even if on that particular afternoon we feel contrary. Not easy, of course.

The Teacher as a Model of Ignorance. The knowledge as information perspective expects the teacher to know it all and pass it along. Knowledge as design not only allows but actually gains from some ignorance in the teacher, albeit not devastating ignorance. The teacher who knows it all and shows it all makes a bad model for students, a model suggesting that the name of the game is knowing the answer — knowledge as information again. We do better in our teacher roles to come across this way: basically competent and reasonably confident, but sometimes puzzled and ready to try to figure something out; sometimes at a loss as to how to proceed but ready to try to invent a strategy; sometimes confused at our own confusion but ready to stand apart from it and probe its source.

The Teacher as a Generic Scaffolder.   As discussed in Chapter 4, scaffolding means supporting the thinking process of a learner by prompting judiciously. There are various gains. One is to keep learners thinking; another is not to let learners feel abandoned in their efforts. Still another is to prompt them as a model of how they might prompt themselves. The latter means that we should try to bias our scaffolding toward the generic, away from the specific.

Suppose, for example, a student of algebra is trying to multiply out the expresssion $(x + 3)(y + 7x)$. You might prompt, "Start by writing down the product of x times y" or "Start by writing down the product of the first term in one parenthesis times the first term in the other" or "Can you remember how you did a similar problem before?" The first prompt is very context-bound; no matter how much it helps the student on this occasion, the student is not hearing a useful general rule. The third prompt models a general problem solving strategy, which may work. If this generic strategy does not help, you can pass to the second prompt, which still has some generality, applying to the multiplication of any algebraic expressions.

Whole lessons or sections of lessons can be taught with the teacher mostly scaffolding rather than presenting. The teacher functions primarily as an organizer of the course of thought, with the students supplying virtually all of the content, for instance, the arguments in critiquing a design or the ideas for a design. In this way, the students both discover that they have substance to contribute to the task at hand and see the strategies of organizing a process of inquiry cast into high relief, since this is all that the teacher does.

Fostering Overt Thinking.   Modeling by the teacher and scaffolding are both ways of making aspects of thinking overt. There are other tactics that serve the same end. For instance, small groups activities press students to communicate with one another in developing and critiquing ideas, and hence cause part of the thinking process to occur in an overt, shared way, rather than privately. Pair problem solving, a technique developed by Arthur Whimbey and Jack Lochhead, asks students to work in pairs. One student thinks aloud while working on a problem, while the other listens and prompts, to help the first student maintain full attention to mental processes. Then the students switch roles. Another pair technique is to have one student function as the guide or manager, designating what questions should be addressed next, while the other functions as the generator, producing ideas, arguments, decisions, and so forth, at the direction of the guide. Again, the students switch roles after a while.

Thinking usually occurs within the silence of our own minds, a phenomenon that stands in the way of our self-awareness of thought processes and our deliberate revision of them. By helping students to make these processes temporarily overt, we can help students to get a handle on them. Although you might think that a debilitating self-consciousness would result, this does not seem to be much of a problem. In fact, it is argued that youngsters learn many aspects of thinking in the first place through conversation with parents, who press them for reasons, ask them questions, and so on. Such patterns of discourse become internalized, so that the youngsters learn to press themselves for reasons, ask themselves questions. The lack of mindful conversations in impoverished homes and in certain other settings seems a likely contributor to the characteristic academic problems of children from such settings.

BRIDGING FROM SUBJECT TO SUBJECT

What does one school subject have to do with another? Whatever answers there might be, it is clear that conventional schooling pays little heed to them. The several subjects run their courses as separately as the rivers on different seaboards. Yet building connections is not hard. By way of example, consider two subject areas chosen for their apparent remoteness, history and biology.

There certainly is a history *of* biology, full of interesting events such as Darwin's development of the theory of natural selection or Harvey's discovery of the circulation of the blood. What about the reverse connection — a biology of history? This one is harder to make sense of, but perhaps the question needs to be interpreted a little. One might read it to ask how biological factors have influenced the history of nations.

For example, arid areas of the Middle East had, in Biblical times, plentiful water and supported fertile crops. What happened? In part, human invention in the form of irrigation upset the ecology. Despite the enormous short-term benefits of irrigation, it has the unfortunate side effect of gradually increasing the mineral content of the soil. In the course of decades or centuries, irrigated lands become too saline to support vegetation. Whole civilizations have changed as a consequence of such effects on the biosphere. And they may do so again. Increasing salinity now poses problems in those parts of the United States where irrigation sees massive use.

Consider some more examples. Both tobacco and the potato originated in the New World. Yet consider how those two products have shaped the economic history of nations and, in the case of the potato, their styles of subsistence. For another, consider how the whaling industry proved a formative force in the economy of the New World for generations. For yet another now in progress, consider how effective use of recombinant DNA techniques might impact on civilization if we come to be able to genetically engineer out birth defects and engineer in qualities such as intelligence or a healthy constitution.

This small exercise in connecting shows that the usual subject matters need not stand so distant from one another. In fact, it might be said that they only stay so because they are left there. Instruction based on knowledge as design need not, indeed should not, accept this status quo. Knowledge as design is a natural bridge builder, pointing up commonalities and inviting contrasts between the various disciplines. In a few paragraphs, here are several sorts of connections that invite exploration and exploitation.

Portable Concepts. A number of important concepts carry across subject areas — either all subject areas or clusters of subject areas. Most central from the present perspective is the notion of knowledge as design and the four design questions, which apply equally well to math, English, physics, history, chemistry, social studies, shop, French, and virtually anything else. The parallel use of these notions in all subject areas will highlight the power and flexibility of the concepts themselves, and also underscore the pervasive involvement humankind has with design at every turn.

To focus on some particulars of knowledge as design, certain kinds of argument as discussed in Chapter 6 and 7 link together certain areas. For example, formal argument involving algebraic notation plays a key role in math, its parent discipline, and physics, chemistry, and other "hard" sciences as well. Statistical methods recur throughout the social sciences, and occasionally in the hard sciences, as well as being another branch of mathematics. The hypothetico-deductive pattern of reasoning appears in formal guise throughout the sciences and in informal guise in many other subject areas such as history or literary criticism, while playing no justificatory role in mathematics. Accordingly, singling out the sorts of argument that suit various subject areas helps to map the commonalities and contrasts among them.

There are many other concepts that cut across all or several subject matters. One is classification. Consider, for instance, such classification systems as the periodic table in chemistry, the taxonomy of life forms in biology, and the taxonomy of verb forms in English or other languages. Or contemplate the similarities and differences from discipline to discipline of a ubiquitous concept like law, as in a moral law, a natural law, a legal law, or a law of grammar. Or compare and contrast the role of definitions as they occur in mathematics, art criticism, and economics. The more such crosscutting themes receive mention and explicit discussion, the more the range of knowledge will seem a coherent terrain rather than a collection of islands.

Portable Skills. If many concepts find application in different disciplines, so do skills provided by high-level strategic knowledge. Especially important and portable are skills of discursive writing. Chapter 3 described how the four design questions can scaffold discursive writing, advice that applies to any field discursive writing suits. Likewise, various strategies for abetting memory, one of them the Chapter 3 strategy of reading with the four design questions, also suit virtually any field.

Of course, the design questions were mentioned earlier, too, under portable concepts. In fact, almost every concept referred to there has associated with it one or more skilled performances, which therefore can be reinforced in parallel in the various disciplines. When, for example, similar sorts of deductive argument prove handy in physics and mathematics, something should be made of this. When problems of insufficient sample size crop up in

making an historical or psychological or linguistic generalization, something should be made of that. When students have developed some ability to design classification systems in the context of English, for instance, and there is an opportunity to carry these abilities over to chemistry or economics,
something should be made of that.

Crossbreeding Subject Areas.   History and biology underwent a shotgun marriage in the introduction to this section, and it worked out well. In general, much of the most provocative intellectual work of this century reflects couplings of disciplines traditionally kept separate. For example, in the meeting of physics and biology we find scientists examining the mechanisms of life at the molecular and submolecular levels, and examining the basic parameters of living systems in terms of factors like heat flow and the ratio of surface area to volume in organisms.   Statistics unites with history in the science of historiometry, where the records of past societies and lives provide raw data for statistical procedures that address such seemingly ineffable issues as "Does history make the person or the person make history?"

Linguistics and history find communality in studies of the evolution of languages and the forces that shape them over the span of centuries. The computer, developed for pragmatic applications of data processing, has proved an illuminating metaphor and model for human mental functioning.   Psychobiologists have devised provocative explanations of behavior and even thought, in terms not of learning or willful action but natural selection. Art has found new media among the paraphernalia of the sciences—lasers, computer displays, plastics, telecommunications equipment, holograms.

It is fair to ask whether these or other pairings have the least application to schools with their appalling difficulties in treating the normal subject areas separately. But such links can be seen as opportunities rather than problems.   Remember the argument advanced in Chapter 4 about the rich variety of meaningful design projects afforded by the disciplines, even though we usually fail to recognize their presence. The same holds all the more so when disciplines are coupled.   Moreover, crossdisciplinary projects can perhaps spark the enthusiasm of students who show some liking for certain disciplines and not so much for others. Students can have their cake and eat it too—and it is a precious cake, since so much of student achievement depends on the delicate texture of intrinsic motivation.

BRIDGING FROM CONTEXT TO CONTEXT

"Use a diagram" is a sound heuristic for many problem-solving situations, a piece of strategic knowledge that in principle has great portability. But portability in principle is not the same as portability in practice. Imagine, for instance, that you learned this principle in a particular context, doing plane geometry problems. Suppose you later find yourself solving a logic problem like those presented in the previous chapter — Bill is no taller than Sam; Jack is no shorter than Sam; the three are different heights; who's tallest and shortest? Will your experience in plane geometry lead you to use a diagram?

This is a question of transfer. It asks whether something learned in one context will transfer to a second context, finding application there. Although you might think that transfer would occur quite automatically between such closely related matters as diagrams in plane geometry and diagrams for logic problems that actually involve an element of geometry, transfer does not necessarily occur. In general, research on transfer of learning discloses that transfer happens far less often and far less readily than people casually suppose. It is a real achievement of the learner, not to be taken for granted.

Teaching and learning based on knowledge as design needs to pay special heed to the problem of transfer. For one reason, some strategic knowledge, like the "make a diagram" heuristic, is in principle general; if in practice it does not transfer automatically to all or at least most contexts of potential application, we need to learn it and teach it in ways that foster transfer. For another reason, knowledge as design finds in even much narrower and more passive knowledge — say historically important dates — a kind of restlessness. Facts are not just for remembering on tests but for applying in diverse ways, as examples, as evidence, as anchor points for other facts, and so on. All such uses involve a degree of transfer. So knowledge as design thrives on transfer and dies without it.

Why is transfer a problem and how can we promote transfer? A classic answer to the first of these questions unfortunately proves not very helpful. The answer proposes that transfer occurs along paths of similarity: You learn a rule like "make a diagram" in one context, and it transfers to another to the extent that the second context resembles the first. Although perhaps roughly true, this account of transfer presents both a theoretical problem and a practical one.

One the theoretical side, how do we define similarity, as vague a notion as one is likely to find? Moreover, maybe contexts that we might intuitively consider similar are not so similar at some deep level, while contexts we intuitively consider disparate may be quite similar at some deep level. On the practical side, the similarity theory of transfer does not help us much as teachers or learners interested in fostering transfer. Presumably, the learning context and the application context are similar to a certain degree no matter how we teach and learn. The similarity theory does not give us any leverage on the transfer problem.

What is Involved in Transfer?

A more fruitful view of transfer has been developed by the Israeli psychologist Gavriel Salomon and me. This view evades the theoretical problem of defining similarity. It seeks to define the mechanisms of transfer, explain why transfer commonly does not occur, and prescribe instructional means to foster transfer.

The key premise is that transfer occurs by means of two rather different mechanisms. In particular, we distinguish between "low road transfer" and "high road transfer." Low road transfer depends on the automatic triggering of well-practiced knowledge or know-how by stimulus characteristics in a new context. For instance, if you know how to drive a car and get behind the wheel of a truck, the likenesses between truck and car engage your car-driving habits which, fortunately, fit driving a truck fairly well, although not perfectly of course. Low road transfer happens automatically given sufficient practice, but usually tends not to reach very far because it depends on common characteristics of the superficial stimulus, as between a car and a truck. To teach for far transfer by way of the low road, one needs to provide *varied* practice that exercises the knowledge or know-how in diverse contexts and so acquaints the learner with a variety of stimulus characteristics that later might trigger its application. Regrettably, most instruction provides practice only on a narrow range of conventional problems.

Whereas low road transfer depends on the automatic triggering of well-practiced knowledge, high road transfer calls for mindful generalization of knowledge from one context and deliberate application in another. For instance, suppose as a chess player you learn that "control of the center" is crucial. Later, as a businessperson, you might say to yourself, "Control of the center — perhaps that principle applies here as well. What might it mean? Well, perhaps control of the sources of raw materials. Perhaps control of key channels of advertising." Such thinking abstracts the principle from the context of chess and seeks potential applications in the domain of business. High road transfer tends not to occur spontaneously because it requires directed mental effort: One has to search out the connections.

What are the implications for designing instruction to foster transfer? Low road transfer benefits from varied practice, as already mentioned. High road transfer requires that the instruction provoke students to invent wide-ranging generalizations and applications. This can happen in a number of different ways — there are really several "high roads." (Alternatively, one might teach directly certain generalizations and applications. The philosophy of knowledge as design favors the more active approach of helping students to find generalizations and applications. That way, the students are more likely to learn how to transfer by themselves.) With these ideas in mind, here are some particular tactics.

Anticipatory Tactics

Instruction designed to foster transfer can teach knowledge or know-how in the first place so as to promote transfer. In particular:

Low Road Transfer by Varied Practice.   Suppose a student confronts exercises that fairly transparently require the use of diagrams, exercises not just in plane geometry, but also in two or three other contexts, perhaps diagramming sentences in English, diagramming atomic interactions in chemistry, and employing flow charts in learning to program a computer. Then perhaps when facing a logic problem the student will think to use a diagram. To generalize, practice of a rule in varied contexts helps to cast that rule into a general form and make it accessible in new contexts.

High Road Transfer by Abstraction of Rules.   Suppose students learning plane geometry are asked to reflect upon their own problem-solving processes and to generalize about elements of that process that seem to help. Some students may formulate the rule "use a diagram." As teacher, perhaps you then ask them, "Is that a rule just for geometry or generally useful, and why?" So they reason about it and conclude that it is a generally useful rule. In other words, deliberate abstraction can result in the recoding of a rule at a more general level, more suitable for transfer to a wide range of contexts.

High Road Transfer by Anticipating Applications. The above scenario can be extended. Suppose you ask the students not just to generalize rules, but to imagine where they might find use. Perhaps you even suggest a range of contexts and ask whether a rule under discussion might prove applicable in those contexts. Possibly you even explore one or two applications. Such activities prime the rule for transfer when learners later find themselves working in one of those other contexts.

Retrieval Tactics

The anticipatory tactics all concern how to prime the learner's learning for later transfer. However, high road transfer can be approached from the other direction: While working in the application context, a person can make a special retrieval effort that will recover knowledge bound to a prior learning context. Here are some ways that instruction can foster such transfer.

High Road Transfer by Generalizing the Problem. Suppose some students working on logic problems are encouraged to reflect on the difficulties they encounter. Perhaps one of them has this to say: "It's hard to keep track of all the information you're given." Maybe with some prompting from you the student extracts a general question: "What ways do I know to keep track of what a problem says?" With this question as a guide, the student may recall such tactics as making lists or diagrams. In general, the practice and habit of reflecting on what is difficult about a problem and abstracting the need will promote retrieval of relevant information originally learned in other contexts.

High Road Transfer by Focused Retrieval. You might also urge learners addressing logic problems to think of specific prior contexts to focus on. Perhaps one student says, "Well, last year we studied geometry. So maybe I can think of something from geometry." After a moment, the student comes up with "Make a diagram." In general, reaching toward a *particular potentially relevant* context of experience should foster transfer.

High Road Transfer by Metaphor-making.   Besides generalizing their difficulties with logic problems, students can also recast the difficulties by asking metaphorical questions. "What have I encountered before that's *like* this in some way?" Perhaps a student posing such a question will think of plane geometry and the make-a-diagram tactic, because "I was always confused there" or because "taller than and shorter than are sort of like geometry" or because "this is a kind of math." The basis for the link hardly matters, so long as a link appears.   In general, the mind's call for likenesses, even sometimes for rather loose and esoteric ones, may yield useful transfers of knowledge.

These six tactics for fostering transfer have been outlined without justifications; here is a brief argument that supports all six. Remember that evidence in plenty shows transfer to be the exception rather than the rule. That is, learning tends to occur in a context-bound way. Every one of the tactics suggested above clearly works to break links to the narrow context at hand by forcing some sort of generalization or other loosening of contextual constraints. For instance, varied practice breaks links to one specific context by providing practice in multiple contexts. Metaphor-making breaks links through a mindset for metaphorical rather than literal retrieval.

With this justification, however, comes a clear problem of pedagogy: Fostering transfer takes time, because it involves doing something special, something extra. With curricula crowded already and school hours a precious resource, it is hard to face the notion that topics need more time than they might otherwise get just to promote transfer. Yet that is the reality. It is actually preferable to cover somewhat less material, investing the time thereby freed to foster the transfer of that material, than to cover somewhat more and leave it context-bound. After all, who needs context-bound knowledge that shows itself only within the confines of a particular class period, a certain final essay, a term's final exam? In the long haul, there is no point to such instruction.

THE DESIGN THAT DESIGNS ITSELF

What is the design that designs itself? In the wide universe this question might have many answer, but so far as we know it has only one: human beings. Human beings design and redesign themselves.

The point has import for education. But before addressing that, ponder this odd practice of self-design. Human beings undertake it without thinking anything of it and, most of the time, without even realizing that they are doing it. For instance, you may decide to attend a trade school and become an automotive mechanic, or to learn computer programming so that you can develop salable software, or to attend a university and become a physicist, or to spend a year out of school in quest of more perspective on life, or to change jobs at age 50 in search of a more meaningful occupation, or to enrich your life with children, or to simplify your life without children, or to jog for cardiovascular health, or to read the ten great books that have been so long left on the shelf. All these decisions involve plans that will change your nature, they all are acts of self-design, and people make such decisions all the time.

Other life forms — paramecia, sharks, mayflies, armadillos, earthworms — are quite properly thought of as designs, but they do no designing of themselves or anything else. A few higher animals such as chimps accomplish a little designing, but not much, and much less self-design. However, we human beings, the only serious designers in sight, are so much taken with design that we not only design and redesign everything around us, but even ourselves.

It is our nature, not an easy one, and for understandable reasons. In many ways designing yourself is harder than other sorts of designing. You cannot perceive yourself as readily as you can externals. You are likely to be more defensive about yourself than about externals. And, perhaps worst of all, you lack the edge of knowing more than what you are designing. Design a door knob, modern dance, or nuclear device and you enjoy the perspective of knowing more than they, since door knobs, modern dances, and nuclear devices know nothing at all. But, as a designer of yourself, you never know more than yourself. How can you ever keep track of yourself? You need help.

Enter the teacher. A teacher, ideally conceived, is a designer who helps learners to design themselves. Consider the alternatives to this notion. One option is the teacher as template, who tries to replicate knowledge into the minds of the students. But this kind of teacher treats knowledge as information rather than design. Another alternative is the teacher as a designer who treats learners as objects and tries to shape them utterly, as sculptors their clay. But people are not objects; such a style undermines intrinsic motivation, provokes rebellion, and deprives learners of practice in self-design. So it seems that teachers must recognize that learners are, or should be becoming, self-designers, and assist them along the way.

How? Not by teachers routinely withholding knowledge. It is not to be thought that students should discover everything for themselves; on the contrary, education often calls for massive and efficient transfer of knowledge. But, for instance, by highlighting design activities that allow individual and even idiosyncratic treatments. For instance, by giving learners room to find their own directions, as in the "problem finding" activities discussed toward the ends of Chapter 4 and Chapter 7. For instance, by encouraging reflection about one's own mental processes.

For instance, by conveying an attitude summed up in this phrase. *You are not what you know.* That is important because, in a sense, we *are* what we know; our specific and general knowledge and know-how channels how we think and act. But to practice self-design, we cannot feel married to our knowledge as it is, protecting it against the world and change. We have to hold our knowledge loosely, not so preciously, no more than toenails you can paint or trim, no more than a tie or a hat.

So teachers, as designers, handle paradoxical clay: the design that designs itself, and is and is not its own knowledge. What sort of reality is this? If reality were a matter of plain truth, I would be in trouble here, for paradox and truth are adversaries. But since reality is our subtlest construction, a matter of design, no matter. For while plain truth cannot be paradoxical, designs delightfully and even designedly can.

Notes

Author (date) entries refer to the complete references under *Sources*.

Introduction: The Giving and Getting of Knowledge.

Reports criticizing primary and secondary U.S. education: for instance, Boyer (1983), Goodlad (1983), National Commission on Excellence in Education (1983), Sizer (1984).

Chapter 1. Knowledge as Design

Natural Selection

For a contemporary and accessible view on evolution and the empirical evidence for it, see the writings of Stephen Jay Gould, for instance Gould (1980).

Knowledge as Design: The Arguments

On the problem of inert knowledge in writing, see Bereiter and Scardamalia (1985); in medical education, see Barrows and Tamblyn (1980); in the context of computer programming, see Perkins and Martin (1986).

The role of understanding the purpose of something in understanding it: Bransford and McCarrell (1977).

Means-end analysis in human problem solving: Newell and Simon (1972). Purposefulness in inventive thinking: Perkins (1981).

The senses of structure and structural learning are many. One includes the acquisition of general logical structures a la Piaget: Inhelder and Piaget (1958); see also Case (1984, 1985). Another includes the acquisition of mathematical structures, as in Jeeves and Greer (1983), Behr, Lesh, Post, and Silver (1983), and Lesh, Landau, and Hamilton (1983). Still another includes the learning of structural elements in poetry, as discussed by Ciardi (1959). One easily could construct a much longer list, the notion of structure being as protean as it is.

Mental models as mediators of understanding: Gentner and Stevens (1983), Johnson-Laird (1983).

Hazards of formal reasoning: Falmagne (1975), Revlin and Mayer (1978), Wason and Johnson-Laird (1972).

Hazards of informal reasoning: Ennis (1969, 1981), Fearnside and Holther (1959), Perkins, Allen, and Hafner (1983), Perkins (1985a,b).

Organization, imagery, and meaningfulness foster memory: See the accessible practically-oriented review of findings by Higbee (1977).

Restoring Connections

Students' misunderstandings of physics: for instance, Clement (1983), McCloskey (1983).

The free-fall problem in particular: Clement (1983).

Computer models of Newtonian motion: White (1984).

Modeling and other modes of symbolic communication in teaching artistic abilities: Howard (1982).

Models and the ambiguity of exemplification: Goodman (1976). Also, see Chapter 5.

The discovery of the genetic code: Watson (1968).

What You Can Do

On the importance of the *explicit* teaching of strategies: Pressley, Forrest-Pressley, Elliott-Faust, and Miller (1985), Schoenfeld (1979).

Chapter 2. Design Colored Glasses

How to Think about Everyday Inventions as Designs

Parts, materials, and shapes, the key question "Why is this the way it is," and the criteria to consider in evaluating a concrete design all are part of the lesson sequence *Inventive Thinking* (Perkins & Laserna, 1986) in *Odyssey*, a one-year course to teach thinking skills. See Nickerson, Perkins, and Smith (1985), Chapter 6, Section 6 on Project Intelligence for a compact description of *Odyssey* and its evaluation.

How to Think about Procedures as Designs

Treating procedures as design is also part of *Odyssey's* inventive thinking sequence (Perkins & Laserna, 1986).

How to Think about Families of Designs

This theme, as well as the example of fasteners, also is drawn from *Odyssey*.

Chapter 3. Words by Design

Reading by Design: Content

Zombie article: from *Time,* October 17, 1983

Research on the effectiveness of the SQ3R plan: Higbee (1977), Robinson (1970).

Reading by Design: Organization

Globe article on arms negotiations: *The Boston Globe,* November 2, 1983.

John Ciardi's discussion of fulcrums: Ciardi (1959), pp. 994–1007.

"The Span of Life" is from Robert Frost, *The Poetry of Robert Frost.* New York: Holt, Rinehart and Winston, 1979.

"Note that neither line . . .": Ciardi (1959), p. 994.

For more on the role of analysis of art in appreciation, see Perkins (1977, 1983).

"A poem is one part against another . . .": Ciardi (1959), p. 995.

"On the Vanity of Earthly Greatness" is from Arthur Guiterman, *Gaily the Troubadour*. New York: E. P. Dutton, 1936.

"My Papa's Waltz" is from Theodore Roethke, *The Collected Poems of Theodore Roethke*. New York: Doubleday, 1942.

"Imagine as a horrible example . . .": Ciardi (1959), p. 1004.

Chapter 4.   Acts of Design

Introduction

Children's theory-making about the physical world: Piaget (1954).

On creativity in educational and other settings: Perkins (1981, 1984, 1985c).

Opportunities for Design

The lesson series on inventive thinking from Odyssey: Perkins and Laserna (1986).

On study strategies, see Higbee (1977), Schmeck (1983).

For research and recommendations on strategies in mathematical problem solving, see Polya (1954, 1957), Schoenfeld (1980, 1982), Schoenfeld and Herrmann (1982), Wickelgren (1974).

On different forms of definition, see Ennis (1969).

On classification, see the lesson series that constitutes Unit 1 of *Odyssey:* Adams, Buscaglia, de Sánchez, and Swets (1986).

Models of Modeling

Reciprocal teaching: Palinscar and Brown (1984).

Intrinsic Motivation

The role of intrinsic motivation in inventive thinking: Amabile (1983).

Problem Finding

Problem Finding in artists: Getzels and Csikszentmihalyi (1976).

On ways to promote problem finding in mathematics instruction: Brown and Walter (1983) and Schwartz and Yerushalmy (in press).

Chapter 5.   Inside Models

What is a Model?

The role of analogy and imagery in scientific discovery and theorizing: Koestler (1964), Miller (1984), Schon (1963).

Exemplification versus denotation and the matter of what properties count: Goodman (1976).

On the Omnipresence of Models

The ubiquity of metaphors in our everyday language and patterns of thought: Lakoff and Johnson (1980).

The role of concrete imagery in encoding abstractions: Arnheim (1969).

Article on the microelectronics center: *The Boston Globe,* April 17, 1984.

On the role of metaphor in thought and perception: Perkins (1978).

Mental Models

Mental models in general: Gentner and Stevens (1983), Johnson-Laird (1983).

Models of courses of action as a basis for reasoning: Johnson-Laird (1985), Perkins (1985), Kahneman and Tversky (1982).

The washing clothes example: Bransford and McCarrell (1977).

Research on chess masters' repertoires of schemes: Chase and Simon (1973), de Groot (1965), Simon and Chase (1973).

Repertoires in computer programming: Schneiderman (1976), Soloway and Ehrlich (1984). In problem solving in physics: Chi, Feltovich, and Glaser (1981), Larkin, McDermott, Simon, and Simon (1980). In problem solving in mathematics: Schoenfeld and Herrmann (1982). In music: Hayes (1981), Slaboda (1976). In art: Gombrich (1961, 1979).

Mental Muddles

Mental modeling in reasoning: The deposit law example: Perkins (1985), Perkins, Allen, and Hafner (1983).

Reframing in psychotherapy: see, for example, Watzlawick, Weakland, and Fisch (1974).

Naive physics in general: Chi, Feltovich, and Glaser (1981), Clement (1983), Larkin, McDermott, Simon, and Simon (1980), McCloskey (1983).

Normal responses to the trajectory of the ball problem: Clement (1983), McCloskey (1983).

Computer models for providing experience with Newtonian motion: White (1984).

Evidence for the Effectiveness of Models

Barbara White's experiment with a computerized Newtonian world: White (1984). The keyword method: Atkinson (1975), Atkinson and Raugh (1975), Raugh and Atkinson (1975).

Learning programming with a mental model of the computer: Mayer (1976, 1981).

Chapter 6. Inside Argument

Formal Patterns of Argument

The more conventional approach, which treats formal argument as the backbone of informal argument, is exemplified in, for instance, Beardsley (1975), Black (1952), Ennis (1969).

The 27 varieties of syllogisms, along with a theory of how people solve them by using mental models: Johnson-Laird (1983).

On the validity of logical forms, see, for example, Kripke (1980) and Quine (1980).

Some Patterns of Informal Argument

On the difficulties of justifying induction, see Goodman (1983).

Numerous problems of critical evaluation are discussed from a philosophical perspective in Beardsley (1958). Educational and empirical perspectives can be found in Perkins (1977) and Perkins (1979).

The influence of vivid models: The Volvo example is borrowed from Nisbett and Ross (1980), who review the influence of vivid instances on reasoning as well as a number of other factors that undermine reasoning.

The presumed representativeness of small populations: Tversky and Kahneman (1971).

Distrust of the predictiveness of large samples drawn from very large populations: Bar-Hillel (1979).

Chapter 7.   The Art of Argument

A Study of Informal Reasoning

The research outlined here is reported in more detail in: Perkins (1985); related articles include Perkins (1985) and Perkins, Allen, and Hafner (1983).

A Quick Argument for This Approach

The merits of explicit instruction: See Pressley, Forrest-Pressley, Elliott-Faust, and Miller (1985) and Schoenfeld (1979).

Tie Breakers

The whole issue of exploring and resolving issues via consideration of expectation values is discussed by Baron (1985) as part of a general examination of the nature of rationality and intelligence.

Summary of several decision making tools: Hayes (1981).

The Challenge of Formal Argument

For further discussion of this theme, see Perkins (1985) and Perkins, Allen, and Hafner (1983).

The Art of Mathematical Argument

The works of Polya: Polya (1954, 1957).

Wickelgren on mathematical problem solving: Wickelgren (1974).

Schoenfeld's managerial strategy: Schoenfeld (1980).

Heuristic Power

Schoenfeld's set of heuristics: Schoenfeld (1980).

No instructional effect without explicit identification of heuristics: Schoenfeld (1979).

Impact of explicit instruction in Schoenfeld's heuristics and managerial strategy: Schoenfeld (1982), Schoenfeld and Herrmann (1982).

On problem posing: Brown and Walter (1983).

On problem finding in geometry: Schwartz and Yerushalmy (in press).

Chapter 8.   Schooling Minds

What Holds Schools Back?

Note again the various reports on the state of U.S. education mentioned in the references for the introduction to this book.

Bridging from Information to Design

A number of contemporary books offer a general perspective on the teaching of thinking strategies and the development of learner's potentials more generally. Here is only a sample.

General survey and review: Nickerson, Perkins, and Smith (1985).

Philosophical and psychological perspectives on human potential: Gardner (1983), Scheffler (1985).

Collections of articles reviewing research and programs concerned with the teaching of thinking: Segal, Chipman, and Glaser (1985), Baron (1985), Lochhead and Clement (1979).

Problem-solving and learning strategies with supporting research: Hayes (1981).

Rationality, intelligence, and decision-making: Baron (1985).

Intelligence and its enhancement: Sternberg (1985), Whimbey (1975).

Resource book for administrators and practitioners collecting many key concepts and ideas for interventions: Costa (1985).

Bridging from Teacher to Students

Pair problem solving: Whimbey and Lochhead (1982).

Internalization of overt patterns of communication is a developmental mechanism emphasized by Vygotsky (1962, 1978). See also Case (1984, 1985).

Bridging from Subject to Subject

Historiometry: see Simonton (1984).

Bridging from Context to Context

The theory of transfer developed by Salomon and Perkins: Perkins and Salomon (in press), Salomon and Perkins (in press).

Sources

Adams, J., Buscaglia, J., de Sánchez, M., & Swets, J. (1986). *Foundations of reasoning* (lesson sequence from *Odyssey: A curriculum for thinking*). Watertown, Massachusetts: Mastery Education.

Amabile, T. M. (1983). *The social psychology of creativity.* New York: Springer-Verlag.

Arnheim, R. (1969). *Visual thinking.* Berkeley: University of California Press.

Atkinson, R. C. (1975). Mnemotechnics in second-language learning. *American Psychologist, 30,* 821–28.

Atkinson, R. C., & Raugh, M. R. (1975). An application of the mnemonic keyword method to the acquisition of a Russian vocabulary. *Journal of Experimental Psychology: Human Learning and Memory, 1,* 126–33.

Bar-Hillel, M. (1979). The role of sample size in sample evaluation. *Organizational Behavior and Human Performance, 24,* 245–257.

Baron, J. (1985). *Rationality and intelligence.* New York: Cambridge University Press.

Baron, J. (1985). What kinds of intelligence components are fundamental? In S. S. Chipman, J. W. Segal, & R. Glaser (Eds.), *Thinking and learning skills, Volume 2: Current research and open questions* (pp. 365–390). Hillsdale, New Jersey: Lawrence Erlbaum Associates.

Barrows, H. S., & Tamblyn, R. M. (1980). *Problem-based learning: An approach to medical education.* New York: Springer.

Beardsley, M. C. (1958). *Aesthetics: Problems in the philosophy of criticism.* New York: Harcourt, Brace, & World.

Beardsley, M. C. (1975). *Thinking straight: Principles of reasoning for readers and writers.* Englewood Cliffs, New Jersey: Prentice-Hall.

Behr, M., Lesh, R., Post, T., & Silver, E. (1983). Rational-number concepts. In R. Lesh & M. Landau (Eds.), *Acquisition of mathematics concepts and processes* (pp. 91–126). New York: Academic Press.

Bereiter, C., & Scardamalia, M. (1985). Cognitive coping strategies and the problem of inert knowledge. In S. S. Chipman, J. W. Segal, & R. Glazer (Eds.), *Thinking and learning skills, Vol. 2: Current research and open questions* (pp. 65–80). Hillsdale, New Jersey: Lawrence Erlbaum Associates.

Black, M. (1952). *Critical thinking: An introduction to logic and scientific method.* Englewood Cliffs, New Jersey: Prentice-Hall.

Boyer, E. (1983). *High school: A report on secondary education in America.* New York: Harper and Row.

Bransford, J. D., & McCarrell, N. S. (1977). A sketch of a cognitive approach to comprehension: Some thoughts about understanding what it means to comprehend. In P. N. Johnson-Laird & P. C. Wason (Eds.), *Thinking: Readings in cognitive science* (pp. 377–399). Cambridge, England: Cambridge University Press.

Brown, S. I., & Walter, M. I. (1983). *The art of problem posing.* Hillsdale, New Jersey: Lawrence Erlbaum Associates.

Case, R. (1984). The process of stage transition: A neo-Piagetian viewpoint. In R. J. Sternberg (Ed.), *Mechanisms of cognitive development* (pp. 19–44). New York: W. H. Freeman and Company.

Case, R. (1985). *Intellectual development: Birth to adulthood.* New York: Academic Press.

Chase, W. C., & Simon, H. A. (1973). Perception in chess. *Cognitive Psychology, 4,* 55–81.

Chi, M., Feltovich, P., & Glaser, R. (1981). Categorization and representation of physics problems by experts and novices. *Cognitive Science, 5,* 121–152.

Chipman, S. F., Segal, J. W., & Glaser, R. (Eds.). (1985). *Thinking and learning skills, Volume 2: Research and open questions.* Hillsdale, New Jersey: Lawrence Erlbaum Associates.

Ciardi, J. (1959). *How does a poem mean?* Boston: Houghton Mifflin.

Clement, J. (1983). A conceptual model discussed by Galileo and used intuitively by physics students. In D. Gentner & A. L. Stevens (Eds.), *Mental models.* Hillsdale, New Jersey: Lawrence Erlbaum Associates.

Costa, A. L. (Ed.). (1985). *Developing minds: A resource book for teaching thinking.* Alexandria, Virginia: Association for Supervision and Curriculum Development.

de Groot, A. D. (1965). *Thought and choice in chess.* The Hague: Mouton.

Ennis, R. H. (1969). *Logic in teaching.* Englewood Cliffs, New Jersey: Prentice-Hall.

Ennis, R. H. (1981). Rational thinking and educational practice. In J. Soltis (Ed.), *Philosophy and education* (Vol. 1, Eightieth yearbook, pp. 143–183). Chicago: National Society for the Study of Education.

Falmagne, R. J. (Ed.). (1975). *Reasoning: Representation and process in children and adults.* Hillsdale, New Jersey: Lawrence Erlbaum Associates.

Fearnside, W. W., & Holther, W. B. (1959). *Fallacy: The counterfeit of argument.* Englewood Cliffs, New Jersey: Prentice-Hall.

Gardner, H. (1983). *Frames of mind.* New York: Basic Books.

Gentner, D., & Stevens, A. L. (Eds.). (1983). *Mental models.* Hillsdale, New Jersey: Lawrence Erlbaum Associates.

Getzels, J., & Csikszentmihalyi, M. (1976). *The creative vision: A longitudinal study of problem finding in art.* New York: John Wiley & Sons.

Gombrich, E. H. (1961). *Art and illusion: A study in the psychology of pictorial representation.* Princeton, New Jersey: Princeton University Press.

Gombrich, E. H. (1979). *The sense of order: A study in the psychology of decorative art.* Ithaca, New York: Cornell University Press.

Goodlad, J. I. (1983). *A place called school: Prospects for the future.* New York: McGraw Hill.

Goodman, N. A. (1976). *Languages of art.* Indianapolis: Hackett.

Goodman, N. A. (1983). *Fact, fiction, and forecast.* Cambridge, Massachusetts: Harvard University Press.

Gould, S. J. (1980). *The panda's thumb: More reflections in natural history.* New York: Norton.

Hayes, J. R. (1981). *The complete problem solver.* Hillsdale, New Jersey: Lawrence Erlbaum Associates.

Higbee, K. L. (1977). *Your memory: How it works and how to improve it.* Englewood Cliffs, New Jersey: Prentice-Hall.

Howard, V. A. (1982). *Artistry: The work of artists.* Indianapolis: Hackett.

Inhelder, B., & Piaget, J. (1958). *The growth of logical thinking from childhood to adolescence.* New York: Basic Books.

Jeeves, M. A., & Greer, G. B. (1983). *Analysis of structural learning.* New York: Academic Press.

Johnson-Laird, P. N. (1983). *Mental models.* Cambridge, Massachusetts: Harvard University Press.

Johnson-Laird, P. N. (1985). Logical thinking: Does it occur in daily life? Can it be taught? In S. S. Chipman, J. W. Segal, & R. Glazer (Eds.), *Thinking and learning skills, Vol. 2: Current research and open questions* (pp. 293-318). Hillsdale, New Jersey: Lawrence Erlbaum Associates.

Kahneman, D., & Tversky, A. (1982). The simulation heuristic. In D. Kahneman, P. Slovic, & A. Tversky (Eds.), *Judgment under uncertainty: Heuristics and biases* (pp. 201-208). Cambridge, England: Cambridge University Press.

Koestler, A. (1964). *The act of creation.* New York: Dell.

Kripke, S. A. (1980). *Naming and necessity.* Cambridge, Massachusetts: Harvard University Press.

Lakoff, G., & Johnson, M. (1980). *Metaphors we live by.* Chicago: University of Chicago Press.

Larkin, J. H., McDermott, J., Simon, D. P., & Simon, H. A. (1980). Modes of competence in solving physics problems. *Cognitive Science, 4,* 317-345.

Lesh, R., Landau, M., & Hamilton, E. (1983). Conceptual models and applied mathematical problem-solving research. In R. Lesh & M. Landau (Eds.), *Acquisition of mathematics concepts and processes* (pp. 263-343). New York: Academic Press.

Lochhead, J., & Clement, J. (1979). *Cognitive process instruction.* Hillsdale, New Jersey: Lawrence Erlbaum Associates.

Mayer, R. E. (1976). Some conditions of meaningful learning for computer programming: Advance organizers and subject control of frame order. *Journal of Educational Psychology, 68,* 143–150.

Mayer, R. E. (1981). The psychology of how novices learn computer programming. *Computing Surveys, 13*(11), 121–141.

McCloskey, M. (1983). Naive theories of motion. In D. Gentner & A. L. Stevens (Eds.), *Mental models* (pp. 299–324). Hillsdale, New Jersey: Lawrence Erlbaum Associates.

Miller, A. I. (1984). *Imagery in scientific thought: Creating 20th-century physics.* Boston: Birkhauser.

National Commission on Excellence in Education. (1983). *A nation at risk: The imperative for educational reform.* Washington, D.C.: United States Department of Education.

Newell, A., & Simon, H. (1972). *Human problem solving.* Englewood Cliffs, New Jersey: Prentice-Hall.

Nickerson, R., Perkins, D. N., & Smith, E. (1985). *The teaching of thinking.* Hillsdale, New Jersey: Lawrence Erlbaum Associates.

Nisbett, R., & Ross, L. (1980). *Human inference: Strategies and shortcomings of social judgment.* Englewood Cliffs, New Jersey: Prentice-Hall.

Palinscar, A. S., & Brown, A. L. (1984). Reciprocal teaching of comprehension-fostering and comprehension-monitoring activities. *Cognition and Instruction, 1,* 117–175.

Perkins, D. N. (1977). Talk about art. *Journal of Aesthetic Education, 11*(2), 87–116.

Perkins, D. N. (1978). Metaphorical perception. In E. Eisner (Ed.), *Reading, the arts, and the creation of meaning* (pp. 111–139). Reston, Virginia: National Art Education Association.

Perkins, D. N. (1979). Are matters of value matters of fact? In C. F. Nodine & D. F. Fisher, *Perception and pictorial representation* (pp. 301–315). New York: Praeger.

Perkins, D. N. (1981). *The mind's best work.* Cambridge, Massachusetts: Harvard University Press.

Perkins, D. N. (1983). Invisible art. *Art Education, 36*(2), 39–41.

Perkins, D. N. (1984). Creativity by design. *Educational Leadership, 42*(1), 18–25.

Perkins, D. N. (1985a). Postprimary education has little impact on informal reasoning. *Journal of Educational Psychology, 77*(5), 562–571.

Perkins, D. N. (1985b). Reasoning as imagination. *Interchange, 16*(1), 14–26.

Perkins, D. N. (1985c). What else but genius? Six Dimensions of the creative mind. In M. R. Raju, J. A. Phillips, & F. Harlow (Eds.), *Creativity in science* (pp. 15–27). Los Alamos, New Mexico: Los Alamos National Laboratory.

Perkins, D. N., Allen, R., & Hafner, J. (1983). Difficulties in everyday reasoning. In W. Maxwell (Ed.), *Thinking: The frontier expands* (pp. 177–189). Hillsdale, New Jersey: Lawrence Erlbaum Associates.

Perkins, D. N., & Laserna, C. (1986). *Inventive thinking* (Lesson sequence in *Odyssey: A curriculum for thinking*). Watertown, Massachusetts: Mastery Education.

Perkins, D. N., & Martin, F. (1986). Fragile knowledge and neglected strategies in novice programmers. In E. Soloway & S. Iyengar (Eds.), *Empirical studies of programmers.* Norwood, New Jersey: Ablex.

Perkins, D., & Salomon, G. (in press). Transfer and teaching thinking. In D. N. Perkins, J. Lochhead, & J. Bishop (Eds.), *Thinking: The second international conference*. Hillsdale, New Jersey: Lawrence Erlbaum Associates.

Piaget, J. (1954). *The construction of reality in the child*. New York: Basic Books.

Polya, G. (1954). *Mathematics and plausible reasoning* (2 vols.). Princeton, New Jersey: Princeton University Press.

Polya, G. (1957). *How to solve it: A new aspect of mathematical method* (2nd ed.). Garden City, New York: Doubleday.

Pressley, M., Forrest-Pressley, D. L., Elliott-Faust, D., & Miller, G. (1985). Children's use of cognitive strategies, how to teach strategies, and what to do if they can't be taught. In M. Pressley & C. J. Brainerd (Eds.), *Cognitive learning and memory in children: Progress in cognitive development research* (pp. 1–47). New York: Springer-Verlag.

Quine, W. (1980). Two dogmas of empiricism. In *From a logical point of view* (pp. 20–46). Cambridge, Massachusetts: Harvard University Press.

Raugh, M. R., & Atkinson, R. C. (1975). A mnemonic method for learning a second-language vocabulary. *Journal of Educational Psychology, 67*, 1–16.

Revlin, R., & Mayer, R. E. (Eds.). (1978). *Human reasoning*. Washington, D.C.: V. H. Winston and Sons.

Robinson, F. P. (1970). *Effective study*. New York: Harper and Row.

Salomon, G., & Perkins, D. N. (in press). Transfer of cognitive skills from programming: When and how? *Journal of Educational Computing Research*.

Scheffler, I. (1985). *Of human potential: An essay in the philosophy of education*. Boston: Routledge & Kegan Paul.

Schmeck, R. R. (1983). Learning styles of college students. In R. F. Dillon & R. R. Schmeck (Eds.), *Individual differences in cognition* (Vol. 1), (pp. 233–279). New York: Academic Press.

Schneiderman, B. (1976). Exploratory experiments in programmer behavior. *International Journal of Computer and Information Sciences, 5*, 123–143.

Schoenfeld, A. H. (1979). Explicit heuristic training as a variable in problem solving performance. *Journal for Research in Mathematics Education, 10*(3), 173–187.

Schoenfeld, A. H. (1980). Teaching problem-solving skills. *American Mathematical Monthly, 87*, 794–805.

Schoenfeld, A. H. (1982). Measures of problem-solving performance and of problem-solving instruction. *Journal for Research in Mathematics Education, 13*(1), 31–49.

Schoenfeld, A. H. & Herrmann, D. J. (1982). Problem perception and knowledge structure in expert and novice mathematical problem solvers. *Journal of Experimental Psychology: Learning, Memory, and Cognition, 8*, 484–494.

Schon, D. A. (1963). *Displacement of concepts*. London: Tavistock.

Schwartz, J. L., & Yerushalmy, M. (in press). The geometric supposer: Using microcomputers to restore invention to the learning of mathematics. In D. N. Perkins, J. Lochhead, & J. Bishop (Eds.), *Thinking: Proceedings of the second international conference*. Hillsdale, New Jersey: Lawrence Erlbaum Associates.

Segal, J. W., Chipman, S. F., & Glaser, R. (Eds.). (1985). *Thinking and learning skills, Volume 1: Relating instruction to research*. Hillsdale, New Jersey: Lawrence Erlbaum Associates.

Simon, H. A., & Chase, W. (1973). Skill in chess. *American Scientist, 61*, 394-403.

Simonton, D. K. (1984). *Genius, Creativity, & Leadership: Historiometric inquiries.* Cambridge, Massachusetts: Harvard University Press.

Sizer, T. B. (1984). *Horace's compromise: The dilemma of the American high school today.* Boston: Houghton Mifflin.

Slaboda, J. (1976). Visual perception of musical notation: Registering pitch symbols in memory. *Quarterly Journal of Experimental Psychology, 28*, 1-16.

Soloway, E., & Ehrlich, K. (1984). Empirical studies of programming knowledge. *IEEE Transactions on Software Engineering, SE-10*(5), 595-609.

Sternberg, R. J. (1985). *Beyond I.Q.: A triarchic theory of human intelligence.* New York: Cambridge University Press.

Tversky, A., & Kahneman, D. (1971). Belief in the law of small numbers. *Psychological Bulletin, 2*, 105-10.

Vygotsky, L. S. (1962). *Thought and language.* Cambridge, Massachusetts: MIT Press and Wiley.

Vygotsky, L. S. (1978). *Mind in society: The development of higher psychological processes.* Cambridge, Massachusetts: Harvard University Press.

Wason, P. C., & Johnson-Laird, P. N. (1972). *Psychology and reasoning: Structure and content.* Cambridge, Massachusetts: Harvard University Press.

Watson, J. D. (1968). *The double helix: A personal account of the discovery of the structure of DNA.* New York: Signet Books, New American Library.

Watzlawick, P., Weakland, J., & Fisch, R. (1974). *Change.* New York: Norton.

Whimbey, A. (1975). *Intelligence can be taught.* New York: E. P. Dutton.

Whimbey, A., & Lochhead, J. (1982). *Problem solving and comprehension.* Hillsdale, New Jersey: Lawrence Erlbaum Associates.

White, B. Y. (1984). Designing computer games to help physics students understand Newton's laws of motion. *Cognition and Instruction, 1*, 69-108.

Wickelgren, W. A. (1974). *How to solve problems: Elements of a theory of problems and problem solving.* San Francisco: W. H. Freeman & Co.